Gridlock

Cities across the world are facing unprecedented challenges in traffic management and transit congestion while coping with growing populations and mobility aspirations. Existing policies that aim to tackle congestion and create more sustainable transport futures offer only weak remedies. In *Gridlock: Congested Cities, Contested Policies, Unsustainable Mobility*, transport consultant John C. Sutton explores how two competing discourses in transport policy and planning practice – convivial and competitive ideologies – lead to contradictory solutions and a gridlock in policy as well as on transport systems.

Gridlock examines current transport and mobility in a geographical, social, political-economy and technological context. The challenges of rising congestion are highlighted through case studies from the UK, the USA and OECD countries. Sutton offers readers a vision of a sustainable mobility future through the concept of mobility management, combining mobile communication and information technology with logistics to match travel demand to the capacity of transport systems.

Suitable for transport professionals and students of transportation planning and policy, *Gridlock* offers a unique manifesto for sustainable mobility settlement, addressing the pressing problems of growing populations and congestion while looking ahead to a more sustainable future.

John C. Sutton, PhD is an independent transport consultant who has worked in the UK, the USA and Asia as a transport planner, manager and developer of transport information systems, including GIS applications. He has published widely, including *Transport Coordination and Social Policy* (Avebury 1988) and as co-editor of *Community Transport: Policy, Planning, Practice* (Gordon and Breach 1995).

Gridlock
Congested Cities, Contested
Policies, Unsustainable Mobility

John C. Sutton

Routledge
Taylor & Francis Group
NEW YORK AND LONDON

First published 2015
by Routledge
711 Third Avenue, New York, NY 10017

and by Routledge
2 Park Square, Milton Park, Abingdon, Oxon OX14 4RN

Routledge is an imprint of the Taylor & Francis Group, an informa business

© 2015 Taylor & Francis

The right of John C. Sutton to be identified as author of this work has been asserted by him in accordance with sections 77 and 78 of the Copyright, Designs and Patents Act 1988.

All rights reserved. No part of this book may be reprinted or reproduced or utilised in any form or by any electronic, mechanical, or other means, now known or hereafter invented, including photocopying and recording, or in any information storage or retrieval system, without permission in writing from the publishers.

Trademark notice: Product or corporate names may be trademarks or registered trademarks, and are used only for identification and explanation without intent to infringe.

Library of Congress Cataloging in Publication Data
Sutton, John C.
Gridlock : congested cities, contested policies, unsustainable mobility / John C. Sutton.
pages cm
Includes bibliographical references and index.
1. Traffic congestion. 2. Urban transportation. 3. Urban policy. I. Title.
HE336.C64S88 2015
388.3′142—dc23
2015001963

ISBN: 978-1-138-85197-9 (hbk)
ISBN: 978-1-138-85201-3 (pbk)
ISBN: 978-1-315-72384-6 (ebk)

Typeset in Sabon
by Swales & Willis Ltd, Exeter, Devon, UK

Printed and bound in the United States of America by Publishers Graphics, LLC on sustainably sourced paper.

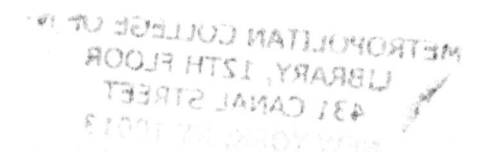

Contents

List of Figures and Tables viii
List of Boxes ix
Preface x
Acknowledgements xii
Preamble: A Vision of Mobility and Transport in 2035 xiv

PART I
Unsustainable Transport: Congested Cities, Contested Policies 1

1 Introduction: The Challenge of Mobility 3

1.1 The Age of Mobility 3
1.2 The Paradox of Transport and Mobility 8
1.3 Expanding Mobility and the Pending Congestion Crisis 11

2 Sustainable Transport and Mobility 15

2.1 Meta-mobility: Assimilating Spatial and Social Mobility 15
2.2 The Mobile City 17
2.3 Balancing Mobility and Sustainability 20
2.4 Transport Obligations under the Kyoto Protocol 24
2.5 Transport, Accessibility and Social Inclusion 26
2.6 The Postmodern City: A Vision of Sustainable Urban Mobility 33

3 Global Transport and Mobility Trends 36

3.1 Mass Mobility: A Global Phenomenon 36
3.2 Trends in the UK 37
3.3 International Outlook 39

vi *Contents*

    3.4 Mobility Trends in the USA 45
    3.5 Congestion Limits to Economic Growth 50

PART II
Transport Technology and Policy Development   55

  4 **Smarter Transport Technology and Innovation**   57

    4.1 Intelligent Transport Systems 57
    4.2 The Impact of Location Technologies on Transport
        Innovation 58
    4.3 Vehicle Technology 60
    4.4 Scheduling Logistics 63
    4.5 Intelligent Mobility: The Future for Transport
        Technology 64

  5 **Sustainable Transport Policy in the UK**   66

    5.1 Paradigm Shifts in Transport Planning 66
    5.2 Bucking the Trend: London Exceptionalism 71
    5.3 New Realism and the Sustainable Travel Agenda 74
    5.4 New Labour and the New Deal for Transport 75
    5.5 Smarter Choices Travel Programme 77
    5.6 The Policy Context: The Stern and Eddington Reports 80
    5.7 The Coalition Government's Transport Policy 84
    5.8 Back to the Future: The Old Realities Reassert
        Themselves (but Not Quite Business as Usual) 87

PART III
The Mobile Society: Political, Cultural and Social
Dimensions of Travel   93

  6 **The Political Economy of Sustainable Transport**   95

    6.1 Sustainable Transport, Unsustainable Politics 95
    6.2 Central–Local Relations in Transport Policy 98
    6.3 Contested Policies, Unsustainable Mobility 102

  7 **Cultural Influences on Transport Discourses**   105

    7.1 Sustainable Transport Discourse 105
    7.2 Automobile Culture 106

7.3 *Gender and Mobility* 114
7.4 *The Culture of Mobility* 118

8 The Sociology of Mobility 122

8.1 *The Mobile Society* 122
8.2 *Mobility Domains* 129
8.3 *Transport Radicalism and Social Movements* 133
8.4 *Future Scenarios for the Mobile Society* 136
8.5 *The Social and Political Implications of Mobility* 138

PART IV
Mobility Management: From Gridlock to Sustainable Mobility 143

9 Mobility Management 145

9.1 *Concept of Operations* 145
9.2 *Travel Demand Logistics Management* 146
9.3 *Congestion Pricing: Monetising Mobility* 148
9.4 *Limitations of Smarter Choices Travel Programmes* 154
9.5 *The Role of Infrastructure Investment* 155
9.6 *Mobility Management: A New Paradigm for Sustainable Transport* 156

10 Manifesto for Sustainable Mobility 160

10.1 *Prospectus* 160
10.2 *Programme* 162
10.3 *Concluding Remarks* 167

Index 170

Figures and Tables

Figures

2.1	Accessibility to Major Centres in Greater Manchester by Road and Public Transport. Travel Time in Minutes.	28
3.1	Index of Global Passenger Transport Activity, 2000–2050, Index of Pkm (2000 = 100)	40
3.2	Index of Global Freight Transport Activity, 2000–2050, Index of Tkm (2000 = 100)	41
3.3	Global Mode Split, 2000 and 2050: Halfway Case between High and Low Scenarios (%)	41
4.1	Transport Technology Potential Model (Adapted from Geerlings & Rienstra 2003)	59
5.1	Paradigm Shifts in UK Transport Policy 1945–2015	70
6.1	Central–Local Decision-Making Cycle	101
8.1	Mobility Domains	131

Tables

2.1	Comparison of STPM, Kyoto Greenhouse Gas and Transport CO_2 Emissions Reduction Targets	24
2.2	Workplace Accessibility: Proportion of Population within 30, 60 and 120 Minutes' Journey Time – Average for Greater Manchester (2006)	30
3.1	Major Findings of the 2012 Urban Mobility Report (498 US Urban Areas)	47

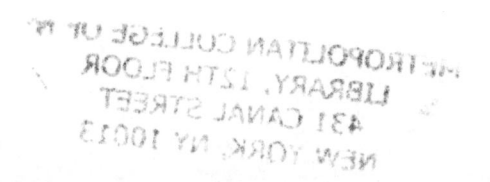

Boxes

1.1	Towards Sustainable Mobility – Three Propositions	7
2.1	City Structure and Transport – Four Typologies (Adapted from Thompson 1977)	18
2.2	Kyoto Protocol and Greenhouse Gas Reduction Targets	25
3.1	Chartered Institute of Logistics and Transport: Vision 2035 Report – Findings and Recommendations	37
3.2	Capital Congestion: Projected Population and Travel Growth in London by 2050	50
8.1	The 'Mobilities' Paradigm	123
8.2	Cycling as a Social Movement	134

Preface

I began thinking about this topic in 2006, soon after returning to the UK following thirteen years working overseas, mainly in the USA. At that time the UK transport sector was focused on the deliberations of the Stern report on climate change and how to reduce carbon emissions. It was an interesting period, and the casual observer may have formed the opinion that sustainable transport was the settled policy; that the UK was embarking on a radical shift that would wean motorists off their car dependency, ushering in a new era of collective transport characterised by more use of public transport, cycling and walking, not to mention new shared mobility models such as car sharing and car clubs.

On closer scrutiny, however, this sustainable transport 'promised land' turns out to be overstated. For the reality is that sustainable transport as a policy has not fundamentally changed how the UK travels or how its transport systems work. There have been some victories and minor changes to travel behaviour, but overall, sustainable transport remains wishful thinking. Despite calls for sustainable travel programmes such as Smarter Choices to go mainstream, the public has not (yet) bought in to the concept and neither has the Government (at least not wholeheartedly). This is because the sustainable transport agenda means little to the general public, who view mobility and transport differently from those responsible for planning and managing our transport services. Briefly, sustainable transport is about curbing travel, or at least channelling it to more energy-efficient modes, whereas most people see their mobility and means of satisfying this via the transport system as an essential element in their lifestyle, which they want to optimise to meet their needs rather than be constrained in their travel choices. The planners and the public are talking in different idioms and end up talking past one another rather than engaging constructively.

This was the situation I observed as a practising transport consultant advising on various transport schemes. It is not all conflict, and in many cases there is a meeting of minds, normally on specific scheme components or over technical matters, but on the bigger policy issues and measures the two cultures are miles apart. I began to research why this is so, and why professional views in favour of sustainable transport do not sit easy with the public, especially motorists, and what if anything can be done to bring the two sides closer together. This turned out to be a bigger and longer task than I had envisaged: the result is this book. It is my contribution to the sustainable transport debate, or as I interpret it, sustainable mobility. There are no easy solutions and the prescriptions I propose are not perfect, only second best. Nevertheless, I believe they are better than the alternatives and will, therefore, be more acceptable to the public and policy makers. My prognosis follows from the diagnosis of the transport and mobility problems facing all societies that desire increased mobility. Transport planners may think mobility is not desirable, but the public take a different view. This may be unpalatable to some but is a reality borne out by the evidence. In coming to a resolution we need to understand the context within which mobility is accomplished – geographical, social, economic and political. My research started out as a study into transport policy and planning, but of necessity has branched into other disciplines and methods as I sought answers to the mobility conundrum.

The focus of the book is primarily on the UK, but I also had in mind an international audience who would be interested in how transport policy and practice was being implemented in the UK, not least because they may be grappling with similar issues of how to deliver sustainable transport with growing demands for mobility. In some respects the UK is leading the debate on how to reconcile these competing objectives, and this book will hopefully offer perspectives and lessons that could be transferrable to other countries. Where appropriate I have used case studies from other nations, including the USA and OECD member states, to compare with the UK. The book's primary audience is students of transport planning but it should also appeal to graduates and researchers in other disciplines who are involved in this area but have only limited knowledge of transport methods and techniques. Transport problems and policy initiatives are rising up the political agenda in many societies and this work should therefore be of interest to scholars of policy making in related disciplines such as urban studies, environmental policy, social policy and political-economics. Some understanding of transport policy and planning issues is assumed, or at least can be deduced from the text. Likewise I have chosen not to bombard the reader with masses of data or statistics that may obfuscate the key points under discussion: rather I have been selective and judicious in using information that elucidates the analysis sufficiently to support the arguments being made. The references and sources quoted in the body of the work provide a wealth of data and information for those interested in more detail.

John C. Sutton
January, 2015

Acknowledgements

The research and discovery phase for this book involved conversations with a number of friends and colleagues, who unwittingly provided a sounding board for some of the ideas and topics that ultimately made it into the contents. I hope the themes explored will resonate with them and that they will forgive me if I have appropriated their point of view over a beer or a glass of wine!

I am indebted to Kris Beuret OBE, Director of Social Research Associates and Commissioner for the Independent Transport Commission (ITC), who through her work on the ITC and in particular the Why Travel? Project, provided valuable insights on how human travel and mobility might be changing in response to technological and social developments. Dr Mark Brown, a friend and colleague from our early consulting days at Halcrow Fox and Associates (and now Business Development Director, Consulting at Amey) shared his knowledge and experience of transport economics and appraisal and their impact on transport policy. The 'Knowledge Centre' at the Chartered Institute of Logistics and Transport lived up to its title and was a mine of information that I used extensively, on-site and on-line, and must be one of the best libraries for material on transport anywhere. I'm also grateful to the TAS Partnership Ltd for providing opportunities to work on a variety of projects that have kept me up to date with transport information technology and its deployment in private and public sector organisations. The draft was reviewed by Dr David Gillingwater, a former mentor and colleague from Loughborough University, who's insightful and forthright comments were much appreciated and are reflected in the final version. I am grateful to Nicole Solano, Commissioning Editor for Planning and Urban Design publications at Routledge and Judith Newlin, Editorial Assistant, for guiding me through the publishing process.

The illustrations were derived from a variety of sources and I'm thankful to the publishers for permission to reproduce the materials here. Figure 2.1 illustrates maps of accessibility by car and public transport prepared by Basemap Ltd using Open Government License including map data from the Ordnance Survey. Other information derived from UK public sector sources is published using Open Government License 3.0. Figures 3.1, 3.2 and 3.3 are taken from the 2011 *Transport Outlook* report prepared by the International Transport Forum of the Organisation for Economic Co-operation and Development. Figure 4.1 Transport Technology Potential Model is adapted from a diagram produced by Geerlings and Rienstra for a paper in *Transport Planning and Technology* (Taylor & Francis 2003). Table 3.1 is extracted from the 2012 Urban Mobility Report produced by the Texas A&M Transportation Institute. The Chartered Institute of Logistics and Transport kindly permitted me to summarise their *Vision 2035* report in Chapter 3. All other illustrations are my own work and, as with the text, any errors or omissions are my responsibility.

Finally, this endeavour would not have been possible without the encouragement and support of my wife, Jean Taylor Sutton, whose forbearance over many months and several re-writes was a source of inspiration. She deserves a lot of credit for remaining true to the project whenever I felt doubts and frustrations with the lack of progress.

Preamble
A Vision of Mobility and Transport in 2035

By 2035 most vehicles are powered by electricity, hydrogen or a hybrid mixture of electricity/hydrogen/natural gas (mostly in the form of compressed natural gas (CNG) or liquefied petroleum gas (LPG), referred to as autogas). Peak oil was reached in the mid-2020s (the point when production went into decline), so while there is still plenty of oil to be extracted it is used primarily for heating, producing electricity and non-fuel products. Autogas and CNG are converted from natural gas, which by 2035 is still abundant but expensive to convert for mass vehicle use; hence their use in heavier goods vehicles and buses. The barriers to public acceptability of electric vehicles, such as range and recharging facilities, have been overcome with charging points installed in most public parking places as well as booster inductive loops installed beneath the road surface that charge the vehicle while 'on the move'.

The switch to ultra-low-emission vehicles powered by renewable energy sourced largely from wind, tides and nuclear power has met the carbon-reduction targets mandated in international protocols but has not solved other transportation problems such as congestion, collisions and affordability. For these, government policy has deployed technology and new travel rules that regulate mobility via a combination of price and rationing to reduce transport demand. A new logistics regime ensures that demand does not exceed the available supply of road space or transit services throughout the day. Trips are booked in advance directly with a supplier or through transport brokers, called mobility managers. New mobility management companies have emerged to manage travel for individuals and firms. Car journeys inside designated travel zones (TZs) are not monitored, but trips crossing TZ boundaries have to be requested and a fee is payable when crossing cordon points on the roads connecting the TZs. As all cars and trucks are equipped with global positioning systems (GPS) and mobile communications, fees are automatically deducted. A fine is levied if trips are made without permission, and can lead to withdrawal of driving license for repeat offences. The number of cars allowed inside the TZ in any time period, typically an hour, is determined based on monitoring and modelling of movements within the zone. This does not always provide a level of service commensurate with free-flow traffic conditions, but fine-tuning normally results in low levels of congestion and travel time reliability between points in the TZs. Transport planning practice builds some redundancy into the network models to allow for perturbations caused by weather, incidents or unauthorised incursions. TZ size varies by urban and rural area (the latter typically much larger). As well as booking trips to an area, requests can be made for parking in car parks wherein the driver is directed to the designated parking space (a time window for arrival and departure is allowed and any violation results in the car being removed and a hefty fine imposed).

Longer distance car trips also require advanced booking for a specified route. Travelling at peak times costs more than in the off-peak. Motorway journeys are semi-automated: cars and trucks join the motorway at specific junctions within a time window (5 minutes at peak times) and drive along the entry/exit lane (formerly called the 'hard shoulder') until instructed to move into the motorway cruise lanes. Once in these lanes the vehicle telematics takes over and cars travel in convoy at a constant speed until the exit junction is reached, where the reverse manoeuvre takes place and the driver is once more in control. While on the motorway, drivers and their passengers can watch TV, use the internet or make calls via their mobile digital e-commerce device or 'console' (which used to be called a smartphone), which now comes in all manner of shapes and sizes from wearable wrist bands and eye glasses to notepads, and are connected via the internet 'cloud' to a myriad of digital services. The telematics in the vehicle also connect to the console and communicate instructions from roadside instruments and overhead drones that monitor traffic. The telematics automatically adjust the vehicle's speed and movement in response to sensors placed around the vehicle that monitor the external environment. These sensors ensure that the vehicle keeps on track and also assist the driver on local roads to avoid collisions or other dangerous situations. It is now law that all vehicles include speed limiters that are activated automatically by the satnav device (a standard feature of all in-car telematics) so that posted travel speeds for the class of road are never exceeded.

Trips that are arranged at short notice, or when there is a need to travel in an emergency, can be accommodated because of the redundancy built into the network. Except for emergencies, these trips are charged a premium price. This system of journey pricing is similar to how it works on the railways and buses. Most journeys on public transport are guaranteed a seat. Commuters no longer have to endure cramped standing conditions. A few standing passengers are allowed, but generally all seats are booked in advance. The only exception is urban bus, metro and London Underground services. Commuters who travel regularly with season tickets have seat reservations on specific services, and because the number of commuters is known in advance train services are provided as limited stop services. More regular stopping services are used by those buying tickets at short notice (if they can't get on a fast service) and by commuters opting to catch a train at a different time. If commuters cannot get a place on a train they may be required to work from home where feasible – something employers are flexible about and the Government encourages. Remote working at home is possible given the broadband connections that all households have. This is also where the mobility manager can assist. Employers engage mobility managers to create a personal travel plan for their employees and make all the travel arrangements; employees can also use these companies for non-work related trips. The mobility managers act like personal travel agents for regular and ad hoc trips.

In major cities the bus services operate as they have always done with no reserved seats. However, fares are now regulated, as they are on the railways, which is part of the compact that the Government reached with the public as part of the new mobility policy. In suburban and rural areas buses no longer run to fixed schedules, except for intercity buses, and are provided by a range of flexible transport services that respond to demands and pick people up at a suitable point near their origin. These flexible services use a variety of providers (bus operators, community transport, carpooling and shared taxis) and like their urban counterparts charge a fixed price based on distance or zone(s) travelling in. They have proved popular, and it is possible to book a door-to-door journey, including connecting to a train or flight with a reserved seat on each leg of the journey. By 2035 information and communication systems are mature and integrated into all business processes, so the traveller has great confidence in the reliability of the system by whichever mode is being used.

Another advance is in how payments are made. Cash or cheques are rarely used in transactions these days, and even credit cards are going out of fashion. 'Money' is stored on the console as a pre-paid stored value or acting as a debit/credit card. The console functions as a personal node on the cloud, to which the traveller has access to a range of services including transferring funds and making payments. The console is also a location device with built-in GPS and transmitter so people's locations as well as vehicles can be monitored. This is used to determine how many passengers are in a car, for example, when calculating mobility points for specific journeys. Delays in individual trip schedules are detected and journeys can be re-scheduled proactively, and the traveller notified accordingly. Thus, if a train is running late and a bus connection is missed, a taxi or other service will be arranged at no extra cost to the passenger (the extra cost is picked up by the provider not fulfilling their part of the schedule). Special transport brokers manage this aspect of the service – referred to as total journey management – and negotiate fees and penalty payments with the transport companies and mobility managers.

Carpooling incurs fewer mobility miles than single occupant journeys, as do trips using shared vehicles organised by car clubs (some mobility managers even run their own car clubs). Hence, collective car ownership or car clubs are popular and fewer households own personal cars. When entering a vehicle (car, bus, train or plane) the console registers your presence with the vehicle's telematics. The console acts like a mobile passport. If you don't have it you may be denied access to the service. It adds up the miles you travel on different modes of transport so that you know how many mobility miles you have used/have left as part of your annual allowance. Mobility quotas can be exceeded but at great expense.

The mobility miles allowance is part of the compact between the Government and people. The trade-off is basically restrictions on freedom of travel and increased surveillance on mechanised modes in return for improved quality and reliability of service at fixed prices, with some flexibility to accommodate last-minute trips. Each adult (aged 16 or over) is given 7000 'mobility miles' per annum, which is calculated by factoring the average car mileage in the UK. These mobility miles can be used to travel by different modes at fixed rates. For travel by private car, for example, the miles are pro-rated 1:1 and 1:2 for using a car club or rideshare service. On buses the ratio is 1:4 (i.e. 4 bus miles uses 1 mobility mile) and on trains it varies from 1:5 for commuter trips to 1:10 for intercity travel. There is thus a big incentive to use those modes that incur fewer miles. At the end of the year, surplus miles can be traded and sold to other people, through a mobility manager, or cashed in with the Government (at below market rates). People who walk or cycle a lot may acquire a significant number of unused miles and therefore be financially rewarded for their environmentally friendly travel behaviour. This policy encourages more active travel with commensurate health benefits. People with disabilities receive a higher mobility allowance, reflecting their mobility needs when travelling independently; taxis and other accessible transport operators receive more miles for carrying people with disabilities, so there is a financial incentive to transport these people. Disabled and elderly people with concessionary mobility miles can also transfer more miles as passengers, which acts as an incentive for family members, friends, car clubs, etc., to include these people in their travel plans.

Summation: Two Hypotheses for a Sustainable Mobility Future

The vision described above is designed to constrain the total amount of mobility to the capacity of the transport system. It is not perfect and it doesn't always work flawlessly, but it is a more equitable means of allocating mobility than one based on rationing by congestion (the current practice) or price alone. As described in the rest of this document, the technologies to enable this vision are already in place or under development. What is problematic is whether this policy of travel demand management will be politically attractive and acceptable to the electorate. Two hypotheses are put forward which suggest that they will be.

The **first hypothesis** is that mobility management is fairer, equitable and more affordable than a system of road tolls or other road pricing solutions and for these reasons will be more acceptable to the majority of the public. As congestion, pollution and other adverse impacts of transport increase, the public and policy makers will become more open to radical solutions. The damage to the economy caused by these ills will also force governments to act boldly. They will look to solutions in other countries and find that traffic control and mobility management is high on the agenda across the developed and developing world, with the latter finding it easier to implement radical solutions using the latest information and communications technologies with fewer political obstacles, especially in countries with less liberal or social democratic forms of government. This will give them an edge in the race to resolve mobility problems to the benefit of their economies.

The **second hypothesis** is that high levels of mobility – of goods and people – are essential for a successful market-oriented economy and in order to preserve this, the polity and the public will be forced to make compromises. Societies that follow the capitalist economic model will be impelled by the forces of globalisation to adopt the mobility practices of those countries with successful economies if they are to compete effectively. In a reversal of economic development trends in the 20th century, when developed countries provided the model for developing countries to follow, in the 21st century developing nations such as Brazil, Russia, India, China and South Africa (referred to as the BRICS countries) will pursue their own political-economic models to manage public policy issues like mobility, and will fare better being less constrained by pluralist political systems. Neo-liberal economies will be forced to adopt practices pioneered in these less democratic nations. They will sacrifice some of their freedom of mobility in order to compete effectively. This will provide a boost for public transport and car-sharing services, which will be planned and regulated as part of the mobility mix.

These hypotheses and the vision that flows from them are justified in the chapters that follow.

Part I
Unsustainable Transport
Congested Cities, Contested Policies

1 Introduction
The Challenge of Mobility

1.1 The Age of Mobility

A little over 50 years ago a report on *Traffic in Towns* was published by the UK Government (Ministry of Transport 1963). Written by Colin Buchanan, it became an influential guide to accommodating the motor car in towns and cities. The report identified the trade-offs required between allowing accessibility by car, the effects on the built environment and the costs involved. It was difficult to accommodate traffic in historic town centres, for example, without costly measures to mitigate their impact; hence cheaper traffic management measures and pedestrianisation schemes were preferred. In other centres where the environment was of lower quality, redevelopment was possible to accommodate cars in multi-storey car parks as part of shopping malls. Thus, the scene was set for the segregation of cars in towns where the environmental impact and cost were justifiable.

Fast forward to the present day and the legacy of *Traffic in Towns* is evident throughout the country. Where traffic constraint has not been applied, car-oriented development and traffic congestion is pervasive. Despite our attempts to re-model the city and accommodate cars, the results are less than impressive. The car has accelerated suburban sprawl, contributed to the demise of some town centres – contrary to what Buchanan intended – increased congestion despite massive investment in roads and traffic management schemes, caused thousands of deaths and injuries and polluted the environment to such an extent that transport is a major contributor to climate change through carbon emissions. It is also recognised as a factor in promoting less healthy lifestyles and obesity. And these problems are chronic, with no sign that they will be alleviated any time soon.

These problems were predicted by some commentators in the years following the Buchanan Report, highlighting that changes in car ownership and mobility would have far-reaching effects on society at large and the political economy of transport, specifically the demand for more road infrastructure and the redevelopment of cities to accommodate the car

(Townroe 1974). The sceptics were prescient in forecasting the wider implications of the car on politics and social culture, and through the 1970s an increasing number of academics and analysts began to question whether car ownership and use was good for society, arguing that more convivial modes of public transport were more appropriate to urban lifestyles (for examples see Plowden 1972, *Towns Against Traffic,* and Bendixson 1974, *Instead of Cars*).

Their concerns, however, rarely resonated with the general public, politicians, opinion formers and the majority of the transport profession, who at that time viewed rising levels of prosperity and mobility in the post-war years as a positive trend and part of the modernisation of society – broadening social mobility and spatial horizons through greater travel freedom and boosting economic performance. In short, auto-mobility was regarded as a liberating force that since the 1950s had benefitted those on lower incomes and not just the middle class. But as mass car ownership spread, so did the problems associated with traffic growth – pollution, congestion, accidents and community severance. In response governments and the auto industry have put into place a range of mitigation measures that have improved the safety and fuel efficiency of automobiles, together with better traffic management. However, they have been less effective in tackling congestion, pollution and wider environmental impacts, the social exclusion of those without access to a car, and the rising cost of transport (public and private) to the individual and the public purse. The outlook does not look good, especially given the rise in population and traffic forecasted for the decades ahead. What was once seen as a liberating mode of transport is now regarded by many policy makers and opinion formers as a nuisance that needs to be regulated and controlled more effectively if we are to make our cities more liveable.

The dilemma facing politicians and policy makers is how to accomplish this. There are solutions on offer – explored in later chapters – but they all present challenges and require hard choices. These are problematic to politicians and arouse suspicions among members of the public, business and other constituencies who fear that they will lose out in whatever bargain is struck. In short, there is no consensus among politicians, professionals or the public: indeed, transport policy and planning has become more contentious and is likely to become more political and contested in future. More than in most other countries, transport policy and planning in the UK has become a battleground among competing ideologies and policy discourses. Transport and mobility has become an arena in which competing political philosophies are put into practice, often behind a veneer of economic theory and environmentalism. The result is gridlock on the streets as well as in policy.

On one side is the sustainable transport narrative, which aims to reduce mobility by improving accessibility by non-auto modes and the remodelling of cities around smarter travel and smarter urban development.[1] We may characterise this as the 'convivial transport' movement, which emphasises public transport, cycling and walking solutions. Juxtaposing this is the automobility culture, which idealises the conspicuous consumption of mobile paraphernalia – cars, air travel and mobile telephony. Sustainable transport is the counterfactual to the mobile lives that most people aspire to in a culture driven by competition and market forces. Convivial philosophies of smarter travel and sustainable transport are the antithesis of a 'competitive transport' system. These two discourses currently dominate transport policy and give rise to contradictory solutions. Convivial transport advocates smarter choices, regulation and public policy interventions to deliver a more sustainable transport system. Competitive transport supports liberalisation and privatisation of transport services with market economics driving transport policy, such as road pricing solutions to choke off excess demand. The contradictions evident in these two approaches reflect different views or ideologies on the role of transport in society. Is it to support economic growth, travel choice and personal mobility? Or is it to promote equal accessibility, environmental justice and more collective transport solutions? The current narrative among politicians, and broadly accepted by the transport profession, is that we can do both, or at least mix-and-match policies sufficiently enough to deliver a (convivial) sustainable transport solution within a (competitive) transport system. This is embedded in current transport practice and the policy discourse of sustainable transport.

This discourse and the accompanying narrative constitutes 'Plan A' for tackling climate change, traffic congestion, pollution, road safety and other transport issues. This plan also includes measures to boost the economy by selective investments in road, public transport, airports and port schemes. As will be discussed later, the Government and some transport organisations see no contradiction between policies that boost mobility with policies that aim to reduce travel demand. If these policies fail to meet CO_2 and congestion-reduction targets, there is a 'Plan B', long advocated by some elements of the transport sector: namely, congestion pricing for road users. This policy, successfully implemented in some cities, is regarded by its supporters as the only feasible solution to matching demand and supply, and providing the revenue stream for more investment in infrastructure. It may be a sound economic solution, at least in theory, but runs into a number of political and cultural barriers, which so far have restricted its deployment in the UK to central London. Perhaps its biggest problem is that it is a regressive tax on people's mobility and would have major impacts on business as well as individuals. Outside the ivory towers of academia, policy think tanks and a few transport lobbies, there is little enthusiasm among politicians or the public.

The policy conflation of convivial and competitive transport measures (in Plan A, Plan B or a combination thereof) is a compromise that falls short of what is required to meet sustainable transport goals or deliver sufficient supply-side improvements to mitigate congestion and gridlock. Integrating the two policy perspectives requires balancing social consumption and social investment. Convivial transport solutions do not adequately address social consumption needs of the population or the political-economic demands of capitalism. A competitive transport system cannot keep up with the demands for social investment, leading to increasing congestion and inefficiency. Eventually the transport system will collapse under the weight of its internal contradiction; that is, investment cannot keep up with congestion (Nair 2011).[2]

The premise of this book is that both Plan A and Plan B are not deliverable for economic and political reasons, and consequently are not robust enough to resolve the transport and mobility challenges the country faces. And these issues are not just confined to the UK but are international in scope. Wherever rising mobility expectations combine with more affluence and population increase, the consequences are insufferable levels of congestion that will become critical in the next decade. This book outlines a 'Plan C', which takes elements of the other two plans and adds a key requirement to limit mobility demand to the transport supply available and thus control the level of congestion. It accomplishes this through the application of information and communication technologies allied to a strategy of mobility management. Unlike the other two plans, this policy is progressive, fairer and more equitable. The rationale for this solution is explained in the chapters that follow.

According to the current sustainable transport narrative, the most pressing problem facing transport is the environmental impact of auto-mobility and specifically the problem of carbon emissions, which are contributing towards anthropogenic climate change. In consequence, agreements have been reached to reduce CO_2 and other emissions from cars by means of improving fuel efficiency, capturing tailpipe emissions, switching to electric propulsion systems, car-sharing schemes and promoting the use of alternative modes. Notwithstanding the reality of climate change, the pending crisis in transport is not environmental pollution but congestion. Congestion will create the conditions for unsustainability mobility, which will impact on communities across the globe before the world's climate reaches the forecast rise of two degrees Celsius by 2050.

My prediction is that congestion is already a factor in economic and social organisation and will become ever more limiting over the next two decades. So much so, that by the 2030s the politics and policies of transport and mobility will alter radically, ushering in a new sustainable mobility settlement. This will contain some of the actions and initiatives advocated by the sustainable transport lobby, with two fundamental differences: firstly mobility freedoms will be sacrificed in order to preserve economic and social stability; and secondly environmental impacts will be mitigated by advances in technology. How this will be accomplished is discussed in the following chapters, which examine the future of transport and mobility through three propositions – see Box 1.1.

Box 1.1 Towards Sustainable Mobility – Three Propositions

The first proposition is that resolving transport and mobility problems related to increasing congestion, travel cost, safety and climate change (based on carbon emissions) will be significant drivers of transport policy and the conflicts between them will produce more radical solutions than has hitherto been contemplated. Smarter travel measures may mitigate some mobility problems but only succeed in delaying the inevitable mobility crisis.

The second proposition is that technology will play an increasing role in managing transport systems and shaping travel demand. Location-aware technologies such as global positioning systems (GPS) will be pervasive in each stage of travel and help to transform how transport systems are managed and travel demands are met.

The third proposition is that, following on from the above, mobility management will supersede accessibility as the principal activity of transport planning. Logistics services that embrace location-aware technologies will be deployed to match demand to the available supply of transport resources. This will be inevitable in order to manage and control excess mobility. In this process, mobility will be rationed by a combination of price and availability. Those suffering from mobility problems or poor accessibility will be compensated by a combination of door-to-door services where transport is required and home delivery of products and services where travel is not essential.

Mobility is too important to be left to market forces. Like education and health, mobility has emerged as a public good that post-industrial capitalism needs in order to sustain economic development, access to resources (especially labour) and to generate the capital (profits, rents) required to reinvest in new products and services. This is why uber-capitalist cities such as London, New York and Hong Kong – agglomerations of capital formation – have invested massively in creating mass transit systems underwritten by government agencies. Without these extensive public transport systems, these centres of capital formation and distribution would not thrive. It is ironic that successful capitalist cities that promote free markets and competition are reliant on 'socialist' transport services for their very survival (with the public sector taking on the risk rather than the private sector). If it were otherwise, the cities, as capitalist enterprises, would not exist in anywhere near their current scale and form, and it is this contradiction that explains why mobility will continue to be subsidised to support the expansion of cities. City expansion – horizontally, vertically and through densification – causes more congestion, which requires further measures to maintain a level of mobility commensurate with the viability of the city.

Mobility, once a symbol of freedom and liberation, is now exploited to maintain a viable urban capitalist economy. The burden of mobility will increasingly be borne by the consumer – as passengers or purchasers of goods – through longer journey times and more expensive travel. Mobility domains or classes will evolve, with those in the lower mobility classes being more constrained than those higher up the mobility ladder. We already see how visceral curtailing people's mobility can be: witness, for example, the furore over plans to raise fuel taxes and airport charges, implement road tolls, increase commuter rail fares, and deploy speed cameras and other measures to restrain mobility. As congestion increases and mobility is threatened, further conflicts over what to do about it can be expected. There are no easy solutions and no single constituency that can claim hegemony over transport policy. A sustainable mobility system will require a coalition of the willing, who are prepared to act in the national interest rather than their own selfish interest. This will not be easy and will require political leadership. It is not just the future of the transport system that is at stake, but the economic and social systems that have come to be dependent on mobility to function effectively.

1.2 The Paradox of Transport and Mobility

One of the intriguing findings of observing traffic in cities is known as the Downs–Thomson paradox, which states that the equilibrium speed of car traffic on the road network is determined by the average door-to-door speed of equivalent journeys by (rail-based or otherwise segregated) public transport (Mogridge et al. 1987). It follows that increasing road capacity can actually make overall congestion on the road worse. This occurs when the shift from public transport causes a disinvestment in that mode such that the operator either reduces frequency of service or raises fares to cover costs. This shifts additional passengers into cars. Ultimately the public transport system may be eliminated and congestion on the original (expanded) road become worse than before.

The general conclusion is that expanding a road system as a remedy to congestion is not only ineffective, but often counterproductive. This is also known as the Lewis–Mogridge Position and was derived by Mogridge following a case study of London (Mogridge 1990) and by Lewis in studying mass transit in the USA (Lewis and Williams 1999). Mogridge coined the phrase 'traffic expands to meet the available road space', which neatly sums up the paradox. It doesn't mean that no road building should occur, only that it will induce demand and the consequences should be fully understood for private and public transport users. The Lewis–Mogridge Position is often used to understand problems such as congested roads in cities and on motorways, as well as the success of schemes such as the London congestion charge, which reduce the level of demand. The position is not confined to private transport. Mogridge concluded that all road investment in a congested urban area will have the effect of reducing the average speed of the transport system as a whole – road and public transport (ibid.).

However, according to Downs this link between average speed on public transport and private transport 'only applies to regions in which the vast majority of peak-hour commuting is done on rapid transit systems with separate rights of way' (Downs 1992). Central London is an example, since in 2001 around 85% of all morning peak-period commuters into that area used public transport (including 77% on commuter rail, the Underground and Docklands Light Railway) and only 11% used private cars. When peak-hour travel equilibrium has been reached between the rail/metro system and the major commuting roads, then the travel time required for any given trip is roughly equal on both modes.

The potential for induced demand was posited as the 'Iron Law of Congestion' by Downs. His book *Stuck in Traffic* detailed the economic disadvantages of traffic congestion and proposed road pricing as the only effective means of alleviating it (Downs 1992). Downs' book was denounced by traffic engineers for its insistence on the futility of congestion relief measures (also known as the Mogridge–Lewis Position). However, enough of his gloomy predictions about congestion were proven right that he subsequently published a sequel, *Still Stuck in Traffic* (Downs 2004). Downs' recommendations are starting to see implementation, largely in the form of high-occupancy toll (HOT) lanes in the medians of crowded US freeways and through congestion pricing, already implemented in several cities around the world, including London, Singapore and Oslo (although not, it should be noted, in North America, where Downs was largely writing about).

Mogridge's observations in the 1980s were during a time when urban public transport was struggling to cope with the demands put upon it, and users were switching to cars but finding that their travel speeds were no greater than when horse-drawn buses were in use a hundred years earlier (about nine miles per hour). The point is that improving travel speeds on public transport, especially metros and commuter rail services, lifts the travel speeds of all transport modes. Since then, major cities such as London and Paris have invested massively in enhancing their mass transit systems with improved travel speeds, and have attracted a lot more passengers. Even so, car journey speeds have not improved significantly in London, despite the imposition of congestion charging in the central area and a reduction in traffic of around 15%. This could be because the road system was so overloaded that it will take a substantially bigger reduction to see any increase in travel speeds; or it could be that despite the improvements in public transport capacity this has not always resulted in faster journey times; and it could also be the case that commuters are travelling longer distances to work to take advantage of faster journey times compared to car users, who follow routes where the travel time advantages of rail and metro are not as great.

For these reasons the travel equilibrium theory is not universally accepted. Interestingly, however, the recent surge in cycling in London, supported by cycling-friendly measures such as designated cycling routes, is attracting commuters who otherwise would have used bus, metro or rail for at least part of their journey, and areas of central London suffer from cycling congestion at peak times of the day. Indeed, congestion is also evident among pedestrians using transport interchanges such as Underground and rail stations, as well as on streets that serve as major pedestrian thoroughfares. Central business districts of many cities have severe congestion to such an extent that mobility is a challenge whatever mode of transport is used. Our cities are literally becoming too crowded, especially at popular tourist attractions, shopping areas, transport interchanges, and other sites at specific times of the day or week. Some of the congestion is acute, but much of it is chronic and does not lend itself to easy solutions. The success of central places feeds on itself and becomes more intense until gridlock prevents further expansion. At this point measures are needed to control the mobility flow into the location, including redirecting demand to alternate destinations if available.

The paradox of mobility – induced demand to fill the capacity available – is a growing problem in cities throughout the world, especially in large cities, which are getting bigger in population size and geographic extent. The potential size of the induced demand as a result of population growth or increases in disposable income is exponential to city scale. This is important, as more than half the world's population now live in urban areas and city scale is continuing to increase. Cities with more than one million people were exceptional in the 20th century but are now commonplace. The number of people living in urban areas is forecast to more than double between 2010 and 2050 (accommodating 70% of the world's population), requiring three times the land area than present (Shlomo 2012).[3] Most of this growth will occur in Africa and Asia.

The concentration of people and activities in cities requires high levels of mobility in order to function effectively. The dilemma or paradox facing the city is that expanding economic activity requires more transport and mobility, which becomes more problematic to deliver: space is in short supply, as is finance to pay for transport systems to support the economic development. In consequence, cities face a crisis of congestion that they are finding increasingly difficult to overcome.[4] We may be facing what Baeton refers to as the 'tragedy of the highways', analogous to Hardin's 'tragedy of the commons', whereby individual actions to maximise their own position ultimately lead to the destruction of the common land, where everyone loses (Baeton 2000). The 'tragedy of the highways' is especially relevant to the debate over carbon emissions from transport, where regrettably some governments and many people are still in denial over the effect of CO_2 build-up on climate change. Failure to tackle CO_2 concentrations in the atmosphere will lead to global warming, with major upheavals in regional climates and some areas getting warmer while others get colder, and ironically could trigger a new ice age.

Just as the debate on climate change has become political, so the debate on mobility will rise up the political agenda. A convivial transport policy suggests that measures that promote access for all and sustainable travel behaviour are desirable, but these are contradictory to a political-economic model that places a premium on travel choice and personal mobility. Mobility provides one of the few mechanisms whereby people can leverage power over their life chances, economic and social wellbeing. Politically this translates into a powerful voice for lobbies supporting mobility, especially by car and train, on issues ranging from taxes on fuel, rail fares, fixing pot holes in the road to strategic road and rail investments. As the majority of voters in the UK live in car-owning and commuter-rail-using households, this represents a large constituency that politicians cannot ignore. Businesses also rely on mobility for their logistics and their workforce to function effectively, so the economic and political power of the mobility lobby is substantial.[5] This is also evident in other countries.

This presents a huge challenge for transport planners and activists who advocate alternative solutions such as smarter choices. They have to use persuasive methods to get people and businesses to change their travel behaviour because coercive measures are likely to run into considerable opposition, as demonstrated in referenda on congestion charging in Edinburgh, Manchester and West London, which were rejected by significant margins. Likewise, attempts to introduce workplace parking levies have been ignored except in Nottingham. The Labour Government of 1997–2001 attempted to introduce coercive measures to curtail car use but backed away in the face of opposition from motorists and other auto lobbies (see Chapter 5 for a fuller discussion).

1.3 Expanding Mobility and the Pending Congestion Crisis

As transport problems worsen – through unbearable levels of congestion and rising cost of mobility expressed in fuel prices and fares – a tipping point will be reached. It will become evident that the impact on the economy and society is unsustainable, and radical action will be required that will unite policy discourses and the political economy in a concerted programme of measures to keep people and freight moving. Some researchers see this point occurring when peak oil production is reached – estimates range from 2012 to the mid-2020s (Gilbert and Perl, for example, claim a transport revolution is required in response to oil depletion (Gilbert and Perl 2010)). However, recent discoveries of shale gas and oil look likely to extend the petroleum reserves for several decades notwithstanding further exploitation of proven fossil fuel reservoirs in challenging environments, such as in the deep oceans and the Arctic. Others point to the effects of climate change, including global warming, and rising sea levels that could threaten many coastal cities, as the catalyst for changing our transport systems and travel behaviour.

The more likely catalyst for change is that current trends in congestion and rising costs of mobility will seriously impact on the ability of society to function efficiently, causing a major re-think on transport policy and measures to keep the economy moving. The pressures will come from the bottom as well as the top. Internal stresses will be felt most acutely by people trying to get to work or other activities; they will experience increasing delays and unreliability in journey times. This is inevitable as the population expands faster than we can increase transport supply, and this applies to public transport as well as to road improvements. Businesses and freight companies will face chronic problems in managing the supply chain and will need to build redundancy (at extra cost) into their warehousing and distribution systems in order to preserve resilience. External pressures will come from trading partners and enterprises beyond our shores who don't experience the same levels of congestion or cost and consequently operate in a more robust and efficient market. Their success in managing mobility will exert pressure on the UK to conform to best practice overseas in order to compete effectively. In conclusion, the only way to preserve a competitive, mobile society is by matching demand to the available supply. The only question is, which is the best method to accomplish this?

The remaining chapters in this book explore this question from a number of dimensions – transport planning and policy, technology, political economy, culture and sociology. Fundamentally, mobility is a key determinant of travel behaviour. We live in a mobile society tuned to satisfying mobility by whatever means we have at our disposal. In western societies this means the car first, buses second, then rail, followed by cycling and walking. Cycling is currently moving up the transport agenda and may challenge the bus for attention and resources, but it is unlikely to seriously challenge rail or car modes. In developing countries mobility is still predominantly accomplished by walking, cycling, bus, various forms of paratransit, trains, motorbikes and scooters, and finally cars for the elite.

The situation there is changing rapidly: each motorcyclist is a potential car owner, and as prosperity expands among the lower classes the demand for mechanised modes of transport will grow. The mobility gap is widening between those with the resources to afford auto-mobility and those dependent on non-auto modes for their mobility. This is exacerbated by dispersed forms of development that de-couple residential and business location, together with changes in culture and lifestyle aspirations that place a premium on mobility. This mobile culture is not sustainable and will reach a crisis point as congestion approaches gridlock. As explored in later chapters, the gridlock we face is not just manifested on the transport systems but in policy discourses and the political economy.

Notes

1 These programmes go under a number of labels, including 'smarter choices', 'active travel', 'transit oriented design', 'new urbanism' and the catch-all 'sustainable transport'. These programmes are not exclusive and include many of the same elements packaged in different formats.
2 Nair argues that emergent economies such as India cannot sustain western levels of economic activity, which are resource-intensive and environmentally destructive. Rather Nair calls for Asia's developing countries to eschew consumerism and adopt a more ascetic economic model that will deliver sustainable development and save the planet from environmental disaster. Nair's vision is for a paternalistic (authoritarian?) style of capitalism, perhaps like Singapore or an Asian Norway, where expectations are managed and resources allocated more equitably.
3 Shlomo's book, *Planet of Cities*, and its companion volume, *Atlas of Urban Expansion*, questions the main tenets of the familiar Containment Paradigm, also known as smart growth, urban growth management, or compact city, that is designed to contain boundless urban expansion, typically decried as sprawl. This paradigm is considered deficient and practically useless in addressing the central questions now facing expanding cities outside North America and Europe. In its place Shlomo proposes to revive an alternative Making Room Paradigm that seeks to come to terms with the expected expansion of cities, particularly in the rapidly urbanising countries in Asia and Africa.
4 The effects of congestion are not just confined to the transport system but impact on housing availability, the provision of public services and the general affordability of living in congested cities.
5 There is also a powerful aviation lobby that supports airport expansion and airline competition. Air travel is enjoyed by many people who have come to think of it as a normal part of their mobility system, like owning a car.

References

Baeton, G. 2000, 'The Tragedy of the Highway: Empowerment, Disempowerment and the Politics of Sustainability Discourses and Practices', *European Planning Studies*, 8, 1, pp. 69–86.
Bendixson, T. 1974, *Instead of Cars,* Temple Smith, London, revised edition 1977: Penguin.

Downs, A. 1992, *Stuck in Traffic: Coping with Peak-Hour Traffic Congestion*, The Brookings Institution, Washington, DC, USA.

Downs, A. 2004, *Still Stuck in Traffic*, The Brookings Institution, Washington, DC, USA.

Gilbert, R. & Perl, A. 2010, *Transport Revolutions: Moving People and Freight Without Oil*, Earthscan, London, UK.

Lewis, D. & Williams, F.L. 1999, *Policy and Planning as Public Choice: Mass Transit in the United States*, Ashgate, Burlington, USA.

Ministry of Transport 1963, *The Buchanan Report: Traffic in Towns*, HMSO, London, UK.

Mogridge, M.J.H. 1990, *Travel in Towns: Jam Yesterday, Jam Today and Jam Tomorrow?*, Macmillan Press, London, UK.

Mogridge, M.J.H., Holden, D.J., Bird, J. & Terzis, G.C. 1987, 'The Downs–Thomson Paradox and the Transportation Planning Process', *International Journal of Transportation Economics*, 14, pp. 283–311.

Nair, C. 2011, *Consumptionomics: Asia's Role in Reshaping Capitalism and Saving the Planet*, Infinite Ideas, Oxford, UK.

Plowden, S. 1972, *Towns Against Traffic*, Andre Deutsch, London, UK.

Shlomo, A. 2012, *Planet of Cities*, Lincoln Institute of Land Policy, Cambridge, USA.

Townroe, P.M. 1974, *Social and Political Consequences of the Motor Car*, David & Charles, Newton Abbot, UK.

2 Sustainable Transport and Mobility

2.1 Meta-mobility: Assimilating Spatial and Social Mobility

Spatial mobility and social mobility have historically been treated as separate areas of study with their own distinctive traditions, rooted in geography and sociology, respectively. The central argument put forward in this book is that we need a more holistic view of mobility in all its manifestations – spatial, social and virtual – to understand its role as integral to the way the economy works and how it impacts lifestyles and life chances. Spatial mobility and upward social mobility are generally regarded as positive features that make people and places more accessible and improve opportunity. However, high levels of spatial mobility achieved by modes of transport that consume excessive amounts of fuel and impact the environment in lots of different ways are increasingly seen as negative influences and a threat to society – principally via their levels of carbon emission, but not exclusively. Hypermobility is also seen by some as undermining community relations by speed and distance, weakening the bonds with people and place, which are best experienced in neighbourhoods at walking pace (Adams 2001). This presents a number of challenges to the way our cities and transport networks are designed, in changing individual travel behaviour and in the institutional arrangements for planning, managing and operating transport services.

City structure has evolved with transport systems, from the walking city through the public transport city to the motorised city characterised by low-density urban sprawl. Urban expansion would simply not be possible without advances in transport technology – trains, buses, cars and planes. Cities are sometimes defined simply as density plus diversity, a concatenation of physical form and social groupings, differentiated by land use, income and ethnicity. We know that density is related to accessibility, reflecting the value of the land, even if this relationship may be weakening. Diversity and social segregation are determined by other socio-economic factors, less well understood, but nevertheless observed and theorised in urban sociology and human geography. Studies of urban economics and the social ecology of cities demonstrate that the city is a dynamic environment that is constantly adjusting its entropy. Some cities are able to exist in a stable, steady state, and change slowly; what we may call entropy-maximising cities. Generally the more stable cities are those with strong central cores and planning regimes to preserve high-density urban form.

Cities attract migrants who contribute to the urban dynamics and the entropy of the city. This entropy – randomness and uncertainty – is characteristic of dynamic cities and is more probable as city scale increases. Thus megacities are likely to be more dynamic than smaller cities, and megacities in developing countries (such as Jakarta, Manila, Mumbai and Lagos) are more chaotic than megacities in developed nations (such as Tokyo, New York and Moscow). No doubt part of this is down to governance, but the entropy exhibited in growing cities can also be attributed to mobility. Mobility is essential for migration, for commuting and the delivery of goods, for financial transactions and the mobility of capital, for creating social opportunities, and providing the means to accomplish interactions in space and cyberspace. The range of mobilities and their involvement in urban dynamics is pervasive. Hence the need for a broader concept of mobility – a meta-mobility, that integrates the socio-economic dynamics of urban entropy with the spatial potential of the transportation system.

The transport system is an essential element of meta-mobility but does not on its own generate mobility. Trip generation is a function of other activities, that is, a derived demand required to satisfy other goals. However, there is evidence that the better the physical connectivity provided by the transport network, the easier the travel opportunities, and therefore the more likely that interactions will take place. Thus, the most dynamic cities are those with extensive transport networks that facilitate the level of interactions and opportunities necessary to maintain their dynamism. In these cities, the density of land use and population requires either an efficient mass transit system or extensive highway network to satisfy mobility demands. People and businesses in these cities are united in their support and use of *their* transport service, and once settled they tend to be relatively fixed and irreversible in their locales and travel patterns.[1] As Kaufmann notes in *Rethinking the City*, 'The most mobile cities are also the most attractive to individual and collective actors' and 'We can observe that policies aimed at strengthening the harmonious development of cities – in other words policies of the city – have largely to do with mobility' (Kaufmann 2011, p. 141). Following Kaufmann, we can add mobility as a critical feature to density and diversity in how cities are defined. As we are considering mobility in the widest sense, thus: City = Density + Diversity + *Meta-mobility*.

There are different city structures for satisfying mobility, and while sustainable mobility seems to favour urban living at higher densities, the trend for urban expansion is into low-density suburbs and exurban locales that rely for their mobility on the car rather than public transport. Even in cities such as London and Paris, with their extensive public transport networks, cycle routes and convivial walking environments, commuters who live in the suburbs or commuter towns switch to using cars as their primary mode in their home neighbourhoods. The flexibility and reversibility of car-based mobility is a major feature of lifestyle and culture in most developed countries and appears to be on a similar trajectory in developing nations. This has important implications for transport systems development and mobility, as explained below.

2.2 The Mobile City

Transport is critical to how a city functions, and from observations of transport movements and land-use patterns, planners have developed sophisticated models to replicate travel behaviour by different modes. These models are used to forecast changes in travel demand resulting from changes in demography, employment and land uses. The models have tended to be reactive in so far as they have been used to 'predict and provide' requirements for new transport systems, especially new roads, which in turn generates additional traffic. Interest has turned, therefore, to modelling different patterns of land use and city structure to constrain traffic growth and promote a new urbanism more favourable to public transport, walking and cycling. So how realistic is it to retro-fit cities with modern urban transit systems and higher density, mixed land uses? This was a key question examined by J.M. Thompson in *Great Cities and their Traffic* (Thompson 1977).

Thompson's major achievement was to describe four typologies of urban structure related to the influence of automobiles (see Box 2.1). The dynamics of car use are such that unless positive measures are taken to contain urban sprawl, retain high-density housing and employment areas together with investment in public transport, the city will disperse towards multi-centre, low-density developments where traffic is persistent and the car is the only realistic way of getting around (Gillespie, Healey & Robins 1998). Thompson argues that without positive intervention, the weak centre cities will morph into auto-dependent cities.

> **Box 2.1 City Structure and Transport – Four Typologies (Adapted from Thompson 1977)**
>
> 1 Type one cities have grown during the automobile era and are largely defined by their reliance on car travel. North American cities such as Los Angeles, Phoenix, Denver and Dallas are archetypes, but examples can be found on other continents, such as Milton Keynes in England and Canberra in Australia. These cities are characterised by having dispersed activity centres with very weak central business districts.
> 2 The second type has weak centres but with average densities and more concentric urban form that may pre-date the automobile era. Examples include Melbourne and San Francisco and provincial cities in the UK, such as Manchester, Leeds and Birmingham. These metropolitan areas are multi-polar with many new developments on the periphery, which act as a centripetal force in urban development.
> 3 The third type is represented by a strong centre with high-density urban centres and well-developed public transport systems. This is characteristic of cities with important commercial and financial functions that grew in the 19th century, such as Paris, New York, Sydney, Hamburg and Edinburgh.
> 4 Lastly, there are cities that have implemented traffic control and modal preference in their structure, with the central areas and inner cities dominated by public transport. They have high land-use densities and aim to preserve the current urban structure as part of their planning regime. This system typifies cities with a long history of favouring public transport, such as London, Hong Kong, Vienna, Stockholm and historic cities such as York, Norwich and Durham.
>
> Source: adapted from Thompson, J.M. 1977, *Great Cities and their Traffic*, Gollancz, London.

While we can assign cities to these categories, they have not always been of that form. For instance, many of the UK cities that today may be weak centres once had strong centres and were oriented around public transport. The process may even be reversed. Los Angeles (LA), a type one megalopolis, is now trying to rectify its auto dependency by building metro lines and commuter rail capacity, and encouraging transit-oriented design around metro stations. Clearly there is a long way to go for LA to regain some form of transportation balance and become a type two city.

The urban sprawl and traffic congestion serves as a reminder of the dangers of allowing transportation systems to develop unfettered without considering urban land use. LA could also be a poster-child for the ultimate consumer capitalist city, free-wheeling (bar the traffic congestion), mass mobility and freedom by car and a hyperactive city gung-ho for making money, celebrity culture (Hollywood and movies) and indulging in excess. Beneath the glitz and gloss there is a deeper reality: the traffic congestion and pollution is strangling and poisoning the city, and parts of the freeway network are in gridlock throughout the day (not just during the peak hours). LA no longer has a peak in the traditional sense, and just as the city never sleeps, so the traffic doesn't stop.

The consequences are that LA is incurring massive congestion costs through travel delay and lower productivity, and is therefore a less attractive place for new investment. According to the Southern California Association of Governments, the population of 18 million in 2007 will expand to 24 million in 2035. The area is now so well developed, albeit at low density, that new development is pushing far into the desert lands to the east of LA, up to 70 miles from the central business district. This staggering rate of development could turn into a Hollywood nightmare, as far as transportation is concerned, unless the authorities get to grips with the transport systems. As noted in the Regional Transportation Plan, 'Southern California is running out of land to support low-density future growth' and 'Nearly all natural locations for urban development have been consumed, leaving us with hard choices about how we are to grow and change to meet the demands of the future'.[2] The development of the metro and commuter rail is part of the solution but it is going to require a lot more investment to create a public transport network that can meet LA's needs.

LA represents the ultimate auto-city, a testament to auto-culture. This hegemony has been observed in other cities with detrimental effects on the economy and vitality of the city and its neighbourhoods. In the US context, Jane Jacobs pointed out in her book, *The Economy of Cities,* that an efficient city uses its scarce resources – land and accessibility – to arrange these in convivial ways that make for diverse neighbourhoods with a range of services accessible by the most efficient means: walking, cycling, public transport and then the car (Jacobs 1969). Vibrant cities such as New York and London attract talent and investment, which is used to add value to services and goods (agglomeration effects) that are then exported to the rest of the world. A successful city exports more than it imports.

Studies such as Downs' *Stuck in Traffic* (mentioned in Chapter 1) make a similar case, that gridlock is undermining the economic viability of cities, and argues for road pricing to adjust demand to supply. The case for road pricing to control auto-mobility will be examined later. The warnings of Thompson and others have been heeded somewhat, and the trend in most cities across the world is towards higher-density development in line with type two or type three cities in order to promote more sustainable travel solutions. However, these developments rarely extend into the suburbs, and urban sprawl has been observed to leapfrog the green belts around cities into exurban communities and 'edge cities' where auto-mobility dominates.

The relationship between transport and land-use development is not straightforward and may not be as strong as perceived. Transport investments do not have a consistent or predictable impact on land use, and the evidence indicates that land-use change does not necessarily follow transportation investments (Guiliano 1995). The shift to an information-based economy and technological trends such as cyber-mobility suggest that the relationship between transport and city form will continue to weaken, impacting the agglomeration benefits of higher spatial accessibility. Car mobility and cyber-mobility allow a growing number of people to work remotely and live urban lifestyles in a variety of locations, including rural areas, a trend first identified by Pahl (Pahl 1965). The city archetypes therefore may only serve as historical exemplars of the relationship between traffic and city structure. Clearly the preservation of cities with a strong core and viable public transport service requires strong planning policies that not all countries have or want. Even with strong planning policies it may not be possible to achieve the desired transportation–land use balance. The centripetal force of information and communication technology, leading to disparate neighbourhoods and aspatial communities of interest, is counterweight to the central places model of urban development. In contemporary society the 'push' of meta-mobility appears to be a greater force than the 'pull' of accessibility in shaping location and movement patterns.

2.3 Balancing Mobility and Sustainability

According to the Brundtland Report, *Our Common Future*, sustainable development is 'development that meets the needs of the present without compromising the ability of future generations to meet their own needs' (United Nations World Commission on Environment and Development 1987, p. 43). It is generally recognised that current transport systems are not sustainable because they are dependent on fossil fuels, which are not only finite but emit greenhouse gases that cause global warming, produce excessive numbers of accidents (fatalities and injuries) and create congestion that borders on gridlock. The challenge is how to balance the demand for mobility against the need for sustainable transport. This is not easy because the measures to deliver sustainability imply restrictions on mobility – using 'carrots' and 'sticks' – that is at odds with a society in which ease of mobility is a key motivator in the travel behaviour of people and businesses.

Physical mobility is simply the ability to move from one place to another by whatever means are available, which could be by different modes such as walking, cycling, bus, train, car or plane. Most trips involve multimodal legs, such as walking to the bus stop or to the car park and ride at train stations, taking a taxi to the airport and so forth. More mobile societies, principally developed economies, make greater use of mechanised modes of travel, which enable longer distances to be covered in a given time. Thus mobility is synonymous with travel speed and distance, and a common measure of mobility among nations is the number of vehicle miles (or kilometres) of travel per capita. Richer countries generally travel further, even if the time spent travelling is similar to that in poorer countries. Advanced economies have become dependent on mechanised modes of travel to transport large volumes of passengers and freight.

As these mechanised modes, especially automobiles, use large quantities of fuel, the sustainability of mobility in developed countries is called into question, as evident in the Brundtland Report and subsequent actions to reduce greenhouse gas emissions contained in the Kyoto Protocol of 1997, which entered into force in 2005. The UK and the European Union (EU) have responded to concerns about the impact of greenhouse gases on climate change by legislating for reductions in emissions and establishing targets to improve fossil fuel efficiency. The UK, for instance, passed a Climate Change Act in 2008, which mandates that by 2050 net carbon use should be at least 80% lower than the 1990 baseline and an interim target of 26% reduction by 2020. The EU has produced regulations that require vehicle manufacturers to adhere to more stringent emissions standards that require greater fuel efficiency as well as incentives to switch to electric vehicles. The EU Commission has also championed the production of Sustainable Urban Mobility Plans (SUMPs) in member states. These are not mandatory, but they provide a toolbox of measures based on best practice in European cities, which urban planners can use to design sustainable travel programmes for their communities. In the UK, the government has created a Local Sustainable Transport Fund (LSTF) to boost local smarter travel measures and alternatives to car use. Developing countries are also set to increase their use of mechanised transport and fossil fuels, and these are likely to be the major areas of growth in greenhouse gases in the period to 2050.

While the targets for reducing carbon emissions and fossil fuel use are clear and measurable, those for congestion are more difficult to define, as is the appropriate level of mobility commensurate with sustainability goals. Road congestion indices, such as the Level of Service (LOS) standard used in the USA (*Highway Capacity Manual*, Ryus et al. 2010), have been developed in some countries. This grades congestion from level 'A' (free-flow conditions) to level 'F' (operating above capacity, resulting in near gridlock conditions). In between these extremes are conditions that approximate to everyday traffic, including reasonably free flow with only slight restrictions on traffic flow (level B), steady flow at or near free flow (level C), approaching unstable flow with speeds slightly decreasing as volumes increase (level D) and unstable flow operating at capacity with irregular flows and variable speeds (level E). Monitoring of traffic congestion in the USA shows that conditions are gradually getting worse in most urban areas and some cities are struggling to cope with levels of service that rarely fall below level D throughout most of the day (American Society of Civil Engineers 2011). The peak spreading of traffic to the shoulders of the peak is extending the morning peak from 07:00 to 10:00 and the afternoon peak from 16:00 to 19:00, but off-peak flows are also increasing in the daytime between the peaks and through the middle evening to 21:00. Even where mitigation measures are put into place such as high-occupancy vehicle lanes, carpooling and transit alternatives, these only seem to slow the rate of increase in traffic rather than reduce it in absolute terms (Schrank, Eisele & Lomax 2012). The chronic problems of traffic congestion in US cities is recorded in an annual *Urban Mobility Report* prepared by the Texas A&M Transportation Institute, which is considered a reliable source of data and a state-of-the-practice analysis of congestion effects in urban areas. Further details are provided in Chapter 3.

Traffic engineers have observed a speed–flow relationship as traffic volumes increase and use this to vary speed limits on managed motorways, which increases throughput. Active traffic management (ATM), or 'managed/smart motorways', as they are referred to in the UK, are enforced by speed cameras, and generally motorists adhere to the variable speed limits and obey lane discipline. The empirical evidence demonstrates that auto-mobility and congestion are incongruous without travel demand measures that constrain the amount of auto-mobility to the capacity of the road network. Even in this case, sustainable urban auto-mobility is only feasible if automobiles are powered by electricity or hybrid fuel technologies that emit ultra-low levels of greenhouse gases.

LOS measures have also been devised for multimodal transport, including public transport, cycling and walking (Dowling 2012; Fruin 1971; *Highway Capacity Manual*, op. cit.). These measures may include factors such as wait times, service frequency, crowding on buses and trains, queuing, as well as capacity to accommodate overtaking vehicles/bicycles/pedestrians and contravening flows (of bicycles and pedestrians) that impede movement.

Sustainable mobility is a broader concept than sustainable transport and includes economic and social aspects of sustainability that are often absent in transport studies (Guers, Boon & Van Wee 2010). This point has been made by Black, who notes that sustainable transport is wrapped up in some type of potential mobility that is seen as fundamental to economic wellbeing (Black 2003). Black has devised an index of sustainable transport and potential mobility (STPM), defined as 'travel and transport that minimise the negative impact on the environment and human health and welfare, and utilise minimal amounts of non-renewable resources *in the presence of comparable economic levels that enable mobility*' [my emphasis] (ibid., p. 318). The reference to economic wellbeing is critical to the STPM index and is what differentiates Black's analysis from other indicators of sustainable transport, which focus on variables such as vehicle fuel efficiency, tailpipe emissions, number of accidents or level of congestion. The problem with these indicators, as Black notes, is how to weight each one against another. For example, are vehicle fatalities more important than congestion? Is emitted carbon more critical than accessibility? And how do we weigh the value of one against the other?

The STPM index combines a measure of travel and transport (vehicle kilometres of travel, VKT), fuel use (FUEL), and potential mobility (gross domestic product, GDP) in the following formulation:

$$STPM = GDP - ((VKT - FUEL)/2).$$

These variables are converted to per capita figures and standardised. The GDP figure is a measure of a state's performance and is used as a proxy for potential mobility because car ownership and travel in general is correlated with economic performance. The sign is changed on the VKT and FUEL variables so that larger values (i.e. lower fuel use and travel) represent more sustainable solutions. Thus a value > 0 indicates high potential mobility and low sustainability and conversely values < 0 have low mobility potential and high sustainability. Not surprisingly, the STPM for developed countries is generally > 0 and < 0 for developing countries. The closer the index is to 0 the more potential mobility is in balance with sustainability. Black calculates the STPM for 104 nations for which data are available. The STPM index for the UK is −3.01, whereas the USA has an overall value of 18.15. The value for the USA is not surprising, but the value for the UK will come as a shock to those who believe that the UK is pursuing unsustainable transport practices. Developed countries of the OECD and Europe have scores that fall for the most part between +10 and −10, broadly indicating a balance between potential mobility (average GDP growth) and sustainability (average levels of fuel use and VKT). Developing countries generally have low negative values (< −10), reflecting low levels of potential mobility against what would ordinarily be viewed as sustainable travel and transport. Kenya, for example, has a score of −30.36, which is an attractive sustainability value but only accomplished as a result of its low level of mobility. In Black's opinion, these nations should endeavour to increase their mobility (GDP) while retaining the higher (desirable) scores on their VKT and FUEL measures.

2.4 Transport Obligations under the Kyoto Protocol

Apart from a few countries, the STPM index is not consistent with other measures of transport sustainability, such as those produced by the United Nations Framework Convention on Climate Change for the Kyoto Protocol in 1997. This is not surprising given that the STPM measure is a broader indicator of mobility potential linked to economic factors compared to the more narrow environmental definitions of sustainability that dominate transport discourse. Table 2.1 compares the STPM scores for a selection of countries with the greenhouse gas emissions reduction targets determined for the Kyoto Protocol – see Box 2.2.

The greenhouse gas reduction targets are more onerous than those implied by the STPM index, especially in the transport sector. In order to stabilise CO_2 emissions at 1990 levels – the Kyoto baseline reference date – substantial reductions in emissions from transport would be required in developed nations, especially as CO_2 emissions from transport are likely to rise by 40% globally with current Kyoto targets (Banister 2005). To achieve a global stabilisation target (zero increase 1990–2020) requires developing and emerging countries to reduce their rate of emissions growth, and the OECD nations would need to modify their targets by −50%. As Banister notes, 'The key question is whether the OECD countries, in particular the USA, would contemplate reductions of 50% in their emission levels. If not, then the global stabilisation target is impossible, at least in the transport sector' (ibid., p. 27). The indications are not good, and so far there is little optimism that the OECD countries will come anywhere near meeting these targets.

Table 2.1 Comparison of STPM, Kyoto Greenhouse Gas and Transport CO_2 Emissions Reduction Targets

Country	STPM value*	Kyoto GHG reduction target (1990–2010) %**	Targets required to stabilise CO_2 emissions in transport (1990–2020) %***
USA	+18.15	−7.0	−50.0
UK	−3.01	−12.5	−50.0
Belgium	+2.79	−7.5	−50.0
Emerging countries (China)	−28.66	–	+50.0
Developing countries (Kenya)	−30.36	–	+100.0

* *Source*: Black (2003), pp. 322–325 and Appendix 20.2.
** These include emissions from all sources, of which transport makes up at least 20% and a growing share.
*** CO_2 stabilisation targets estimated by Banister (2005), Table 2.4.

This is confirmed in subsequent international conferences on climate change under the auspices of the United Nations, such as those in Copenhagen (2010), Cancun (2011) and Doha (2012), which have made slow progress on agreeing actions to limit carbon emissions to avoid a 2°C rise in global temperatures by 2050. The latest annual summit, held in Lima in 2014, has at least struck a deal – dubbed the Lima Call for Climate Action – which paves the way for a new international protocol to supersede Kyoto, to be agreed in Paris in 2015. It remains to be seen whether this represents a real breakthrough, or another delaying tactic by countries posturing to protect their national interests.

Box 2.2 Kyoto Protocol and Greenhouse Gas Reduction Targets

The Kyoto Protocol lists forty Annex 1 countries (including the UK), which collectively are expected to reduce their CO_2 equivalent emissions of six specified greenhouse gases by 5.2% below 1990 levels. There is a mandated emissions reduction target that each country is expected to meet by the first commitment period of 2008–2012. Britain's target reduction is −12.5%, within a range of −21% (Germany) to +27% (Portugal). The USA, the world's biggest energy consumer per capita, was given a target of −7% and Canada −6%, whereas Australia was allowed +8% growth in emissions. The second commitment period extends from 2013 to 2020 and incorporates more ambitious targets to be reached in 2030, the Doha Amendment to the Protocol agreed in 2012.

Some countries, including the UK and the Netherlands, have committed themselves to greater reduction targets, which is now framed in national legislation, and the EU has also taken a lead in promising 15% reduction overall by 2010 (compared with the −8% target mandated by the Kyoto Protocol). The USA failed to ratify the protocol, and this has weakened the status of the global treaty. Achieving these targets has proved challenging for many countries, especially as emissions from transport have continued to grow.

Developing and emerging countries are allowed to grow their emissions in order to enable their economic development. This includes accommodating growth in emissions from transport as a result of increasing car ownership (about 6% per annum) and use of trucks for moving larger volumes of freight.

At least the increases in CO_2 emissions allowed in emerging and developing countries are more in line with the STPM scores. The difference between the STPM scores and the targets set in the Kyoto Protocol targets (and the more ambitious targets estimated by Banister) represent the value gap between those who view the problem as an environmental imperative and those who see sustainability in a wider socio-economic context. The question is, to what extent should we prioritise economic, social and environmental goals for sustainability?

One possible solution is to increase 'transport intensity', that is, achieve higher throughput on the transport systems with fewer inputs such as oil and other non-renewable resources. For example, by substituting automobility with mass transit, cycling or walking for the majority of trips, and living at higher densities, especially in advanced economies where suburbanisation with low-density housing and high car ownership is the norm. Higher density of activities enhances network connectivity opportunities, thus enabling high mobility by convivial modes of transport. In contrast, lower density favours auto-mobility. Increasing transport intensity is seen by its proponents as a mechanism to de-couple transport development from economic growth, for example, improvements in freight logistics that are independent of economic factors but that have resulted in more efficient and effective use of transport resources and environmental benefits (Banister 2005).

Banister acknowledges that there is an empirical correlation between GDP and mobility as measured by VKT but argues that this link needs to be broken to accomplish a sustainable transport future. He is not excluding the economic dimension but instead proposes a framework to integrate the 'strong' (environmental and social) and 'weak' (economic) sustainability concepts, with an emphasis on the strong elements. The proposed measures to increase transport intensity present tough targets, which may not be socially acceptable within each country, requiring different combinations of the measures to be effective. We can observe that, 'transport is becoming more sustainable, but this optimism needs to be tempered with a note of caution, as some of the major countries are still a long way from the thresholds and the high energy costs of long distance travel are difficult to reduce' (Holden, Linerrud & Banister 2013).

2.5 Transport, Accessibility and Social Inclusion

The strong concept of sustainability conflates environmental and social elements as complementary features. The assumption is that creating a more environmentally friendly transport system will benefit those on lower incomes and socially marginalised groups who depend more on collective transport services. Thus strong sustainability policies are perceived to be progressive in promoting economic and social equity. This is a big assertion to make and may not always be the case. As discussed in later chapters, road-user charging schemes to reduce traffic are generally regressive in their impacts and affect the poor more than the rich. It is important therefore to measure the social aspects of transport, as well as quantify the environmental impacts.

Broadly, the social element is interpreted as the accessibility opportunities provided by the transport network. Accessibility is simply defined as proximity to facilities in space and time by whatever transport resources are available. Thus, people living in rural areas generally have to travel further to access activities, and if they are reliant on public transport their destination choices may be limited. In contrast, cities have more facilities available locally, which can be accessed by a variety of modes and thus offer more choices. Traditional accessibility analysis focuses on proximity, whereas contemporaneous notions of mobility are about opportunity and potential in the broader social sphere: what sociologists refer to as *motility*. This includes the non-spatial aspects of mobility opened up by the new opportunities accessible in the virtual mobility of cyberspace. Advances in telecommunications and the internet have extended access to a range of goods and services. There has been speculation that remote access via computers could substitute for the need for travel for work and other activities, but as yet the evidence is mixed (Metz 2012). Indeed, the web may encourage more travel by showing people travel opportunities that they had not previously considered. Information is a necessary input to activating behaviour (although it doesn't have to be acted upon). It is possible that the flexibility to search for goods and services on-line is changing people's travel behaviour in that they explore places via cyberspace, and use the time saved to travel to more disparate places (often at greater distance). Thus mobility in cyberspace may be complementary to mobility in geographic space.[3]

As cities decentralised in the 20th century it was recognised that suburban, low-density living required more time to access distant facilities, encouraging car mobility at the expense of other modes. The position is summarised in *Access for All* (Schaeffer and Sclar 1975): 'The problem of modern urban transportation is not congestion or speed, but access. Equal access to all, or nearly all, can be an urban reality if transportation and land-use projects are evaluated and ranked by the access they offer. In practical terms this implies that public transit should be given priority over private transportation, and that land-use patterns would be arranged to minimise travel distances' (ibid., p. 171). Around this time a number of other publications, from independent researchers as well as public institutions, drew attention to the links between land-use planning and transportation to accomplish more equal accessibility in rural as well as urban areas (Independent Commission on Transport 1974; Moseley 1979). As the Independent Commission on Transport put it succinctly, 'Mobility, in the sense of having the facility to move or perform great amounts of travel, is not in itself desirable. It is access to people and facilities that matter' (ibid., p. 127). This viewpoint has prevailed among transport planners despite trends in the opposite direction, which is problematic, and juxtaposes planners against the desires of the majority for increased mobility.

The changes in city structure and car ownership have had profound effects on the economy, culture and lifestyles. We may lament the loss of the walking/cycling/public transport city to the automobile, but this has been the direction of travel in economic and social policy despite the reservations of transport planners and attempts to constrain, and in some cases even reverse, these trends. Such has been the concern with the domination of mobility by cars, that government has identified social exclusion (through lack of accessibility) as a major public policy issue. In the late 1990s the UK Government set up a Social Exclusion Unit to examine policies to improve social inclusion and social mobility including the role of transport in accessing services. The Department for Transport mandated that local transport plans (LTPs) should analyse accessibility to a range of facilities such as employment sites, schools, doctor's surgeries and shops (and produce maps where appropriate). An example is illustrated in Figure 2.1.[4]

In this case travel times to major centres in Greater Manchester by car and public transport (bus, rail and urban metro) is mapped, and the accessibility advantage by car is clear. Access from some areas by public transport is difficult, especially sparsely populated rural areas on the periphery. Accessibility to major centres within 60 minutes' travel time is generally good in urban areas and along major corridors, but suburban locales and even some inner city neighbourhoods have relatively poor access by public transport. In contrast, car accessibility provides much greater travel opportunities within the area and for longer distance commuter travel. This is significant because of the way it has changed the transport geography of the region. Prior to mass car ownership, public transport would have given most people access to the facilities they need, which were largely contained within the towns of Greater Manchester. Since the rise of car mobility, people and places have become more disparate and footloose. The job–housing balance, for instance, is now a regional planning issue across North West England and North Wales rather than a sub-regional matter within Greater Manchester, with the travel to work area extending up to 50 miles from the city. Access opportunities for those reliant on public transport have broadly remained stable or even declined, especially in the smaller centres, whereas access opportunities by car have increased with the development of the motorway network.

The impact is evident in Table 2.2, which measures average travel time to workplaces by car and public transport, and shows the clear advantage of accessibility by car. Only about one-fifth of the population are within 30 minutes' travel time of their workplace by bus or rail, compared with nearly three-quarters who travel by car. Within 60 minutes' travel

(a)

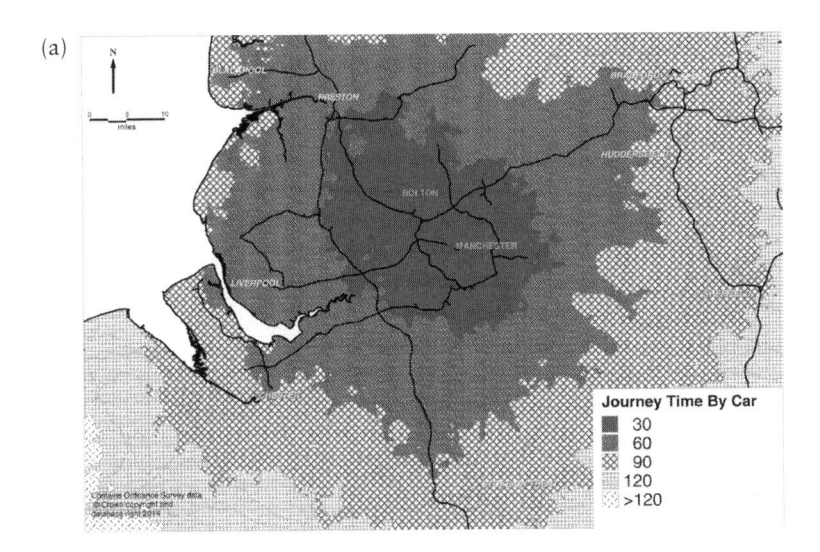

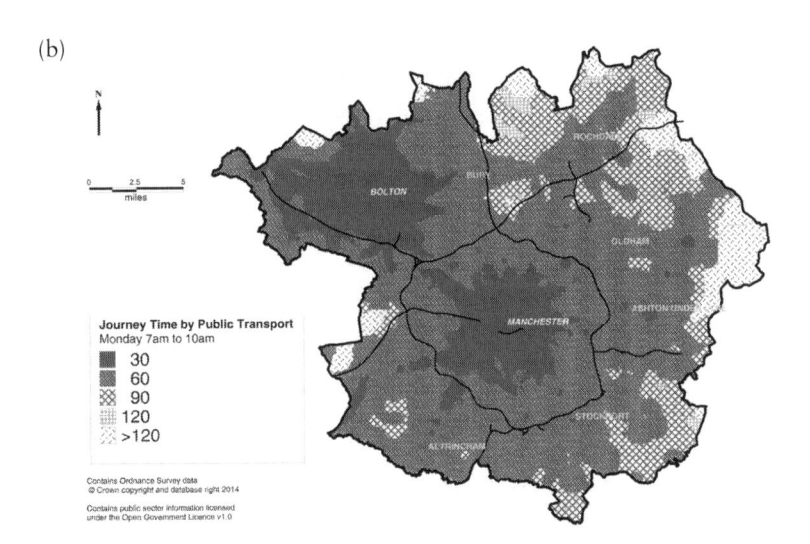

(b)

Figure 2.1 Accessibility to Major Centres in Greater Manchester by Road (a) and Public Transport (b). Travel Time in Minutes.

time – often regarded as the maximum time that most people are prepared to travel to activities – only about half the population are able to access workplaces by public transport, compared with 93% of car users. Even at 120 minutes' travel time, workplace accessibility by public transport is achievable by less than 90% of the population. The high accessibility zones

Table 2.2 Workplace Accessibility: Proportion of Population within 30, 60 and 120 Minutes' Journey Time – Average for Greater Manchester (2006)

Travel mode	Proportion of population within		
	30 min	60 min	120 min
Car	0.72	0.93	0.99
Public transport AM	0.21	0.49	0.83
Public transport PM	0.22	0.52	0.88

Source: Workplace accessibility data derived from NWRA Accessibility Study, report for the North West Regional Assembly, MVA Consultancy, October 2006. Contains public sector information licensed under the Open Government Licence v3.0 (http://www.nationalarchives.gov.uk/doc/open-government-licence/version/3 [accessed April 2015]).

on the commuter accessibility map indicate the area that has most potential or attractiveness for activities such as distribution, retail and services, which can reach customers within easy travel time (and vice versa). More peripheral zones offer less potential. The areas of high car access may be in places where public transport access is low. Over time the relocation of activities and residential locations to more car-accessible locations encourages car dependency, which in turn feeds into further concentration of activities in high car-access zones, such as adjacent to motorway junctions and on major trunk roads.

Mapping accessibility in this way enables us to identify access-poor zones and evaluate remedies. These could include enhancing public transport services or zoning development in areas with good public transport. The reality is that planners have few powers to intervene to improve accessibility beyond supporting bus services or reaching planning agreements with developers. The results, however, are not encouraging, and social exclusion for those on low incomes or with a disability remains a significant challenge. These disadvantaged groups suffer the multiple deprivations of low income and limited travel choices. Public transport provides a low-cost way of supporting mobility, especially among low-income groups, and is more efficient in delivering transport solutions in urban areas (Lewis & Williams 1999). However, local authorities have seen their budgets for public transport support cut since 2010 and under the deregulated bus market have few tools to address accessibility issues.

Accessibility may be the maxim of planners, but mobility is the mantra of the public. During the last 50 years, peoples' horizons have broadened with travel and exposure to consumer-advertising culture, levels of affluence have increased, and the constraints of social class on behaviour have loosened. These changes are associated with greater mobility – spatial and social – and feed a desire for greater access to different experiences and choices, which can only be satisfied through more mobility. Thus a circular process is set in motion, whereby mobility is the means to satisfying these wants, which creates more demand for mobility. As a result, a 'mobility gap' has opened up between, for example, access-poor and access-rich areas, and between the mobility disadvantaged and mobility privileged.

The ability to overcome accessibility constraints is related to social and institutional factors as well as access to transport resources (Hagerstrand 1970, 1973), namely:

- capability constraints, such as the physical mobility of an individual or their domestic set-up, for example the need to look after children at specific times of the day;
- coupling constraints related to the transport system, such as proximity to public transport or access to a car for personal use; this is the component of accessibility used in transport planning to measure network connectivity; and
- institutional constraints, such as times of attendance at school or work, opening times of shops and other facilities.

The ability to overcome accessibility constraints lies in the social and institutional domains, not just geography and transport. Institutional and social factors have changed significantly since the rise of mass car ownership, in a symbiotic manner. Examples include the move towards the 24-hour society for shopping and entertainment, the dependence on cars to meet family and household commitments, especially children's activities, and the use of the internet to make arrangements and order goods and services that previously required face-to-face contact. Auto-mobility has enabled adults to loosen the capability and institutional constraints, and when combined with coupling opportunities this provides a significant advantage over other modes of transport. As these examples demonstrate, the social and institutional dimensions of accessibility need to be understood alongside the space–time dimension.

A good example of the social and institutional barriers to accessibility alongside the spatial aspects is provided by the physical access to transport services by people with disabilities. Laws and regulations exist to promote equal access to buses, trains, taxis and planes for those with mobility impairments. This is a growing problem as the number of elderly people increases in developed countries. Transport modes are becoming more accessible and operators are mandated to cater for people with special needs, such as wheelchair access, but significant barriers still remain. If only one link in the travel chain is missing then a journey may be impossible; seamless travel across all modes is still problematic. Apart from the physical barriers there are other impediments that discourage travel by disabled people, such as lack of adequate training of staff to assist passengers and the psychological feeling of being powerless and dependent on others

(Chartered Institute of Logistics and Transport 2013). With the numbers of elderly and disabled people increasing, these problems will get worse and are likely to attract more attention.

Accessible transport for disabled people is recognised by the Government and transport planners as an issue that needs addressing, but to date it has been compartmentalised into a separate 'accessibility box' from spatial accessibility analysis. The mobility and transport problems of people with disabilities are associated with the physical accessibility of the mode of transport rather than a wider social policy issue of transport coordination (Sutton 1988). Thus, paratransit or special transport services for those with mobility impairments have been set up by community transport organisations and local governments, including dial-a-ride and other demand-responsive services. In this respect, the disenfranchisement of disabled travellers who cannot access the range of transport services exposes the weakness of accessibility analysis that does not address mobility issues. Elderly and disabled people are eligible to use local bus services free of charge and rail services at one-third discount as part of the Government's national concessionary fares schemes. These schemes, which cost over £1 billion per annum, recognise the important role that mobility and transport plays in keeping elderly people active. Indirectly these subsidies are supporting local bus services, although there are some in the bus industry who believe the money would be better spent by supporting bus services directly, which benefits all bus users, not just those over retirement age. Universal benefits such as concessionary fares have been criticised for poorly targeting those who need them most, and they are worthless if local public transport services are poor or non-existent. Nevertheless, they are highly valued by the recipients, and an effective lobby of elderly persons' organisations has been successful in arguing for their continuation. The Government justifies the policy because of the mobility benefits it confers on those who might otherwise not have access to any other mode of transport, that is a social benefit, rather than an environmental benefit to encourage concessionaires to use local buses rather than their cars (if available).

Accessibility and mobility may have been regarded hitherto as dichotomies in transport planning, but it's time that accessibility underwent a re-think, just as mobility has in recent years. This is not simply a technical question of updating our models or analytical techniques but requires a more fundamental reconsideration on the zeitgeist of mobility in contemporary society. Planners traditionally have taken a dim view of mobility, preferring to measure transport performance in terms of accessibility. However, as mobility aspirations form an important influence on travel behaviour it is time for planners to re-connect with mobilities in the broadest sense – that is, meta-mobility, and integrate mobility and accessibility in a new methodological framework. Mobility is a key driving force in how our economy and society is organised, augmented by the new mobile capabilities in cyberspace and social networking. These new technologies will change the character of spatial and social interactions in the future meta-mobility landscape, with both positive and negative effects. The challenge facing transport planners and policy makers is making sense of these developments, the opportunities and threats they present, and integrating them into transport epistemology.

2.6 The Postmodern City: A Vision of Sustainable Urban Mobility

In response to the sustainability agenda, architects and planners have investigated alternate urban structures to accommodate population growth together with a convivial transport system. In a sense, there is an attempt to develop a fifth typology of city structure and sustainable transport as an additive to those described by Thompson, the difference being that the sustainable transport system determines the urban structure rather than traffic. These models of urban design have antecedents in the town and country planning movement from the 19th century onwards, and in the works of modern architects such as Le Corbusier and Mies van der Rohe in the mid-20th century, followed by postmodernist urban planners with their visions of multicultural, eclectic city neighbourhoods.

In this vision, the transport system is arranged hierarchically, reflecting a central-place system of local neighbourhoods with local shops and services accessible by walking or cycling, connected to larger centres by intermediate transport systems such as buses, light rail and personal rapid transit, and high-speed rail providing the links between the larger centres for longer distance travel supplemented by planes. It's a nice vision, and note that the car does not figure highly (if at all!) in some of these plans. However, it assumes that people will comply with this arrangement and be satisfied to travel in the way the planners ascribe; businesses and government services would also be required to conform to the plan. It may have some chance of being realised in totalitarian states that can order their citizens to behave in particular ways but is unlikely to be popular in democratic nations. Besides, most people reside in cities with historical built environment and it is difficult to re-model these to optimise the transport system, as Buchanan discovered 50 years ago.[5] A balanced solution that can provide mobility by different modes that compete on journey times may offer a solution in rich cities that can afford the high levels of investment required, but this is beyond the financial reach of most cities and governments. The cost is too high, and in established cities there is not the space to build new transport infrastructure without impacting on neighbourhoods and businesses as well as the natural environment. Locally, good urban design that provides attractive neighbourhoods and shared space schemes among different road users may offer a viable solution, but these have not yet been scaled up to cover an entire city. Where blanket traffic restrictions have been proposed, such as the 20 miles per hour '20's Plenty for Us' campaign, they have faced resistance from the communities affected.

While there is widespread agreement on the need to develop a more sustainable transport system, there is less concurrence on how to deliver an appropriate solution. Current policy espouses the idea that we can have the duality of sustainable transport and economic growth, without any constraints on mobility. Politically this may be astute to appease the various interests but ultimately the reality of congestion and climate change will become apparent. The evidence indicates that a strong sustainable transport policy that gives primacy to environmental and social objectives is required if we are to achieve the targets specified in the Kyoto Protocol. However, the challenge is balancing this with economic sustainability goals associated with mobility and travel choice. Are the two sides reconcilable? Is a sustainable mobility solution a practical proposition or a contradiction?

Notes

1 Reversibility is the notion of being able to adjust travel patterns without moving home or business. For example, switching work from one location to another is possible if within an acceptable driving time. For those without a car or access to flexible transit the opportunities are more constrained, i.e. irreversible.
2 *Regional Transportation Plan: Making the Connections*, Southern California Association of Governments 2008.
3 Metz has observed that people have fairly stable travel budgets for journeys to work and other activities, averaging 1 hour per day. It could be that people are using their travel budgets to search on-line and using the web to locate services within their travel horizon, thus travelling less to non-essential activities but when doing so travelling longer distances to widely dispersed destinations.
4 As well as assessing equality of access to services, LTPs assess the impact on the strategic environment, natural habitats and health, and what mitigation measures, if any, to apply.
5 An exceptional case, often quoted in transport circles, is the Netherlands, where the Government has prioritised cycling and public transport over roads, at least in urban areas. Some other countries, such as Denmark, are pursuing similar strategies. While bicycle mode share is impressive, this is at the expense of public transport as much as cars, and bicycle congestion and conflicts with pedestrians are a problem, as anyone who visits Amsterdam soon discovers.

References

Adams, J. 2001, *The Social Consequences of Hypermobility*, RSA Lecture, 21 November 2001.
American Society of Civil Engineers 2011, *Failure to Act: The Economic Impact of Current Investment Trends in Surface Transportation Infrastructure*, ASCE, Washington, DC, USA.

Banister, D. 2005, *Unsustainable Transport: City Transport in the New Century*, Routledge, Abingdon, UK.
Black, W.R. 2003, *Transportation: A Geographical Analysis*, Guilford Press, New York, USA.
Chartered Institute of Logistics and Transport 2013, *Empowering Staff: Enabling Passengers. The Role of Training in Delivering Accessible and Inclusive Transport Services*, Guide produced by the Accessibility and Inclusion Forum, CILT (UK), Corby.
Dowling, R. 2012, *Multimodal Level of Service Analysis for Urban Streets*, NCHRP Report 616, Transportation Research Board, Washington, DC, USA.
Fruin, J.J. 1971, *Pedestrian Planning and Design*, Metropolitan Association of Urban Designers and Environmental Planners, New York, USA.
Gillespie, A., Healey, P. & Robins, K. 1998, 'Movement and Mobility in the Post-Fordist City', in *Transport Policy and the Environment*, ed. D. Banister, E & FN Spon, London, pp. 243–266.
Giuliano, G. 1995, 'Land Use Impacts of Transportation Impacts: Highway and Transit', in *The Geography of Urban Transportation*, ed. S. Hansen, Guildford Press, New York, pp. 305–339.
Guers, K.T., Boon, W. & Van Wee, B. 2010, 'Social Impacts of Transport: Literature Review and the State of the Practice of Transport Appraisal in the Netherlands and the United Kingdom', *Transport Reviews*, 29, 1, pp. 69–90.
Hagerstrand, T. 1970, 'What About People in Regional Science?', *Papers of the Regional Science Association*, 24, pp. 7–21.
Hagerstrand, T. 1973, 'Impact of Transport on the Quality of Life in Transport in the 1980–1990 Decade', *Proceedings of the Fifth International Symposium on Theory and Practice in Transport Economics*, ECMT, Paris, France.
Holden, E., Linerrud, K. & Banister, D. 2013, 'Sustainable Passenger Transport: Back to Bruntland', *Transportation Research Part A*, 54, pp. 67–77.
Independent Commission on Transport 1974, *Changing Directions*, Coronet, London, UK.
Jacobs, J. 1969, *The Economy of Cities*, Random House, New York, USA.
Kaufmann, V. 2011, *Rethinking the City: Urban Dynamics and Mobility*, Routledge, Abingdon, UK.
Metz, D. 2012, *The Limits to Travel: How Far Will You Go?* Routledge, Abingdon, UK.
Moseley, M.J. 1979, *Accessibility: The Rural Challenge*, Methuen, York, UK.
Pahl, R.E. 1965, *Urbs in Rure: The Metropolitan Fringe in Hertfordshire*, Wiedenfeld & Nickelson, London, UK.
Ryus, P., Vandehey, M., Elefteriadou, L., Dowling, R. & Ostrom, B.K. 2010, *Highway Capacity Manual 2010*, Transportation Research Board, Washington, DC, USA.
Schaeffer, K.H. & Sclar, E. 1975, *Access for All: Transportation and Urban Growth*, Penguin, Baltimore, USA.
Schrank, D., Eisele, B. & Lomax, T. 2012, *2012 Urban Mobility Report*, Texas A&M Transportation Institute, Texas, USA.
Sutton, J. 1988, *Transport Coordination and Social Policy*, Avebury, Aldershot, UK.
Thompson, J.M. 1977, *Great Cities and their Traffic*, Gollancz, London, UK.
United Nations World Commission on Environment and Development 1987, *Our Common Future*, Oxford University Press, Oxford, UK.

3 Global Transport and Mobility Trends

3.1 Mass Mobility: A Global Phenomenon

A milestone was reached in 2011 when the world's one-billionth car was produced, possibly destined for China, which has now overtaken the USA as the world's largest market for new cars. More than thirty-five million cars were made in 2011, a new world record, and most industry analysts expect the growth in car ownership to continue for the foreseeable future, with most growth occurring in emerging economies such as Brazil, Russia, India, China and South Africa (known as the 'BRICS' countries). The growth of auto-based mobility across the globe should perhaps come as no surprise – after all, the car companies are the epitome of multinational enterprises with global reach. But the mass mobility by car that is desired and even planned for by the BRICS and other developing countries confronts a reality that the more advanced nations have begun to recognise: namely, that auto-mobility is unsustainable from an economic (congestion) and environmental (energy and emissions) point of view. It also has adverse effects on safety (road-related deaths and injuries) and social cohesion, which tends to decline as personal mobility takes precedence over collective mode sharing.

Mass mobility – the movement of large numbers of people and goods – is a characteristic of development and modernity. From London to Lagos, San Francisco to Sao Paulo, Berlin to Beijing, people and goods are on the move, and lots of them. Whether making daily commutes to work or journeys for business, tourism or migration, it seems that our world is more connected than ever. Mobility is a key ingredient to satisfying personal lifestyles as well as the functioning of our increasingly interconnected society. Travel tourism as an adventure into serendipity is growing exponentially and counteracts the economic theory that the journey is simply a means to an end.[1] The quality of the journey, however, is important, whether surfing the net, cruising the boulevard or riding the train. Expectations of the travel experience have changed as horizons have broadened through international travel and the internet.

The mobile society – of trains, planes, automobiles, mobile phones and the internet – comprises the physical time–space realm and the virtual reality of cyberspace. The convergence of these two orbits to create a 'hypermobile' society is one of the phenomena of the 21st century, and is one of our biggest challenges as well as opportunities. About half of the world's population of six billion already live in cities, and this is expected to increase to 70% by 2050 or thereabouts, when the global population is expected to exceed nine billion. Further evidence of the impact of these trends on transport and mobility looking ahead to 2035 and 2050, respectively, is provided in three reports published by the Chartered Institute of Logistics and Transport in the UK (CILT), the Organisation for Economic Co-operation and Development (OECD) and the Texas A&M Transportation Institute (TTI) in the USA. These are described in the following sections.

3.2 Trends in the UK

The CILT is the UK's leading professional organisation for logistics and transport, with over 17,000 members. It is an international institute with branches in thirty-one countries. I should declare an interest as a Chartered Member of the UK organisation. CILT is active in the debate on sustainable transport. For example, it has backed plans to introduce road-user charging to reduce congestion and broadly supports the sustainable transport agenda. CILT produced a report in 2011 titled *Vision 2035*, which outlines the future for logistics and transport in the UK (CILT 2011). The context for the report is a projected increase in the UK population of ten million (15%) by 2040, with the prospect of an additional seven million cars on the road (plus a proportionate increase in vans and trucks). Most of this growth will occur in existing towns and cities, and as well as worsening traffic congestion, it will lead to more overcrowding on commuter rail and metro systems. *Vision 2035* examines the forces for change in transport and the wider society to develop a vision for 2035, which are set out in a series of findings and recommendations. These are summarised in Box 3.1.

Box 3.1 Chartered Institute of Logistics and Transport: Vision 2035 Report – Findings and Recommendations

CILT's Vision 2035 reaches more than twenty key conclusions and recommendations to guide future transport policy. Rather than list these individually, they are grouped into eight themes below.

1   The UK will never have sufficient *capacity* to meet all potential demands for transport services. Even doubling the capacity of public transport would do little more than maintain its current market share.

(continued)

(continued)

2. Transport must be *planned* and administered together with economic and spatial planning regionally and in the devolved nations. More imaginative solutions need to be found for rural transport, to enable it to be managed effectively and efficiently. Discontinuities between spatial policies to regenerate and sustain rural economies and transport policies must be resolved. Similarly there are growing problems with serving outer suburban and extra-urban areas that require similar consideration to rural areas.
3. *Information technology* (IT) has the potential to revolutionise the way we use and manage transport and logistics services. IT will help make better use of capacity at a time when spending on infrastructure will be hard to justify and fund and environmental pressures will continue to grow.
4. Provision of effective *freight transport* capacity and reliable journey times must be key priorities to support recovery and growth. Investment in ports, waterways and rail should be considered in order to transport freight more sustainably as part of an integrated network complemented by road haulage activities. Long supply chains that are liable to disruption and high cost increases need to be reconsidered, moving production and distribution, where practical, nearer to the point of consumption.
5. In *passenger transport*, decisions should be based on peoples' mobility and access requirements rather than focusing on separate modes. Indicators based on economic and social performance rather than crude cost per passenger should be used to justify both investment and operating subsidies. Meeting necessary passenger requirements will need investment in roads, rail infrastructure and airport capacity.
6. Aspirational (but achievable) targets should be set and promoted to assist with achieving transport policy objectives and *national carbon-reduction obligations*. The UK's contribution to reducing CO_2 via the transport sector should be a high priority objective. Walking and cycling should be encouraged to help reduce carbon use, and provide health benefits.
7. More use should be made of *pricing mechanisms* to achieve transport policy objectives. In particular road user charging should be used to expose the external as well as internal costs of vehicle use. Government must recognise that economic recovery can only be achieved if sufficient capacity can be released or created in transport networks.

> 8   The *logistics and transport sectors* should take the lead in promoting a reduction in both freight and passenger traffic by supporting alternatives to travel, reduced commuting distances and shorter, more localised supply chains. This needs behavioural change as well as additional infrastructure.
>
> Source: *Vision 2035* Report, Chartered Institute of Logistics and Transport 2011.

There are contradictions between these objectives and measures, which reflects the competing constituencies in logistics and transport, for example: between freight haulier interests, which advocate more investment in infrastructure, versus environmental campaigners, who oppose any expansion that will damage the environment; between the aim of promoting economic growth while delivering on sustainability objectives such as reducing carbon emissions; and relying on technology to reduce the need to travel or enable travel in less polluting vehicles, which does not in itself resolve the problem of traffic congestion. As the report notes, 'there are tough challenges ahead and we may not find all of the options palatable' (ibid., p. 6).

The CILT report is a good reflection of the current debate in transport. It raises awareness of the issues and is an important contribution to thinking about future policy. It is not a manifesto for change or a polemic prescribing ideological solutions. Rather, the intention is to provide a foundation for more focused initiatives to be developed by CILT's industry forums. It tries to be balanced and succeeds in this, but could equally be accused of sitting on the fence. Transport campaigners will be disappointed that it doesn't offer more radical solutions. Planners will be frustrated that it doesn't prescribe specific policies or programmes (although some of these may emerge as the various forums produce their own sector visions in line with the overall themes). The key questions are whether the recommendations go far enough to deliver a sustainable transport system, meet the carbon reduction requirements mandated by the Kyoto Protocol and tackle the growing levels of congestion.

3.3 International Outlook

It is interesting to compare the UK outlook with international trends. For this I have chosen the *Transport Outlook 2011* report produced by the International Transport Forum (ITF) at the OECD (OECD/ITF 2011). The ITF is an intergovernmental organisation with fifty-two member countries. Its stated aims are to 'act as a strategic think tank with the objective of helping shape the transport policy agenda on a global level and ensuring that it contributes to economic growth, environmental protection, social inclusion and the preservation of human life and well-being'.

Transport Outlook 2011 reviews recent developments in the transport sector and discusses future scenarios. It is a 'focused-Outlook', meaning that it does not provide a comprehensive treatment of the transport sector but instead discusses selected topics seen as critical to the future outlook for the sector. This section summarises their long-term view of the likely changes in transport through to 2050, which they see as continuing existing trends only lightly constrained by policies to ameliorate the growth in demand combined with technology fixes to decarbonise transport. The key trends are depicted in Figures 3.1 and 3.2. These charts show the projected increase in passenger and freight volumes between 2010 and 2050. The upper and lower estimates reflect high- and low-growth scenarios modelled by the ITF.

The charts illustrate that even under low-growth scenarios a 306% increase in passenger travel is expected and a 260% increase in freight volumes. This is a tremendous rate of growth, the majority expected to occur in developing countries and in trade between developing countries and developed nations. If correct, this presents a huge challenge to global transport systems that will need to cope with these increases, especially if transport continues to rely on fossil fuels.

Figure 3.3 shows the projected changes in mode shares by mechanised modes (excluding walking and cycling). These forecast increasing share of

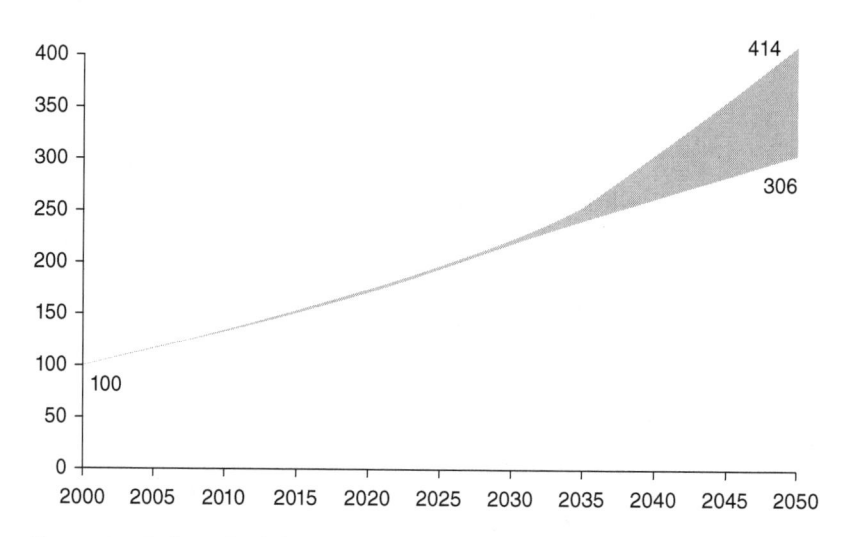

Figure 3.1 Index of Global Passenger Transport Activity, 2000–2050, Index of Pkm (2000 = 100).

Source: Adapted from OECD/ITF (2011), Transport Outlook 2011: Meeting the Needs of 9 Billion People, <http://www.internationaltransportforum.org/pub/pdf/11outlook.pdf> [accessed April 2015].

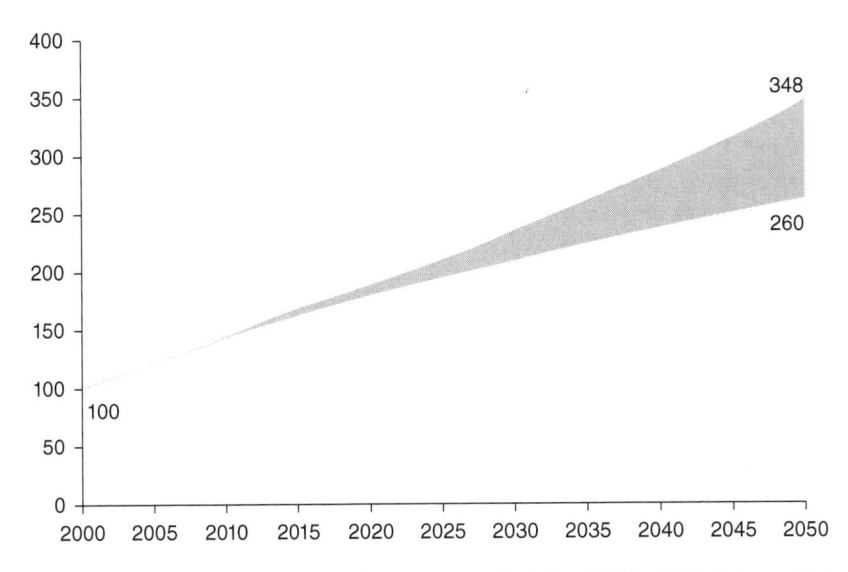

Figure 3.2 Index of Global Freight Transport Activity, 2000–2050, Index of Tkm (2000 = 100).

Source: Adapted from OECD/ITF (2011), Transport Outlook 2011: Meeting the Needs of 9 Billion People, <http://www.internationaltransportforum.org/pub/pdf/11outlook.pdf> [accessed April 2015].

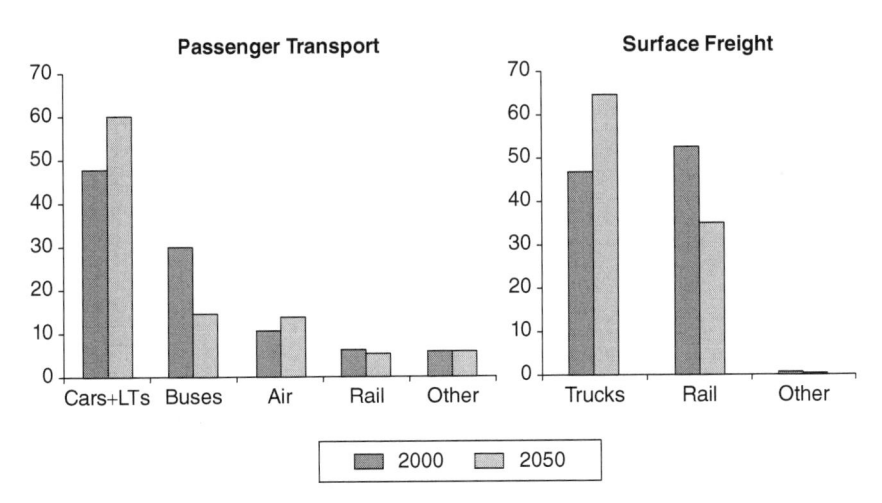

Figure 3.3 Global Mode Split, 2000 and 2050: Halfway Case between High and Low Scenarios (%).

Source: Adapted from OECD/ITF (2011), Transport Outlook 2011: Meeting the Needs of 9 Billion People, <http://www.internationaltransportforum.org/pub/pdf/11outlook.pdf> [accessed April 2015].

passenger travel by automobiles and planes with declining share for buses and rail (note, the actual volumes increase on buses and rail but not as much as the other modes). This is contrary to the trend required if climate change and other environmental impacts are to be minimised. The position regarding freight is also negative from an environmental point of view, with trucks predicted to take an increasing share of the market from rail. These forecasts, if correct, provide a reality check to the transport emissions targets under the Kyoto Protocol and go nowhere near achieving a sustainable transport system analysed by independent experts. The ITF is aware of the Kyoto targets and wider concerns on the environmental impacts of transport and mobility, and evaluate some mitigation measures as described below.

The Long-Term Evolution of Global Transport Demand

The growth in the world's population coupled with rising incomes will lead global mobility to expand strongly through 2050. If infrastructure and energy prices allow, there will be around 3 to 4 times as much global passenger mobility (passenger-kilometres travelled) as in 2000 and 2.5 to 3.5 times as much freight activity, measured in ton-kilometres. Growth will be much stronger outside the OECD region, where passenger-kilometres could increase by a factor of 5 to 6.5, and ton-kilometres by a factor of 4 to 5. The high end of these ranges would be reached only if mobility aspirations in emerging economies mimic those of advanced economies and if prices and policies accommodate these aspirations. Full realisation of such a development path may be unlikely, but this illustrates the significant upside risk associated with the lower, baseline projection. Accounting for population growth, passenger mobility per capita outside the OECD grows three-fold in the ITF baseline scenario or four-fold in the high growth scenario. Consequently, like economic mass, the centre of gravity for mobility will shift to non-OECD economies. In 2000, half of all passenger-kilometres were driven in OECD countries. According to ITF scenarios this declines to around one-fifth in 2050. For ton-kilometres, the OECD share declines from half to around one-third.

It is unclear to what levels car ownership per capita will rise in emerging economies. Very high levels, characteristic of the USA, are unlikely; somewhere between European and Japanese levels is conceivable. The range between these reference points is large, but in either case the share of car-trips in total passenger mobility seems set to increase strongly; for example, from less than 10% at present in China to more than 50% in 2050.

Peak Car Travel in Advanced Economies

Travel by passenger vehicles has not grown much recently in a number of the highest income economies, and has even declined. The 'peak car' travel hypothesis holds that this is because of a saturation effect, where more income no longer translates into more car travel when incomes are very high

(Goodwin 2012; Litman 2012; Madre et al. 2012). But peak car travel is just one among several potential explanations for the observed levelling off of car travel, so projections of future car travel demand should not take peaking for granted. Other potential explanations include increases of fuel prices and uncertainty over future disposable income. Moreover, rising inequality in the distribution of incomes has meant that large parts of the population benefitted little from average growth in income, and this may explain part of the stagnation in travel by car in some countries. For the future, demographics (population size and age structure) will be increasingly important in influencing car travel demand. While the CILT report accepts a levelling off of growth in car travel in its vision, the ITF takes a different position and sees traffic growth returning to long-term trends once real incomes begin to grow again. The UK Department for Transport takes a similar view in its National Road Traffic Forecast (NRTF), which predicts 44% growth between 2010 and 2040; this is the central forecast between the low growth of 34% and the high growth of 55% (Department for Transport 2012). These forecasts have been challenged by transport campaigners and some academics as being unrealistic and if achieved could bring parts of Britain to a standstill.[2]

To try and bring some clarity to this debate, a review of car and train travel trends in the UK was commissioned by a number of interested parties including the RAC Foundation, the Office of Rail Regulator, the Independent Transport Commission and Transport Scotland. The review was undertaken by a team of independent university researchers (Le Vine & Jones 2012). The study identifies significant underlying changes over the past 15 years in several areas, some of which point in opposite directions. Notably, licence-holding among young men has declined, while it has grown rapidly for women in most age groups. Significant gender differences are also apparent in mileage figures: all age groups of women over twenty have increased their use of the car, yet in tandem car use has declined strongly among men between the ages of twenty and fifty. Most of the latter is attributable to dramatic falls in company car usage. And while London has experienced sharp falls in car use, the picture is the opposite in many other areas. In contrast, the growth in rail travel is remarkably evenly spread across the population of Great Britain. It is striking that it has resulted from a larger proportion of the population using rail services over time, rather than more intensive use among the existing users. The authors conclude that 'the notion that car traffic peaked in the mid-2000s is at best an oversimplification' (ibid., p. ii).

The study also looked at the implications for future travel under four scenarios if observed changes in travel behaviour were to continue.

- Scenario 1: company cars. Company car mileage dropped by nearly 40% between 1995/7 and 2005/7. If company car mileage were to disappear completely, without any corresponding increase in personal car mileage, then this would cut total national car mileage per person by a further 10%.

- Scenario 2: gender comparability. If women's car use rose over time to the same levels as men's in 2005/7, right across the age spectrum, then this would add 35% to the average national car mileage per person.
- Scenario 3: generational change. If those currently in their twenties (and younger) preserve their lower mobility characteristics as they age, then over time this would eventually imply a decrease in per-person driving mileage of approximately 20%, once it had worked its way through the population as all cohorts aged.
- Scenario 4: increases in rail market penetration. How far can the base of the rail market keep increasing? In 2005/7, 18% of Londoners used surface rail during their diary week, up from 15% in 1995/7; outside London, this figure grew from 4% to 7%. If these proportions grew to, say, 20% of Londoners and 10% of those living in the rest of Great Britain, then per-person rail mileage would increase by around 40% from its 2005/7 level.

These scenarios do not take into account forecast growth in the population or the effects of an aging profile in the population. They illustrate trends moving in opposite directions, and at best the case for 'peak car' use is weak and largely confined to London. Studies in other countries also present a mixed picture, with no concrete evidence that car use has peaked in developed countries.

CO_2 Emissions

The OECD expects that CO_2 emissions will rise less strongly than mobility because of improving fuel economy. By 2050 global emissions from vehicle use might be 2.5 to 3 times as large as they were in 2000. For emissions from cars and light trucks to remain at the 2010 level, average fleet fuel economy would need to improve quickly and strongly, from around 8 litres/100 kilometres in 2008 to 5 litres/100 kilometres in 2030 and less than 4 litres/100 kilometres in 2050, that is, a two-fold improvement in fuel economy. To meet Kyoto commitments will require even greater fuel economy, to such an extent that the conversion to electric or hybrid electric vehicles is the only feasible option (see below).

The Market for Electric Vehicles

To decarbonise transport radically a large proportion of the road vehicle fleet would have to use alternative energy propulsion systems, including electricity, probably with an accompanying change in models of vehicle ownership and patterns of vehicle use. Part of the strategy for opening up the possibilities for change is to subsidise the purchase of general-purpose passenger cars by the public. Vehicle manufacturers need to count on such subsidy programmes being in place long enough to support investment in electric technologies. In the longer term, however, vehicles will have to become competitive without subsidy, as the cost to public budgets would be excessive if subsidised electric vehicles were to become a large part of overall car sales. At the same time, prices for some of the electric vehicles now on the market suggest that they are financially advantageous in some high-mileage markets, such as delivery vans and taxis, even without subsidies. Policies to promote uptake through non-financial incentives and partnerships might make more sense than subsidies in these markets.

Neither CILT nor OECD challenge the domination of auto-mobility – but they suggest that this can be ameliorated somehow through tweaking existing policies or mitigated through alternative technologies. Is this realistic, or are they living in a transport make-believe? Environmentalist and some transport experts would argue that their policy prescriptions fall short of what is required. If correct, this begs the question of what else needs to be done and how this can be accomplished, especially in non-OECD countries where most of the growth in auto-mobility and CO_2 emissions is occurring. Or are the CILT, OECD and other professional bodies correct, and the environmental imperative can be met with a mixture of technology and changes in behaviour? This is the crucial question for the future of mobility and transport.

3.4 Mobility Trends in the USA

Mobility is a key indicator of the economic health of US communities. It is not surprising, therefore, that US institutions and individuals pay a lot of attention to facilitating auto-mobility and planning improvements to accommodate demands. The predominant planning ethos is still 'predict and provide', despite some attempts to promote transit-oriented design, new urbanism and other approaches to planning that aim to improve accessibility by non-auto modes. It is interesting to compare, for example, the local transport plans (LTPs) prepared in the UK with the equivalent regional transport plans (RTPs) in the USA. The UK LTPs focus on travel demand management, travel planning and smarter choices programmes to meet accessibility targets prior to investing in new infrastructure, unless the infrastructure supports the sustainability goals (such as new cycle paths, rail/bus interchanges and the like). In contrast, the RTPs, prepared by the Metropolitan Planning Organization (a coalition of local governments), use traditional transport modelling techniques to predict future demands and review options to meet these through new infrastructure and the deployment of intelligent transport systems (ITS) to make better use of the existing infrastructure. In some cases the plans may include transit options and demand management measures, but the ethos is generally geared towards expansion and accommodating growth rather than constraining travel.

The planning regime in each country reflects the prevailing political-economic culture. The UK favours restraint and exploration of sustainable options, while the USA is more open to new development and anchored less to historic sentimentality towards townscape and conservation. Thus, travel plans that promote sustainable transport at the expense of car mobility may be politically correct in the UK but would cause apoplexy in many US communities. Likewise, regional transport plans in the US that propose building multi-lane highways, bridges to 'nowhere', and other road improvements which are considered in the policy mainstream would create political revulsion in the UK from a broad swathe of the public, transport planners and politicians. These examples are extremes of the spectrum, and there are many areas of overlap, but it is nevertheless true that auto-mobility is seen as a positive feature by Americans whereas in the UK motoring is perceived as a problem to be tamed and substituted by other more environmentally friendly modes wherever possible.[3]

2012 Urban Mobility Report

In this spirit, the TTI produces an annual mobility index that rates 101 US cities on their level of mobility and congestion (Schrank et al. 2012). The index is eagerly anticipated by the transport profession as well as the media. The professionals pour over the statistics to analyse trends. The media use it to report on how well their city is doing in comparison with others. No doubt politicians and policy makers use the report to promote their transport policies or justify changes. The Urban Mobility Report (UMR) has been published for more than 20 years and has acquired an authoritative status for the reasons just explained. It pushes the buttons of a number of constituencies, and its results are widely quoted in academic publications as well as the popular press. The data are compiled in an extensive research programme and the authors employ a range of methods and techniques to validate the data and produce results that are robust and defensible. It is a seminal document in this respect that touches both professional and layperson interests. The major findings from the 2012 report are summarised below (analysing 2011 data) and in Table 3.1.

The UMR observes that travel is becoming more unstable, journey times are unpredictable and increasing congestion is having an impact on the times that people choose to travel (for those with a choice) and the routes they take. But as the network approaches saturation level, diminishing returns on finding route alternatives kick in and users (people and businesses) become resigned to lengthy journeys (with increased planning time), which has a knock-on effect on commuter stress, productivity and efficiency (Shinkle, Rall & Wheet 2012). While the indices of congestion have improved slightly in the period 2006–2011, including CO_2 emissions, the report authors believe this is a temporary hiatus due to the recession, and

Table 3.1 Major Findings of the 2012 Urban Mobility Report (498 US Urban Areas)

Measure	1982	2000	2005	2010	2011
Individual congestion (per auto user)					
Average yearly delay (hours)	16	39	43	38	38
Travel Time Index	1.07	1.19	1.23	1.18	1.18
Planning Time Index (freeway only)	–	–	–	–	3.09
'Wasted' fuel (gallons)	8	19	23	19	19
CO_2 produced (lbs)	160	388	451	376	380
Congestion cost (2011 $)	$342	$795	$925	$810	$818
National congestion					
Travel delay (billion hours)	1.1	4.5	5.9	5.5	5.5
'Wasted' fuel (billion gallons)	0.5	2.4	3.2	2.9	2.9
CO_2 produced (billion lbs)	10	47	62	56	56
Truck congestion cost (billions of 2011 $)	–	–	–	$27	$27
Congestion cost (billions of 2011 $)	$24	$94	$128	$120	$121

(continued)

Table 3.1 (continued)

Measure	1982	2000	2005	2010	2011
Impact of mitigation measures					
Yearly travel delay saved by:					
Operational treatments (million hours)	9	215	368	370	374
Public transportation (million hours)	409	774	869	856	865
Yearly congestion costs saved by:					
Operational treatments (billions of 2011 $)	$0.2	$3.6	$7.3	$8.3	$8.5
Public transportation (billions of 2011 $)	$8.0	$14.0	$18.5	$20.2	$20.8

Source: adapted from Texas Transportation Institute's 2012 Urban Mobility Report, Exhibit 1, p. 1.

Notes: *Definitions of measures*:

- Yearly auto delay per commuter – the extra time spent travelling at congested speeds rather than free-flow speeds by private vehicle drivers and passengers who typically travel in the peak periods.
- Travel Time Index (TTI) – the ratio of travel time in the peak period to travel time in free-flow conditions. A TTI of 1.30 indicates a 20-minute free-flow trip takes 26 minutes in the peak period.
- Planning Time Index (PTI) – the ratio of travel time on the worst day of the month to travel time at free-flow conditions (freeways only). A PTI of 1.80 indicates a traveller should plan for 36 minutes for a journey that takes 20 minutes in free-flow conditions (20 minutes × 1.80 = 36 minutes).
- Wasted fuel – extra fuel consumed during congested travel.
- CO_2 per auto commuter during congestion – the extra CO_2 emitted at congested speeds rather than free-flow speed by private drivers and passengers who typically travel in the peak periods.
- Congestion cost – the yearly value of delay time and wasted fuel.

traffic and congestion will increase once the economy returns to growth. The UMR also includes estimates on the effect of mitigation measures – operational treatments such as ITS technology deployment, high-occupancy vehicle lanes, freeway ramp meeting, and public transport services. These are shown to have significant impacts on mitigating the cost of congestion, especially public transport. The implication is that without these alternatives traffic congestion and the associated costs would be a lot worse.

The 2011 data are consistent with past trends, namely the following:

- First, the problem is very large. In 2011, congestion caused urban Americans to travel 5.5 billion hours more and to purchase an extra 2.9 billion gallons of fuel for a congestion cost of $121 billion.
- Second, in order to arrive on time for important trips, travellers had to allow for 60 minutes making a trip that takes 20 minutes in light traffic.
- Third, while congestion is below its peak in 2005, there is only a short-term cause for celebration. Prior to the economy slowing, just 5 years ago, congestion levels were much higher than a decade ago; these conditions will return as the economy improves.

Approximately 37% of total delay occurs in the midday and overnight (outside of the peak hours) times of day when travellers and shippers expect free-flow travel. Many manufacturing processes depend on a free-flow trip for efficient production and congested networks interfere with those operations.

Not surprisingly, congestion is forecast to continue to get worse as travel demand grows faster than the supply of new infrastructure. The UMR forecasts that:

- the national congestion cost will grow from $121 billion to $199 billion in 2020 (in 2011 US dollars);
- delay will grow to 8.4 billion hours in 2020; wasted fuel will increase to 4.5 billion gallons in 2020;
- the average commuter will see their cost grow to $1010 in 2020 (in 2011 US dollars); they will waste 45 hours and 25 gallons in 2020; and
- if the price of gasoline grows to $5 per gallon, the congestion-related fuel cost would grow from about $10 billion in 2011 to approximately $22 billion in 2020 (in 2011 US dollars).

TTI recommend a balanced and diversified approach to reduce congestion – one that focuses on more of everything. As the authors comment, 'It is clear that our current investment levels have not kept pace with the problems. Population growth will require more systems, better operations and an increased number of travel alternatives . . . In all cases, the solutions need to work together to provide an interconnected network of transportation services'.

The UMR examines a range of solutions to mitigate congestion but does not advocate any overarching policy to achieve carbon emissions targets, as is the case in the UK and Europe. Its balanced approach includes a blend of 'predict and provide' and 'new realism' measures that will disappoint environmentalists and transport activists but reflect the dominant mobility culture in the USA. The UMR has been criticised by Litman for placing too much emphasis on the costs of congestion and the benefits of auto-mobility rather than evaluating strategies that would improve accessibility by more sustainable modes (Litman 2013). The objections to mobility indices such as the UMR and sustainable transport and potential mobility (STPM) are both methodological and ideological. The UMR authors reject most of the criticisms and point out that their analysis is based on examining actual travel behaviour (Lomax 2013). In response to some of these criticisms, TTI is undertaking research to incorporate access measures into the mobility index and plans to weight trips that use non-auto modes more appropriately in future reports.

3.5 Congestion Limits to Economic Growth

Since 2010 the UMR has used traffic data collected by INRIX, a commercial traffic data collection company, which crowd sources real-time data from vehicles and other devices. INRIX provides a similar service to customers in Europe and produces statistics on traffic congestion in European countries and the major metropolitan areas.[4] In 2014 Belgium was ranked as the most congested country in Europe, followed by the Netherlands and then the UK. The least congested countries, not surprisingly, are those more sparsely populated such as Hungary and Portugal. The most congested cities are Milan, followed by Brussels and Antwerp (both in Belgium), then London and Greater Manchester, ranked fourth and fifth, respectively. The UK has six of the top twenty-five most congested cities in Europe.[5] Box 3.2 illustrates the magnitude of the challenge ahead for a city such as London.

Box 3.2 Capital Congestion: Projected Population and Travel Growth in London by 2050

London's current population of 8.4 million is forecast to increase to 11.3 million by 2050 (and to 9.5–10.0 million by 2030), and these extra people will place huge additional demands on the capital's transport networks. Transport for London estimates that £200 billion of new infrastructure (excluding airports and national rail schemes) will be required by 2050 to meet the projected travel demand on public transport (a rise of 50–60%) and roads (35–40% increase). This is far in excess of current expenditure, and the Mayor of London has called for greater fiscal devolution as well as powers to raise taxes locally for transport projects, perhaps along the lines of the 'Versement Transport' tax applied to wages in the Paris region (Ile de-France). Similar, if less extreme, challenges are faced by mayors of other cities in the UK who, like the Mayor of London, would like to see more taxes devolved. Cities such as London have to devote more resources to tackling transport demands of a growing population and rising mobility aspirations. These demands are outrunning the ability of governments to deliver additional capacity. The scale of the costs to sustain mobility is a drain on the finances of local government as well as the wider economy. Congestion is already a factor in limiting economic growth and will only get worse unless mobility demands are curtailed. The London Infrastructure Plan, for instance, calculates that if the central London economy were to be constrained because of transport problems this could result in an annual loss to national output of approximately £70 billion, or 5.4% of gross domestic product (GDP).

Source: Greater London Authority 2014.

The European index has not attracted the same level of interest or debate that the UMR has in the USA. The results are occasionally published in newspaper articles and in the professional press but to date it has not had the same impact as the UMR. Perhaps this is because the transport debate in Europe is framed less by concerns about congestion than climate change, air pollution and safety. The INRIX scorecard, however, demonstrates what a real and present problem this is becoming and how it is getting worse in most countries. It would be useful to see a similar study such as the UMR produced for each European country, including the effect of mitigation measures such as investments in public transport and smarter choices travel programmes.

The review of current trends in the UK, USA and OECD member countries does not look promising for tackling issues such as congestion, climate change and costs to users of transport systems. The growth of world population and mobility by mechanical modes presents a number of challenges that each country with its own development goals and political culture will address differently. There does not appear to be a simple prescription, even if we agree on the diagnosis of the problem. There are a range of policy solutions that have been advocated by transport specialists and interest groups, but there is no consensus among the political class and the public towards these. Sacrifices and compromises will be necessary to deliver an environmentally sustainable transport system, but inevitably the question comes down to who bears the cost and who gains most from actions to tackle transport ills. We have a 'tragedy of the commons' type situation, in which society loses by not taking collective action but individuals and groups do not associate with the common good and only see their own interest. It will require political will and perhaps a major environmental catastrophe to convince the public of the need to change our behaviours enough to avoid a collapse in our transport systems.

This pessimistic scenario is not shared by everyone, and there are more optimistic views that point to advances in vehicle technology and communications to resolve many of our transport problems. Perhaps this will happen, but it is something of a leap of faith to put all our options in the technology basket. We can hope for the best, but we should plan for the worst. Technology has a part to play but we need to address the social, economic and political elements that shape transport demand and supply. There needs to be a better alignment between the economy, mobility and congestion. We will never satisfy all needs or meet all demands, but through a combination of utilitarianism and Pareto optimality we may just be able to ensure that most requirements are met with the most efficient use of resources in as sustainably manner as possible.

Notes

1 Except for essential trips to work, school, etc., where the institution determines the participation times. Travelling by car at one's leisure – the quintessential 'road trip' – is a form of escapism exercised by the motoring masses. Even on essential journeys, the car offers the possibility to enjoy some 'quality time'.
2 The NRTF has been the topic of much debate and discussion among transport professionals, as reported in the magazine *Local Transport Today* (LTT 592 and LTT 593) 2012.
3 A caveat needs mentioning regarding the UK 'progressive' outlook contained in LTPs, which will be influenced in future by the new local transport bodies (LTBs) created by the Coalition Government – these take over responsibilities for transport investment decisions in their areas. This is likely to lead to conflicts with local authorities and LTP goals. LTBs appear to be more interested in capital investment to promote economic growth, including road infrastructure, rather than focusing on accessibility and social inclusion objectives. If so, they will move transport planning back towards the 'predict and provide' approach.
4 The INRIX Traffic Scorecard is available from: http://scorecard.INRIX.com/scorecard/default.asp [accessed July 2014].
5 The data are compiled from records of real-time traffic on every road segment during peak hours (06:00–10:00 and 15:00–19:00, Monday to Friday) to see how the actual speed every 15 minutes related to how fast traffic would have been if the road were free-flowing. INRIX adds together all the congested segments in a given city and averages it to create a score for that city. To calculate the wasted minutes in traffic, the estimated typical commuter trip length is factored by the number of trips taken each year. The score card is updated monthly.

References

CILT 2011, *Vision 2035: A Report on the Future of Logistics and Transport in the UK*, CILT (UK), Corby.

Department for Transport 2012, *Road Traffic Forecasts 2011: Results from the Department for Transport's National Transport Model*, HMSO, London, UK.

Goodwin, P. 2012, 'Peak Travel, Peak Car and the Future of Mobility: Evidence, Unresolved Issues, Policy Implications, and a Research Agenda', *Long-Run Trends in Travel Demand, Discussion Paper 201–13*, OECD Roundtable, Paris, France.

Greater London Authority 2014, *London Infrastructure Plan 2050: Transport Supporting Paper*. Available from: https://www.london.gov.uk/sites/default/files/transport_supporting_paper.pdf [accessed 14 August 2014].

Le Vine, S. & Jones, P. 2012, *On the Move: Making Sense of Car and Train Travel Trends in Britain*, RAC Foundation, London, UK.

Litman, T. 2012, *The Future Isn't What It Used To Be: Changing Trends and Their Implications for Transport Planning*, Victoria Transport Policy Institute, British Columbia, Canada.

Litman, T. 2013, *Congestion Costing Critique: Critical Evaluation of the 'Urban Mobility Report'*, Victoria Transport Policy Institute, British Columbia, Canada.

Lomax, T. 2013, *Congestion Measurement in the Urban Mobility Report Response to Critique by Mr Todd Litman*, Mobility Analysis Program, Texas A & M Transportation Institute, Texas, USA.

Madre, J.L., Bussiere, Y.D., Collet, R. & Villareal, I.T. 2012, 'Are We Heading Towards a Reversal of the Trend for Ever-Greater Mobility?', *Long-Run Trends in Travel Demand, Discussion Paper 2012–16*, OECD Roundtable, Paris, France.

OECD/ITF 2011, *Transport Outlook 2011: Meeting the Needs of 9 Billion People*, OECD, Paris. Available from: http://www.internationaltransportforum.org/pub/pdf/11Outlook.pdf [accessed 14 October 2011].

Schrank, D., Eisele, B. & Lomax, T. 2012, *2012 Urban Mobility Report*, Texas A&M Transportation Institute, Texas, USA.

Shinkle, D., Rall, J. & Wheet, A. 2012, *On The Move: State Strategies for 21st Century Transportation Solutions*, National Conference of State Legislatures (with support from the Rockefeller Foundation), Denver, USA.

Part II
Transport Technology and Policy Development

4 Smarter Transport Technology and Innovation

4.1 Intelligent Transport Systems

Just as concerns were emerging in the early 1990s around the 'predict and provide' model to meet growing demands for auto travel, transport researchers and developers were experimenting with the latest advances in information and communications technologies (ICT). They were exploring how ICT could be used to produce a more efficient transport system, reduce congestion, make the roads safer and provide better information to travellers in cars and on public transport. The umbrella term applied to this activity in the early 1990s was intelligent vehicle highway systems (IVHS), reflecting the focus on producing smarter cars and highways that could interact more intelligently.

IVHS later evolved into the broader realm of intelligent transportation systems (ITS), which has grown to be a significant sector in transport. The name change reflected a desire to encompass all transport modes, not just automobiles, and the multimodal nature of travel. It also served a political purpose in embracing all transport constituencies so that no sector felt left out. ITS deployments generally fall into two camps: commercial development of technologies such as satellite navigation, automatic vehicle location, in-car telematics (such as Bluetooth wireless communications for mobile phones), adaptive cruise control and cameras to assist in parking, avoiding collisions and such like (Zhao 1997); and public sector schemes to manage traffic and incidents such as the managed/smart motorways (active traffic management) concept developed by the UK Highways Agency (Department for Transport 2005). In some cases the public and private sectors cooperate to produce an ITS service, such as real-time traffic updates and public transport information apps.

As these examples show, the purpose of ITS was to either improve the efficiency – throughput – of the existing transport network or enhance the journey experience, which the traveller would value and pay for (such as satnav devices) or the provider would pay for as part of its service (e.g. real-time journey information). ITS is promoted as a means to make better use of existing transport capacity and avoid costly new infrastructure

(Branscomb & Keller 1996). Commercial companies were looking to add value to their customers' experience of driving, by making driving safer, more comfortable, reliable and exciting – and of course profitable.

Planners and engineers – in the private and public spheres – saw ITS as a technology fix to transport that would revolutionise traffic control and transportation systems management. Other disciplines such as biology and physics were being revolutionised by new discoveries such as DNA sequencing and new sub-atomic particles, and ICT was seeing major advances in computation and data processing that was affecting all aspects of business, government and society, especially when the internet entered the public domain and became a mass media in the mid-1990s. Compared to these innovations, transport developments appeared pedestrian. Transport institutions needed something new and exciting to reinvigorate the sector and hold out the promise of a better future built around the latest technologies. ITS fulfilled this idea and was sold as such. It was embraced by governments as well as business, and there was a belief among many practitioners that ITS could deliver a new 'DNA' for understanding traffic and travel behaviour and how to manage it more effectively. It hasn't quite delivered on this promise, but it has spurred the development of several new transport-related technologies.

4.2 The Impact of Location Technologies on Transport Innovation

Probably the most influential location technology has been the global positioning system (GPS) for vehicle tracking and navigation. GPS was a technology developed for cruise missiles and other military uses that needed equipment to be guided to a target location. Its use for non-military purposes was restricted and only possible to calibrate a day or two after the event (such as mapping the location of assets on a road) when the correct signal was made available by the military. President Bill Clinton removed this 'selective availability' restriction in 2000, so that users with GPS receivers could locate their position in real time. This led to the development of commercial satnav devices that soon became ubiquitous in cars and on public transport systems. Indeed, satnav devices have become the most successful face of ITS among the general public. Allied to GPS is the advance in mobile telecommunications to the extent that most smartphones now contain location technologies including access to digital maps and satellite images for numerous applications. Internet companies such as Google (and later Microsoft) created on-line mapping and imaging applications that bring digital mapping and simple geographic information system (GIS) capabilities to the mobile consumer market.

GPS accuracy has improved over time and the next generation of GPS satellites, launched by the European Union and other countries, will remove the dependence on the USA to provide the signals and allow lots of other uses, for example tracking of vehicles in road-user charging schemes, which otherwise would be risky to deploy. There is no doubt that GPS and allied technologies have improved transport from the users' and managers' perspectives. The jury is still out, however, on whether these constitute a transformational technology, like DNA sequencing, or is instead an influential technology that is important but not ground-breaking.

One way of looking at this is to consider technology potential. In the traditional model of innovation (the familiar 'S curve'), early adopters are followed by the mass take-up of the innovation, which then matures and continues in a steady state until a new invention takes its place. This innovation model explains the adoption process, but doesn't explain why or when an innovation is adopted or how it influences other technologies that may follow.

Another way of looking at technology potential is depicted in Figure 4.1. Here a new invention may stumble along incrementally without becoming widely adopted; it may remain dormant for a while; or it may become influential or transformational on its own merits or in combination with other technologies (Geerlings & Rienstra 2003). Influential technologies trigger a makeover in products and services. For example, GPS took off

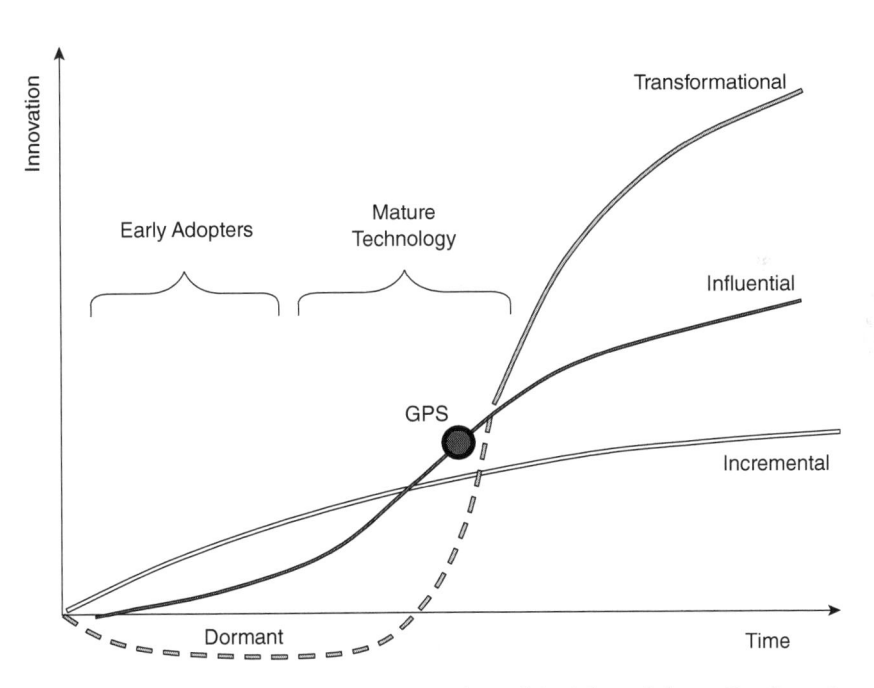

Figure 4.1 Transport Technology Potential Model (Adapted from Geerlings & Rienstra 2003).

when government restrictions on its availability in real time were lifted, but this also coincided with advances in digital mapping and GIS that allowed satellite navigation to be visualised on maps. GPS without the digital maps would not be successful, at least in the consumer market. Since then GPS has been integrated with light detection and ranging (LIDAR), radar and cameras to assist in navigating driverless cars (Google and some car companies have been experimenting with these self-drive systems). It is not yet clear whether GPS will continue its trajectory as an influential technology or transition to become a transformational technology that causes a re-think of business processes rather than just a makeover. GPS appears to be the only current candidate that could transform the transport scene, yet it is not per se a transport technology. This is not uncommon, and to be transformational a technology has to transgress across disciplinary boundaries. DNA, for instance, is as well known for its use in criminal justice as in life sciences.

In transport history transformational technologies are few, beginning with the wheel, followed by the boat and navigation, harnessing animals (horsepower), the steam engine, the internal combustion engine, the aeroplane and most recently the jet engine. Some of these started out as incremental or niche technologies and only became transformative through advances in production methods (Ford's Model T, for instance) or the integration with other technologies (such as materials to support aeroplanes). Contemporary transport technologies such as hybrid/electric vehicles may become influential but are hardly transformational. One other possible contender is fuel cells, which can harness hydrogen to power vehicles. Fuel cells were discovered in the 19th century and are an example of a dormant technology that if allied to other technologies may yet be transformational in delivering an alternative power source and ultra-low emissions vehicles, thus mitigating the impacts of transport on climate change.

If GPS and location technologies develop into powerful means of tracking and controlling movement, their transformative qualities will not necessarily be used in benign ways, and indeed what makes them revolutionary may not be the technology itself but how it is harnessed. To date, GPS has been used to assist in activities such as navigation but could be used to control movement rather than facilitate it. The social and political pressures on future mobility may create conditions whereby mobility rationing (by price or availability) may be imperative to control congestion and preserve a competitive economy. Thus a convergence between transport technology and political-economy would create the conditions for a transport revolution.

4.3 Vehicle Technology

Much has been made of the potential for electric propulsion to replace the internal combustion engine, and most vehicle manufacturers are investing significant amounts in creating hybrid gasoline-electric automobiles or purely electric vehicles.[1] These are supported by government grants and growing infrastructure to support these modes, such as electric charging points. The chief limitation in the operation and appeal of electric cars, in particular, is their range and lack of supporting infrastructure. On both counts the future looks brighter than it was when the first hybrid cars were introduced in the 1990s. Hybrid cars were deployed in preference to all-electric models because of these limitations and have proved reliable in operation and popular among motorists seeking a more environmentally friendly form of car travel.

There are a number of reasons to be optimistic about the future of automobiles. Firstly, advances in electric propulsion technologies are making these vehicles more efficient and economical to manufacture and operate. The next generation of cars will be ultra-low-emission vehicles powered by electricity generated from batteries, fuel cells, liquid petroleum gas or a combination of these that will meet stringent emission targets. This development is not just confined to cars but extends to vans and buses. Secondly, the infrastructure for re-supply of batteries, charging points, service stations and the like is increasing and there is even the prospect of recharging while on the move over smart pavements. Thirdly, the attitude of motorists towards electric vehicles is changing and as utilisation increases the psychological barriers will recede. The inducements to use 'greener cars', promoted through government programs and grants, will also entice consumers to consider this option over a conventional internal combustion engine.

All the signs, therefore, point to a rosy future for more environmentally friendly cars that will ultimately replace the internal combustion engine, supporting the maxim that it is easier to take the internal combustion engine out of the car than the driver. The only serious technical limitation on the horizon is the ability of the energy producers and the national grid to deliver the vast quantities of electricity that will be required. If these are provided by renewable energy sources, such as wind generation, nuclear power and fuel cells, then the electric vehicles will truly be sustainable in terms of their energy use.

This, however, is not music to the ears of the sustainable transport lobby or environmentalists who consider the impact of cars undesirable whatever form of propulsion is used. As already noted, car culture and auto-mobility has many indirect effects on urban sprawl, social exclusion, promoting hyper-mobility, etc. which is antithetical to the concept of a convivial transport system. Electric vehicles may make cars less polluting but otherwise perpetuate the existing car culture and do nothing to solve congestion. In response, car companies, car rental firms and a new breed of car-sharing enterprises are experimenting with collective consumption business models, including pay-as-you-go car hire by the hour, shared vehicle ownership and ridesharing services. The hope (expectation?) is that these will attract more motorists, especially in urban areas, who will see the advantage of shared use of cars rather than outright ownership. These car clubs also provide access to a wider range of vehicles, giving greater flexibility to users. Car-sharing services and car clubs are growing and attracting the interest of large commercial companies but it remains to be seen if they can demonstrate a viable business model. At present, they receive little in the way of government support, but if they show that they can be effective in increasing average car occupancy and lower carbon emissions, there may be a case for government incentives similar to those provided to electric car users. Thus, car sharing should be considered part of the mix for future sustainable mobility.

The automobile of the future will incorporate advanced telematics to assist in vehicle control and navigation. Even today the average car contains more computing power than a standard personal computer, and this is likely to grow as more mobile telecommunications services are added into the vehicle. Vehicle-to-vehicle and vehicle-to-remote sensing device communications will increase dramatically to improve the safety, control and tracking of the vehicle to such an extent that by the 2020s the instrumented highway will enable cars to be driven autonomously in convoys on motorways and other segregated highways. Already, firms such as Google have been experimenting with self-driving cars, and in the USA a demonstration project for an automatic highway that takes over the control of vehicles in platoons has been show-pieced.[2] Research and development in these areas is continuing, and deployment of ITS technologies in-vehicle and remotely will continue to gather pace.

These enhancements are not confined to road traffic. Public transport systems will benefit from many of these developments, including more reliable monitoring and tracking of vehicles in real time, advance notification of service delays, alternate routing options and bookings when disruption occurs, integrated ticketing via smartphones, and other measures to improve the quality of the journey. The cost of these services will decline while the availability of information will increase, and developers will produce user-friendly applications geared towards specific users that will make travelling by public transport more seamless and comfortable.

Perhaps the greatest impact of the ITS and telematics technologies is the ability to track individual vehicles and users (travel objects) across the transport systems in real time. It is already possible to track mobile phone users in cars and use crowd-sourcing techniques to monitor their movements. Currently these are anonymous and aggregated to measure travel speeds or delays, but in future, with the user's permission, location-aware technologies could be personalised to guide the user through transport systems and services, whether by single mode or multimodal systems. The possibility exists to dynamically route individuals once a destination is set, with continual monitoring and feedback on progress, including redirection if a problem ahead is identified. To some extent, the satnav devices in cars that connect to traffic management services already perform these functions, but for the most part the apps are more static than dynamic.

Once these capabilities are deployed and proven, they could be used to manage vehicle and passenger movements in aggregate. For instance, travel by car to a distant destination would entail a review of the routes available, the capacity and estimated travel time, and a place on the route selected would be reserved within a given time window. Route selection and reservation would guarantee that demand does not exceed supply, thus avoiding congestion and travel time unreliability.

4.4 Scheduling Logistics

Another area that has seen significant advances, without getting the attention it deserves, is the scheduling and monitoring of vehicles in transport logistics and supply chain management. Advances in scheduling software together with faster computing power have enabled the scheduling and routing of multiple vehicles and trips to optimise performance, with impressive savings in journey times, costs and the number of vehicles required to meet the transport objective. Allied to this are enhancements in location allocation algorithms that can optimise the location of depots to minimise transport costs or meet just-in-time delivery schedules. When combined, the advances in scheduling, routing and location allocation amount to significant advances in the logistics of carrying goods and people (Sutton & Vissar 2004). To date, progress has been most evident in the movement of goods through the supply chain, and logistics or supply chain management has become one of the fastest areas of growth in the transport industry. Moving people is not as straightforward or malleable as moving goods but the methods and techniques deployed in the freight industry are being adapted to moving passengers, and seem set to continue in the future.

The logistics sector is one of the leading users of ICT in transport – GPS, automated vehicle location (AVL) technologies and geographic information systems (GIS). Routing and scheduling is a complex problem, especially when managing multiple vehicles, organising complex tours, trying to accommodate intermediate stops on-the-fly, or routing with backlogs (Bodin et al. 1983). Real-time data can be used for dynamic routing and scheduling. A range of dynamic information can potentially be incorporated, such as traffic news, roadworks and accidents, travel speeds or travel time, weather conditions and customer information. The internet can be used to distribute information to users' mobile data terminals or smartphones.

These techniques are being transferred into the passenger transport arena, in cars and on public transport systems. Fixed scheduled services will continue to play a role in mass transit, but demand-responsive services, ranging from shared taxis and car clubs to dial-a-ride bus services, will employ logistics techniques to match the demand to the transport supply in the most efficient manner. This includes feeder services to fixed route buses and trains with coordinated schedules at interchange points. Even services with fixed schedules will benefit by 'knowing' in advance the number of passengers to expect, either from pre-booking or sharing of information from upstream providers. The customers will be kept informed of progress through the journey, especially if there are delays or disruptions. When these occur, they will be directed to alternate routes or services with the assurance of a guaranteed ride home.

4.5 Intelligent Mobility: The Future for Transport Technology

While there have been significant advances in transport technology, mobile apps and the provision of real-time information, the hoped-for technology breakthrough that would transform travel has not materialised. Visionaries dream of the flying car or personal rapid transit systems, but these remain as elusive as ever. Rather, we are on an evolutionary path from the internal combustion engine to electric propulsion, in cars and high-speed rail; from mode-specific information and booking systems to multimodal journey planning with enhancements to the journey experience whether travelling by car or public transport. There is much to celebrate and look forward to as we progress towards more integrated and multimodal transport systems, joined up by technology as well as transport infrastructure.

The integration of transport services and technology is sometimes referred to as 'intelligent mobility' as distinct from ITS, with its focus on ICT equipment and services. Intelligent mobility is defined as the efficient and cost-effective movement of goods and people using intelligently methods – in a coordinated and collaborative way – to develop improved transport systems that unlock latent capacity.[3] The focus is on harnessing technology to meet future mobility needs and through the deployment of commercial products and services. The vision outlined for intelligent mobility signifies the ambition to squeeze more capacity onto the transport system to alleviate congestion. It is questionable, however, whether this can be accomplished without reducing demand, for example by tolls or other means of charging road users. We have the technology to deploy road-user charging systems but not the political will outside of a few pilot cities.

Technology may at least solve one of the major concerns with automobility, namely the contribution that vehicle emissions make to greenhouse gases, including CO_2. Assuming that electric vehicles prove to be viable and are recharged from renewable energy sources, the target of reducing CO_2 emissions by 80% by 2050 looks doable. Technology will also play an increasing role in vehicle control and communications that will reduce collisions and improve safety for all road users. And as already mentioned the scheduling and routing of vehicles to optimise road use and improve journey time reliability will become a standard feature of traffic management for freight and passenger movements. We can be confident, therefore, that technology will play a key role in how we manage and operate transport systems in the future, but it needs to be implemented appropriately to specific products and services. Technology on its own will not resolve the problem of congestion. The only long-term solution is to curtail demand to the capacity of the transport systems that we can afford to build. We may be able to squeeze some more capacity out of the current systems and use ICT to manage mobility more intelligently, but ultimately we need to match demand to supply. This can only be accomplished by using a range of policy measures complemented by appropriate technologies. The next chapter describes some of these measures in more detail.

Notes

1 Magnetic levitation powered by electricity was once seen as a possible future technology but has since become dormant due to the amount of energy required to propel the personal travel pods or train sets, as well as the construction costs of dedicated infrastructure.
2 A section of Interstate 15 in San Diego County was used to test the feasibility of driver-assisted technologies, implemented by the National Automated Highway System Consortium (NAHSC).
3 Transport Systems Catapult, available at https://ts.catapult.org.uk/ [accessed April 2014], one of seven technology and innovation centres established and overseen by the Technology Strategy Board, funded by the UK Government and private companies.

References

Bodin, L., Golden, B., Assad, A. & Ball, M. 1983, 'Routing and Scheduling of Vehicles and Crews: The State of the Art', *Computers and Operations Research*, 10, 2, Special Issue, pp. 63–211.

Branscomb, L.M. & Keller, J.H. 1996, *Converging Infrastructures: Intelligent Transportation and the National Information Infrastructure*, MIT Press, Cambridge, UK.

Department for Transport 2005, *Intelligent Transport Systems: The Policy Framework for the Roads Sector*, HMSO, London, UK.

Geerlings, H. & Rienstra, S. 2003, 'Exploring "Weak Signals" in Transportation; An Inventory of Potential Future Trends and Developments in Transportation', *Transportation Planning and Technology*, 26, 6, December, pp. 469–489.

Sutton, J.C. & Vissar, J. 2004, 'The Role of GIS in Routing and Logistics', in *Handbook of Transport Geography and Spatial Systems, Handbooks in Transport, Volume 5*, eds D.A. Hensher, K.J. Button, K.E. Haynes & P.R. Stopher, Elsevier, Oxford, pp. 357–374.

Zhao, Y. 1997, *Vehicle Location and Navigation Systems*, Artech House, Boston, USA.

5 Sustainable Transport Policy in the UK

5.1 Paradigm Shifts in Transport Planning

The history of post-war transport planning can be divided into five phases, described below. These are not discrete boundaries, and overlaps between the different ages occur as one ideology is superseded by another. They represent the predominant hegemony in each period as reflected in policy, legislation and investment in different sectors of transport. Countervailing discourses were present but generally suppressed or dismissed until the conventional wisdom was successfully challenged, for example through political action in response to deteriorating transport conditions or following changes in technology.

1   **Age of Road Infrastructure (1945–1970).** Following the Second World War priority was given to re-building the country's infrastructure, including new roads and motorways to meet the demands of a rapidly motorising society (goods vehicles and cars). In contrast, the extensive railway network was cut back to reflect falling demand. It was during this period that the influential Buchanan Report, *Traffic in Towns*, was produced which highlighted the conflicts between traffic, pedestrians and the urban environment, and pointed out the economic costs of accommodating traffic in historic town centres. In response planners and engineers set about segregating traffic where feasible, including the wholesale re-modelling of some cities. The policy favoured competitive transport over convivial transport solutions.
2   **Age of Transport Revisionism (1970–1980).** Not surprisingly, the destruction of many city environments led to protest movements, most notably in London, where activists were successful in opposing the proposed ring of motorways. Locally and nationally campaigners against motorways and trunk roads emerged and developed arguments not dissimilar to the 'new realism' paradigm of today. An influential book at the time was *Changing Directions*, produced by the Independent Commission on Transport, which, as the title indicates, proposed an alternative approach with more emphasis on environmental impacts in

transport appraisal and more support for public transport (Independent Commission on Transport 1974). Publications like this, and growing concerns about traffic impacts, led to a re-appraisal of the trunk road programme, and in 1977 the Government published a White Paper on Transport Policy that proposed a more balanced approach with more support for public transport, cycling and walking and greater emphasis on environmental impacts (Department of Transport 1977). One practical outcome was the statutory obligation on county councils – the transport authorities at that time – to prepare a public transport plan for their area, including support for bus and rail services. These were first mandated in 1978 but were withdrawn in 1986 following the Conservative Government's deregulation policy. This signified the end of comprehensive transport planning in the shire counties. Public transport planning in the metropolitan areas and London continued under powers granted in the early 1970s, but these were watered down by the mid-1980s. This era laid the foundations for the convivial transport discourse.

3 **Age of Contestability (1980–1997).** The Conservative Government led by Prime Minister Margaret Thatcher had an ideological objection to public services that could be provided by private enterprise. This included municipal bus companies and the regulation of bus services. The Minister for Transport in the early 1980s, Nicholas Ridley, was an enthusiastic supporter of privatisation and deregulation and sponsored the 1985 Transport Act, which ushered in the deregulation and privatisation of local bus services outside London in 1986 (excluding Northern Ireland). This was followed later by the privatisation of the railways in 1993. This age of contestability was a reaction against the revisionist policies of the 1970s and completely changed the landscape for public transport planning and operations, while reverting to a more sympathetic approach to road building and traffic schemes (Button & Gillingwater 1986). There was some acknowledgement of the environmental impact of road building reflected in the appraisal of trunk road schemes, but the bias towards capital investment over revenue support prevailed during this era. Bus services were contested in the market place, with the result that services and ridership declined outside of the major cities and eventually bus operations came to be dominated by large companies. Only in London did municipal planning via franchising remain, and there ridership has held up and even increased. Most other areas have seen a fall in passengers. The shake-up in bus operations has had some beneficial effects, such as more innovative services and better-quality buses, but the long-term effect has been to drive more people into using cars rather than buses. Mrs Thatcher believed in a 'car owning democracy' and substantially achieved this during her term of office. A competitive transport ethos prevailed during this period.

4   **Age of New Realism (1997–2010).** The idea for a different approach to transport policy was first mooted in the early 1990s and gained support among transport academics, practitioners and New Labour politicians. 'New realism' was a backlash against the 'predict and provide' model that had hitherto prevailed and been fervently adopted by the Conservative Government. When the Labour Government entered office in 1997 they took on board the 'new realism' model and had an enthusiastic champion in the Minister for Transport, Environment and Regions, John Prescott. Labour sought to modify the contestable market for public transport with more convivial policies such as franchising that had worked well in London, and gave public transport a boost by switching expenditure into buses, rail, cycling and walking. The big idea was to create a sustainable and accessible transport system that could meet climate change targets (lower carbon emissions) by reducing dependence on cars. The *New Deal for Transport* (DETR 1998) ran into a number of roadblocks – political and institutional – which derailed its full implementation. 'New realism' measures are still part of official government policy but are no longer given the priority they once enjoyed.

5   **Age of Austerity (2010–Present).** The Coalition Government of Conservatives and Liberal Democrats elected in 2010 introduced a programme of cutbacks in public expenditure that has impacted all transport modes. The sustainable transport aims remain but the Government is applying more weight to economic development goals, including some major projects such as high-speed rail, rail electrification and local road schemes. Concern has been expressed by environmentalists and transport campaigners that the Government is reneging on its pledge to meet carbon-reduction targets and its commitment to local bus services. At the same time the 'peak car' hypothesis (described in Chapter 3) is being debated on whether this constitutes a temporary blip in car ownership and use trends or a more fundamental shift to lowering auto use in response to rising costs and environmental concerns. The competitive transport ideology is once again back on the agenda.

The ages of transport described above show how transport policy in the post-war years has swung between competitive and convivial paradigms. It's not quite as simple as this, but generally each age has emphasised either transport system management (TSM) 'growth' or travel demand management (TDM) 'restraint' measures to tackle transport problems. The *New Deal for Transport* was supposed to usher in a period of comprehensive planning with a more integrated approach to land-use transport planning. That hasn't happened, and we are faced with the prospect of a return to disaggregated and disjointed approaches to transport policy and planning.

Figure 5.1 illustrates the swings around a central policy axis between the competing paradigms. These include trade-offs between efficiency and equity, development and sustainability, and personal and collective modes of transport. The 'policy track' traced in the diagram depicts the extent to which policy in the different eras veered away from the central axis towards extremities of the conventional policy domain and sometimes broke through the boundaries of conventional wisdom to pursue more radical policies and outcomes. Examples are the nationalisation of public transport services in the aftermath of the Second World War and the contrary policy of deregulating and privatisation of bus and rail services in the Age of Contestability (1980–1997). The policy shifts are not quite as sharp as those depicted in the diagram, nor were they exclusive: for instance, the Age of New Realism continued previous market-friendly policies simultaneously with policies that promoted equity, sustainability and public transport. These contradictions ultimately led to the watering down of the 'new realism' policy agenda – shown in Figure 5.1 as tracking toward the central policy axis. Despite these simplifications, the diagram conveys the general trend of policies and the political preferences that existed during these periods.

Interestingly, the transport policy consensus did not always equate with the political philosophy of the government in power. So, for example, the Age of Road Infrastructure was supported by Conservative and Labour administrations, despite the latter being more left wing than the New Labour Government that governed during the Age of New Realism. This reflects the political culture and priorities of the day, and perhaps signifies that communities of interest exert power alongside political parties and may even coalesce around a specific issue to mobilise bias that politicians feel unable to challenge. Until the Thatcher-led Government politicised transport policy for ideological reasons, transport policy had hitherto not been high on the policy agenda of political parties or the public. Occasionally, transport issues came to prominence when changes were proposed that impacted people directly, such as drink-driving legislation, urban motorway building and cuts in bus services. Otherwise the nuances of transport policy had been left to the civil servants, professional bodies and lobbies with a special interest in transport issues. The market-led approach to transport policy introduced in the Age of Contestability did not extend to privatising roads or the sale of these assets. This was recognised as a step too far in pursuing a free-market agenda in transport.

One important feature not represented in Figure 5.1 is development in technology, particularly the changes in information and communications technology (ICT) that have transformed many aspects of society for people and businesses. The impact of transport technology was described in Chapter 4 and is central to how transport systems and mobility will be managed and controlled in the future. At this stage we need only note that

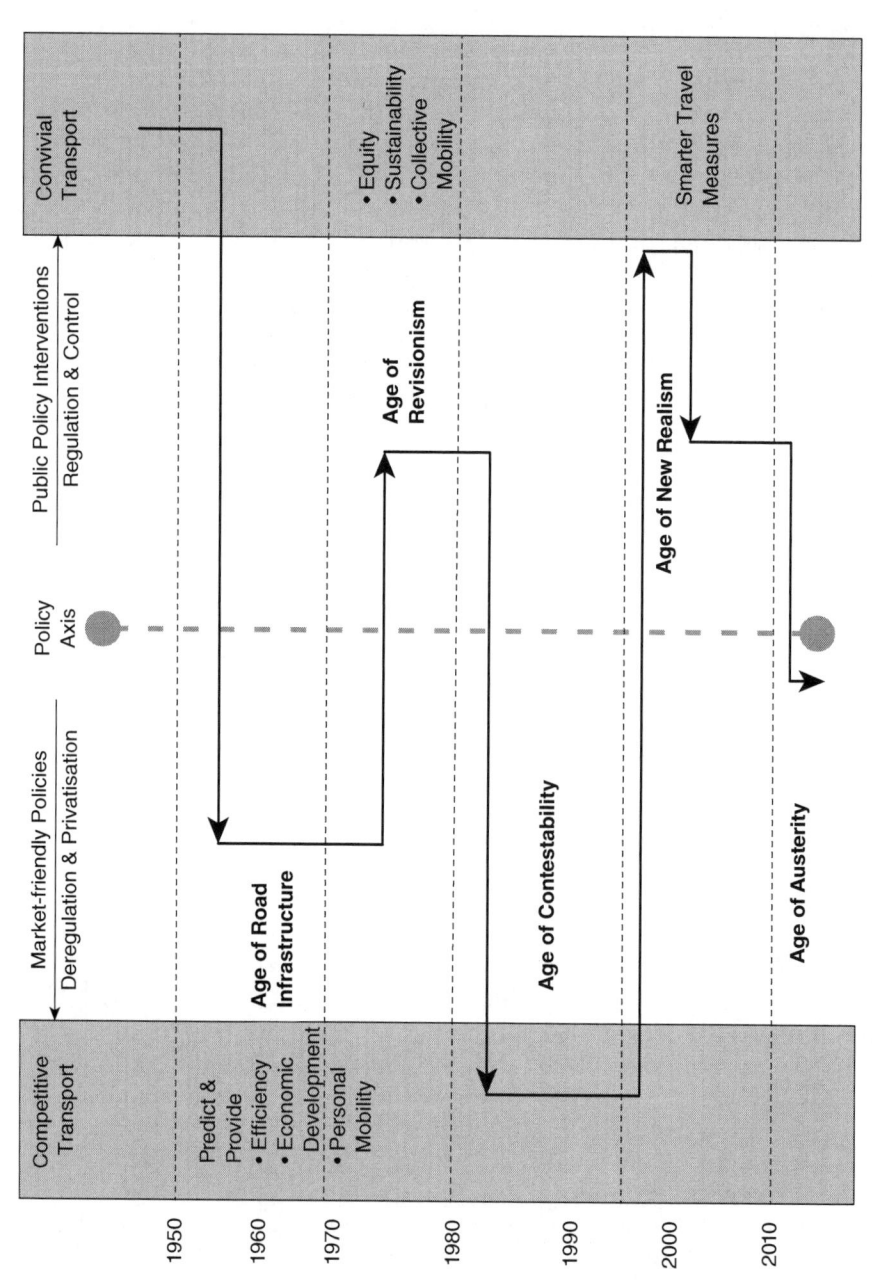

Figure 5.1 Paradigm Shifts in UK Transport Policy 1945–2015.

the ICT revolution, which started in the 1970s, gained momentum in the 1980s with the advent of the personal computer, became ubiquitous during the 1990s (internet) and 2000s (mobile communications), and forms part of the 'mobilities' paradigm (described later, in Chapter 8). Some see this as being more relevant and in tune with contemporary lifestyles and, therefore, superseding the two prevailing paradigms. There is a sense that the countervailing paradigms of 'predict and provide' and 'new realism' are too focused on the transport elements of mobility and consequently out of date and out of touch with the role of mobility in a mobile society.

5.2 Bucking the Trend: London Exceptionalism

Since the Age of Contestability, London has been protected from these swings in policy and has benefitted from stable and consistent approaches to transport governance supported by generous subsidies from central government. London was excluded from the deregulation of bus services in 1986 and instead plans and delivers bus services through franchises let to private bus companies via Transport for London (TfL). London was treated separately because of its size, complexity of transport systems, and its unique position as the nation's capital and status as a world city. TfL sets the fares and determines the routes and frequencies, and the standards that bus operators have to conform to, as well as the vehicle types and common branding (the iconic red buses). This consistency and good route planning by TfL has paid dividends in establishing public transport (on buses, underground and rail) as the primary mode of travel in London, with more than 90% mode share of mechanised modes in inner London. This impressive result is cited by proponents of sustainable transport as demonstrating the feasibility of this approach, which should be adopted by other cities.

Some metropolitan areas outside of London would like to implement the 'London model' but are limited by the regulations and resources available. The transport regulations outside London were amended in Transport Acts in 2000 and 2008 to allow local transport authorities to introduce Quality Partnerships and Quality Contracts, which mirror the arrangements in London. However, to date no Quality Contract schemes have been implemented due to opposition from bus companies (including the threat of a legal challenge) and the financial risks involved at a time of budget cutbacks and austerity in local government finances. In contrast, Quality Partnership schemes, which involve lighter touch regulation, have proved more popular. Quality Partnerships allow local authorities and bus operators to reach agreement on routes, service levels, frequencies, ticketing products and bus operating standards while still leaving fares to be determined by the operators. The Passenger Transport Executives in North East England (Nexus – Tyne and Wear) and West Yorkshire Combined Authority are the only two authorities to have explored setting up Quality Contract schemes in preference to a partnership arrangement. Both of these areas have seen declines in bus patronage, prompting service cutbacks on the commercial network, with knock-on effects on the level of support needed for tendered services. This also affects accessibility and social inclusion of those reliant on bus services, as well as efforts to regenerate their local economies. Maintaining and enhancing bus services is seen as a key policy initiative in improving travel choice, meeting low-carbon sustainable transport targets and enhancing employment opportunities.

In 2014 the Government offered to change the transport regulations in Greater Manchester to the franchising model successfully deployed in London, in exchange for the Greater Manchester Combined Authority adopting the London mayoral model with associated powers and responsibilities. The details have yet to be finalised and the new mayor is unlikely to be elected before 2017. Even so, this represents a change in government policy which may ultimately feed through to other combined authorities in England. The change is part of the Government's attempt to re-balance the economy and create a northern powerhouse centred on Manchester, but stretching from Liverpool in the west to Hull in the east (incorporating Leeds and Sheffield city regions) as a counterweight to London. Part of the plan is to improve connectivity across the region through new road and rail infrastructure, which has lagged behind investments in the South East.

The generous support provided to London and its hinterland in South East England is highlighted in a report by the Institute of Public Policy Research (IPPR; Cox & Schmuecker 2011). They calculate that total transport spending on all modes is £2731 per head in London, followed by £792 per head in the South East, with the other regions trailing far behind. The North West, for instance, receives £134 per head and the South West receives just £19 per head. The worst affected area is the North East, at £5 per head, less than 0.2% of the London per capita allocation. The IPPR analysis of the Government's Autumn Expenditure Statement in 2011 shows that almost half of major transport projects involving public funding benefit only London and the South East, accounting for 84% of planned spending. This is compared with 6% in the north of England as a whole and only 0.04% in the North East. The planned expenditure is skewed because of the London Olympics in 2012, but even so the historic trends show that London receives a disproportionate level of public expenditure. Much of this goes into subsidising fares on bus, rail and underground services. It is questionable whether the public transport systems serving the Greater London region would be sustainable without these subsidies and level of investment. In effect, London is pursuing a supply-side solution to its mobility demands, employing 'predict and provide' methodology to expand its public transport services.

Further evidence of the disparity in funding for sustainable transport schemes can be seen in the expenditure in cycling provision. Cycling has become a popular mode of travel to work and non-work activities in London championed by Boris Johnson – a keen cyclist – elected London's Mayor in 2008, and re-elected in 2012 until 2016. London has led the way in deploying cycle lanes and cycle 'super-highways' as strategic cycle routes across London, alongside a bicycle hire scheme in Central London. In 2013 the Mayor announced his vision for cycling in London with a budget of £913 million over 10 years (TfL 2013). This compares with £148 million expenditure on cycling across the rest of England in 2014–15. Central government funding is targeted on a few locations where cycling potential is perceived to be greatest. Thus, £77 million of government funding will be divided between Manchester, Leeds, Birmingham, Newcastle, Bristol, Cambridge, Oxford and Norwich, while the New Forest, Peak District, South Downs and Dartmoor will each share a slice of £17 million funding for national parks. Local contributions of £55 million make up the balance of the planned expenditure.

The Government has also set up a Local Sustainable Transport Fund (LSTF) to fund projects outside London (including cycling projects), with allocated spending of £600 million between 2011 and 2015 topped up with local contributions worth another estimated £400 million for a total expenditure of around £1 billion. Combined, the funding of LSTF projects and cycling schemes outside London amount to approximately £1.15 billion pounds, which sounds impressive, but the per capital allocation paints a different picture. The London cycling budget alone almost matches the total planned LSTF expenditure across the rest of the country, which comprises six times the population of London. This is why advocates of 'smarter choices' travel programmes have campaigned for greater per-capita funding of LSTF and associated initiatives, suggesting that £40 per head should be allocated from revenue and capital budgets in order to mainstream smarter choices programmes outside the capital (the current spend is about £10 per head on these initiatives, so the higher rate would represent a four-fold expansion).[1] This would certainly give a boost to spending on these initiatives and reduce the gap identified in the IPPR research, but there appears to be little appetite for this apportionment within the Government and the Department for Transport (DfT).

If other regions were to follow the London model, a huge increase in public expenditure would be required, which seems unlikely in the foreseeable future. Even if the funds were available, the geography of cities outside London (more type 2 than London's type 4 morphology on Thompson's classification; see Chapter 2) does not easily lend them to the London solution without massive re-modelling and densification. Not only is this unlikely for financial reasons, there is no evidence that it commands the support of local populations, who are sceptical of 'London' solutions for their area. While public transport systems development is the preferred model in most cities – typically a mixture of light rail, bus rapid transit and bus priority measures, alongside improvements in commuter rail services – the levels of investment are modest compared with those in London, reflected in their mode share of work and non-work trips. In cities such as Birmingham, Manchester, Leeds and Newcastle, car travel to work and other activities is the dominant mode, so there is as much pressure on the need to alleviate traffic congestion as investments in public transport. This illustrates the conflicts between economic and environmental sustainability (identified in Chapter 2) that need to be resolved for a sustainable mobility settlement to be achievable.

5.3 New Realism and the Sustainable Travel Agenda

The authorship of the 'new realism' approach in transport is attributed to Professor Philip Goodwin, who together with colleagues at the Transport Studies Unit at Oxford University, wrote a report for the Rees Jeffreys Road Fund (RJRF), titled: *Transport: The New Realism* (Goodwin et al. 1991). The RJRF had commissioned the report as part of a fundamental reappraisal of the direction of transport policy, which was felt to be necessary in the light of unsustainable traffic growth forecasts and concerns about whether the 'predict and provide' model is fit for purpose. It was pointed out by Goodwin and others that the predicted growth in travel demand could not be met by increasing the supply of road space. Further, the analysis showed that road building induced additional traffic because of external effects on changing land-use patterns as well as catering for non-essential trips that took advantage of the improved traffic conditions (the Downs–Thomson paradox).

The critique of the 'predict and provide' model demonstrated its fallibility. It was widely accepted in the academic and professional community, and subsequently by politicians (especially by the Labour and the Liberal Democratic parties) and by most, but not all, transport correspondents in the media. 'New realism' proposed a number of new principles to guide transport policy that de-emphasises reliance on car use and instead stresses the need to balance demand to the available supply, strengthen land-use planning to improve accessibility by non-car modes, and develop public transport. These components, it was hoped, would create a level playing field where non-car modes could compete effectively with the car and provide efficient solutions.

'New realism' has had a big impact on transport policy and planning and can, without understatement, be said to be a paradigm shift.[2] The timing of the new approach helped to gain support and credence, for it came at a time when many people were questioning the logic and efficacy of the Conservative Government's policies towards transport and the environment.

In 1989 the Conservative Government had produced a White Paper called *Roads for Prosperity* (DfT 1989), which forecast large increases in traffic in the decades ahead and a road-building programme to match. It produced a storm of protest from many different sections of the public and the media, and the credibility of the forecasts and the country's ability to meet them was brought into question. At the same time, awareness of environmental issues and sustainable development was on the rise, as was support for green policies. Thus a confluence of concerns in the scientific, political and social arenas created the conditions for the new paradigm to take hold, and the case for 'new realism' was skilfully articulated by Goodwin and his supporters, who were able to exploit the policy vacuum to good effect.

One outcome was to change the planning policy guidance (PPG) notes to ensure that land-use planning contributed to sustainable development goals. In particular, the 'PPG13' planning guidance for transport was crafted to encourage developments in areas that could be more easily served by public transport (mainly in existing urban areas) and thereby reduce reliance on car trips. This was a reversal from previous Conservative Government policy, which had encouraged suburban and exurban development served by new access roads. The Government was keen to ensure that the PPGs were not seen as being anti-motorist but part of a strategy to regenerate urban areas that are accessible by different travel modes. The change in policy was generally welcomed by the planning profession but not everyone was happy, especially the development industry for whom 'PPG13 represented a radical, probable unrealistic and certainly unwelcome change since it ran against the obvious logic of market forces in a mass car-owning society' (cited in Headicar 2009, p. 116).

5.4 New Labour and the New Deal for Transport

Perhaps the biggest achievement of 'new realism' was selling the approach to the re-modelled Labour party ('New Labour') while they were in opposition, the principles of which they incorporated into the transport policy White Paper, *New Deal for Transport: Better for Everyone*, a year after they were elected in 1997 (DETR 1998). The White Paper laid out the consensus for radical change and made the case for a sustainable transport system that improved the quality of life and the environment rather than accommodating growth of car traffic and its attendant problems of congestion, pollution and CO_2 emissions. It aimed to accomplish this through an integrated transport policy that would: 'integrate transport delivery across all modes, as well as with the environment to minimise harmful impacts, with land-use planning to improve accessibility by non-car modes, and with other government policies in health, education and welfare to address issues of social exclusion' (ibid.).

A number of specific actions to implement the new approach were proposed that subsequently made it into the Transport Act 2000, including: the preparation of local transport plans for a 5-year period, supplemented by annual progress reports; the establishment of a Strategic Rail Authority; support to bus operators through a Rural Bus Fund and Fuel Duty Rebate scheme; Quality Partnerships between local authorities and bus operators to encourage improvement in bus services (later enhanced by Quality Contracts in the 2008 legislation); endorsement of a National Cycling Strategy (inherited from the Conservatives); changes in the calculation of Vehicle Excise Duty related to engine size; the linking of fuel duty to annual inflation plus 1%; and perhaps most radical of all the empowering of local authorities to introduce road-user charging and workplace parking levies. The latter was seen as a means for local authorities to reduce traffic levels and retain any revenues to fund policies adopted in their local transport plan.

In total, the *New Deal for Transport* proposed a comprehensive package of measures that the Government admitted was a challenging programme. To assist implementation and monitoring, an independent Commission for Integrated Transport was established, which also provided a forum for reviewing contentious issues. Further, a Transport Ten Year Plan (to 2010) was published alongside the Transport Act 2000. While the Transport Act 2000 included most of the schemes in the *New Deal for Transport* White Paper, it also specified a number of road infrastructure projects such as motorway widening, trunk road bypasses and other local road improvements that seemed to contradict the overall thrust of the White Paper and the 'new realism' approach. Other policies that proposed re-regulation of public transport and the integration of transport planning and land-use policies were either weakened or jettisoned.

The reasons why are explored by a number of commentators from the field of politics as well as transport. Among the latter, two general themes are articulated. Firstly, some commentators (Docherty & Shaw 2008; Headicar 2009) criticised the Labour administration for not being bolder in pushing through the *New Deal* policies, even if this meant confronting orthodox transport interests, as the Thatcher-led Government had done in the 1980s. However, in doing so it is by no means clear that Labour would have won a second or third term in office. Advisors to the Labour Party while in opposition in the mid-1990s talked up the prospects of a return to the days before bus deregulation, of municipal ownership of bus companies and renationalisation of the railways, as well as stronger planning powers. None of these ultimately happened. Secondly, the influence of institutions and lobbies associated with road building and infrastructure were able to influence the sustainable transport discourse and steer policy in ways that weakened the *New Deal* in favour of a more 'balanced' approach, blending sustainability with economic growth. While in office the Labour Government were confronted with the realities of power and the need to respond to public opinion.

As Headicar observes, two significant events in 2000 and 2001 demonstrated the limitations of political power and how unforeseen events can throw a policy off course. The first, which was induced by the Government, was a blockade by road hauliers of fuel depots and refineries in 2001 in protest at the rise in vehicle fuel prices. Rather than face down the hauliers, as Mrs Thatcher did against the miners, the Government acquiesced and made concessions that undermined one of its central planks in curbing car use, namely the rise in the real cost of fuel. Second, the credibility of the Government's transport strategy was stretched further following a major rail accident at Hatfield station in 2000, which was found to be the result of inadequate maintenance of the rail tracks and signalling. The Government, via Railtrack, had to invest a huge amount of time and resources bringing the rail infrastructure up to standard, which diverted attention away from the broader transport policy agenda. With an election looming in 2001, the Government curtailed its ambitious transport programme in order to regain credibility among the electorate (ibid., pp. 132–133). These two events on their own were not the cause of the revision in transport strategy but sent a warning shot across the Government's bows about the dangers of implementing a programme that was far reaching and stretching the capabilities of the administration. It resulted in a revision, not a U-turn but a J-turn, a half-turn back to the old orthodoxy while retaining the softer smarter choices measures.

The unravelling of the *New Deal for Transport* between the Transport Acts of 2000 and the next White Paper on Transport, in 2004, *The Future of Transport*, was a set-back for the integrated approach to transport and the sustainable travel agenda. 'New realism' still provides the intellectual framework but is couched more in terms of specific soft measures of local travel demand management rather than tough national policy initiatives such as road-user charging. This was a set-back for advocates of 'new realism', including many in the transport profession. Two elements, however, were retained and still form part of official government transport policy: smarter choices travel measures that encourage more sustainable travel locally, and the carbon-reduction targets agreed in the Kyoto Protocol that are enshrined in UK law in the Climate Change Act 2008.

5.5 Smarter Choices Travel Programme

In the years that followed the Transport Act 2000, 'new realism' has been reduced to a sustainable travel agenda referred to as *Smarter Choices* (Cairns et al. 2004). 'Smarter choices' comprise a range of 'soft measures' that fall into four categories:

- workplace and school travel plans;
- personalised travel planning, travel awareness campaigns, and public transport information and marketing;
- car clubs and car-sharing schemes; and
- teleworking, teleconferencing and home shopping.

The aim is to provide practical advice and guidance to local authorities, organisations and individuals to choose more sustainable ways of travel. The DfT supported demonstration projects in three 'Sustainable Travel Towns' – Darlington, Peterborough and Worcester – from 2004 to 2009, to evaluate the effectiveness of these measures (Sloman et al. 2010).

The results show that car trips only declined slightly, by around 9% compared to a 1% reduction in other medium-sized towns (0.5–1% reduction is attributed to the economic downturn that began in 2008). More impressively, bus (10–22%), cycling (26–30%) and walking (10–13%) trips increased substantially, and the report concludes that 'the current evidence base is sufficient to justify a substantial expansion of implementation of smarter choice programmes' (ibid.). The authors assessment of the success of the schemes is that: 'Overall, the Smarter Choice Programmes in the towns contributed positively to objectives of supporting economic growth, reducing carbon emissions, increasing health, promoting equality of opportunity, and improving quality of life', and estimated the benefit-to-cost ratio to be in the order of 4.5.

This would certainly justify the expansion of the programme, but the reduction in car trips is somewhat disappointing and led the DfT to question the efficacy of smarter choices measures. A review of twenty-four schemes across the UK and Europe for the DfT (Cairns et al. 2004) found that if intensely applied, smarter choices measures could lead to an average reduction in car trips of 11%, but perhaps only 2–3% in a low-intensity scenario. Even so, the measures were supported in the DfT's guide to local authorities published in 2009. Significantly, the package of smarter choices measures is left up to the local authorities to decide on what works best locally to be implemented as part of the local transport plans. The programme is not mandatory, and since the election of the Coalition Government in 2010 many authorities have back-tracked on their commitment to smarter choices travel measures in the light of cutbacks in public expenditure (the DfT subsequently created an LSTF to finance local smarter choices programmes). Even before the spending reductions there was some doubt and cynicism as to whether the results seen in the demonstration towns were sustainable in the longer term or transferable to other towns.

In a review of the Transport Ten Year Plan, Goodwin suggests that 20% of car trips are non-car-dependent and therefore susceptible to substitution by other modes (Goodwin 2002). This level of traffic reduction is possible if combined with a range of measures to encourage use of non-car modes (mainly public transport), together with road-user charging of motorways and trunk roads as suggested by the RAC Foundation to deter inter-urban car travel. This would go a long way to accomplishing the goals of changing travel behaviour and reducing traffic, and together with changes in vehicle technology such as electric cars, may be enough to meet CO_2 reduction targets for the road transport sector. Moreover, Goodwin points to peak car use as evidence that the correlation between car traffic growth and growth in the economy no longer holds and there is potential to lock in these gains even when the economy expands if smarter choices measures are pursued. This is the rose-tinted scenario that many in the transport profession hope are achievable. It suggests there can be gain without pain (or only a little pain), achieved through voluntary actions and mildly coercive measures; the resistance, therefore, will be muted. It's the Pandora's box of transport policy, the combination of 'soft' measures and technology that will deliver a near-perfect transport solution.

Following Goodwin some environmental organisations have suggested similar targets for reducing car travel and switching to alternative travel modes. For example, the Campaign for Better Transport in a submission to the Government on its carbon-reduction strategy (drawing on a report by Buchan commissioned by the CBT) suggested that CO_2 emissions could be cut by 26% by 2020 (the interim target established in the Climate Change Act) if car traffic is reduced by 15%, improving car fuel efficiency by 25% and reducing freight and aviation emissions by 19% and 30%, respectively (CBT/Buchan 2008). These targets were proposed as doable within existing policy and without new legislation, drawing on evidence from the Smarter Choices Programme and the Sustainable Travel Towns Demonstration project.

The targets proposed by the environmental lobby and academics such as Professor Goodwin appear modest and achievable without too much disruption to transport systems or to people's travel behaviour. However, the changes, while appearing to be modest, would have a dramatic impact on public transport and on the Government's revenue stream from fuel duties. As the RAC has pointed out, a switch to public transport of this magnitude would more than double the number of trips on the rail and bus networks. As rail is approaching capacity, and most trips are local anyway, most of the mode switch would be to buses unless cycling and walking could fill the gap. Assuming that most of the 15–20% of car trips would switch to bus, this would require a massive increase in bus capacity and a major extension of the bus network to cover areas currently not served or served poorly.

The CBT/Buchan analysis is more optimistic and suggests this is feasible if a package of smarter choices and other measures is implemented, with a target of 50% more rail travel, 25% more local bus travel, 30% increase in walking journeys, a three-fold increase in cycling and trebling journeys made by light rail and bus rapid transit. The analysis, using data compiled from a range of sources including the National Travel Survey (NTS) and Transport Statistics Great Britain, assumes the same number of passenger journeys, and predicts that:

- car occupancy improves;
- mode switch occurs through Smarter Choices/Land Use package;
- average passenger journey length falls by about 7% (back to NTS 1997 level) but varies by purpose;
- as journey length falls, mode switch to walk and cycle; and
- longer distance mode switch to rail and coach.

While this may be technically feasible, the chances of it happening under a deregulated bus regime with limited public subsidy for non-commercial services seems remote. CBT/Buchan also assumes a sympathetic regulatory regime, political support and public acquiescence to the proposed changes. Buchan's analysis is interesting as an estimate of the type and magnitude of the required changes to accommodate a 15% reduction in traffic. Buchan comments: 'The overall picture here is one of travel patterns which are not unknown in terms of recent years, which [are] capable of being achieved through the policy package, and which are capable of being accommodated on the transport system with the land use, smarter choice, and infrastructure changes which are also proposed.' (ibid., p. 166).

This is a big set of assumptions, and with these in mind the results should be interpreted cautiously. Nevertheless, it may provide a benchmark for future models to compare with. It's worth pointing out that the proposed package meets the target 26% reduction in emissions by 2020 but by 2050 an 80% reduction in emissions is mandated, more than three times the level achieved in Buchan's modelling, which raises the question of whether the trajectory described is extendable beyond 2020. Note, also, that Banister's analysis of CO_2 reductions to meet the Kyoto target requires a 50% reduction by 2020 (see Table 2.1), which is substantially more than the CBT/Buchan benchmark.

5.6 The Policy Context: The Stern and Eddington Reports

The search for policy levers to meet the climate change targets has been given added impetus by the Stern Review on *The Economics of Climate Change* in 2006 and the 2008 Climate Change Act, which enacted Stern's recommendations for CO_2 emission reduction targets (Stern 2006). These mandatory targets will provide a severe test for transport policy and practice over the period to 2050.

The Stern Review says that developed countries need to cut their CO_2 emissions by 60–80% by 2050. Stern says there is an economic case for this, and perhaps a moral one. Unchecked global warming would have a huge impact on the UK and the global economy. The option of being 'rich and dirty' does not really exist. But nor is it necessary to make ourselves poor in order to avert irreversible climate change, so long as we begin taking action to decarbonise our economy now. Reducing CO_2 emissions does have an economic cost but Stern estimates this at a global cost of 1% of gross domestic product (GDP), if we tackle the challenge in the most economically efficient manner, although for developed countries such as the UK this cost could be higher. The Stern Review is not about sacrificing all economic growth to reduce CO_2 but tackling climate change in the most cost-effective way possible, in order to deliver future economic and social objectives.

For the transport sector of the economy, Stern recommended that the externalities produced by transport should be fully accounted for, and specifically called for carbon pricing to be introduced through taxation, trading or regulation. Stern also called for more research into low-carbon transport solutions, and the Government subsequently commissioned the King Review to examine the potential for low-carbon cars. Stern found that transport accounts for 14% of global greenhouse gas (GHG) emissions, behind the power and land-use sectors and the same as the agriculture sector. The majority of these emissions are from road transport (76%) and aviation (12%). Further, transport was the fastest growing sector in Organisation for Economic Co-operation and Development (OECD) countries and the second fastest growing sector in non-OECD countries between 1990 and 2002 (emissions increasing by 25% and 36%, respectively). Under business-as-usual conditions, transport emissions are expected to more than double from 1990 to 2030. Transport emissions are expected to grow fastest in non-OECD countries, such that their share of global emissions grows from one-third to half by 2030. As noted in Chapter 3, car ownership and use is rising rapidly in the BRICS nations and other developing countries.

In 2050, transport emissions are expected to be double those in 2005 with aviation contributing a bigger share. However the sector's contribution to climate change is likely to be significantly greater than this because of the use of synthetic fuels (synfuels), such as oil produced from coal and gas, which is twice as polluting as conventional oil because of emissions released in the production process. By 2050, the rising cost of conventional oil could mean that one-quarter of transport energy demand would be met by synfuels. These are major challenges for the transport sector and by extension for the global economy. Stern notes that transport is one of the more expensive sectors to cut emissions from because the low-carbon technologies tend to be expensive and the welfare costs of reducing demand for travel are high. Transport is also expected to be one of the fastest growing sectors in the future and, therefore, 'transport will be among the last sectors to bring its emissions down below current levels' (Stern Review, 'Annex 7.c. Emissions from the transport sector').

Cost-effective emission savings from transport are initially likely to come from improvements in the fuel efficiency of oil-based transport vehicles, behavioural change, and use of biofuels. There are limits to the role that biofuel could play in transport as land availability and technological constraints could drive up the cost, so efficiency improvements account for about three-quarters of the potential carbon saving: for example, by more use of hybrid cars. The other quarter will therefore have to come from behavioural changes such as those induced by smarter choices measures and road-user charging. The CBT/Buchan analysis referred to earlier places more emphasis on behavioural measures to achieve the carbon reductions by 2020, which may reflect a more realistic policy choice in the short term and allow fuel-efficiency improvements to be obtained later through technology advances. Conversely, it could be that Stern recognises the political difficulties and economic consequences of behavioural change policies and therefore puts more faith in the ability of technology to deliver the desired outcome.

Stern accepts that transport is still likely to be largely oil-based in 2050, hence it is important for it to decarbonise in the longer term if stabilisation at 550 parts per million (ppm) CO_2 equivalent is to be achieved. He concludes that: 'Road transport is likely to be decarbonised before aviation. Biofuels and hybrid electric/gasoline technologies are already feasible for roll out in road transport vehicles and biofuels may be ready for use in aviation in the longer term. Road transport would probably be the first transport mode to adopt hydrogen technology, although as the technology develops it could potentially be ready for use in other modes. Rail could be decarbonised by electrifying the service and generating the electricity in a renewable way' (the TGV high-speed rail network in France already uses electricity generated by nuclear power).

At the same time as the Stern Review the Government commissioned the Eddington Transport Study to examine the long-term links between transport and the UK's economic productivity, growth and stability, within the context of the Government's broader commitment to sustainable development (Eddington 2006). The study confirms that there is a vital link between transport and the economy and advocates a focused approach, targeted on congested and growing cities and their catchment areas, and key inter-urban links and international gateways, where congestion poses the most serious threat to economic growth. Eddington concludes that national connectivity is good, so there is no need to add many new links or to seek dramatic reductions in journey times between cities. Also, he makes it clear that although investment in new infrastructure will sometimes be the only answer to a transport problem, there are other options that should be explored, including pricing, regulation and traffic management, encouragement of smarter choices, travel planning and development of new technologies. Although Eddington is clear that transport capacity will have to increase, the study's prescription is not for wholesale 1989-style road building. Rather he recommends a new systematic decision-making framework to determine transport improvements that will relieve blockages in air, port, rail and road capacity to sustain economic growth. However, this will need to ensure that transport supports all the key elements of sustainable development as described in the Stern Review.

The Government's response to Stern and Eddington is contained in a discussion document entitled *Towards a Sustainable Transport System* (TaSTS) (DfT 2007) that was subsequently turned into *Delivering a Sustainable Transport System* (DaSTS) (DfT 2008) policy following a consultation period. DaSTS currently forms the department's official policy and advice to local authorities on transport issues pending reforms proposed in the 2011 Local Transport White Paper referred to below (DfT 2009). While the Eddington Study paid notice to the Stern Review, transport campaigners and commentators have criticised the conflicting remedies offered by the two reports. On the one hand, Stern provides a robust argument in favour of far-reaching and long-term actions to reduce carbon consumption, which seemingly justifies radical changes in transport policy and practice to meet the CO_2 targets. On the other hand, Eddington makes the business case for targeted investment in transport infrastructure, including road schemes and airport expansion, that arguably contradicts the decarbonisation policies advocated by Stern. Even so, there are several initiatives proposed by Eddington that have been broadly welcomed in transport circles, including the need for a national road-pricing scheme (which Eddington believes could reduce traffic demand by as much as 50% in congested urban areas), the review of transport appraisal methods and a new approach to strategic transport planning so that short-term plans (5–10 years) reflect medium-term options (10–20 years) and a long-term outlook (20–30 years).

The Government's attempt to reconcile Stern and Eddington in the DaSTS policy agenda laid out five broad goals for transport policy, namely: (1) maximise the competitiveness and productivity of the economy; (2) address climate change, by cutting emissions of carbon dioxide (CO_2) and other greenhouse gases; (3) protect people's safety, security and health; (4) improve quality of life, including through a healthy natural environment; and (5) promote greater equality of opportunity through reducing social exclusion and improving accessibility. These goals are interpreted by environmental campaigners and some professionals as a shift towards a more radical transport planning, which gives priority to carbon-reduction measures (such as smarter choices), road pricing and the new approach to assessment over congestion reduction requiring new infrastructure (like airport expansion and road building) or issues of governance (Parr 2008). While these policy initiatives generally support a greener approach to transport issues, they lack a lot of detail and are short on specific measures other than describing long-range targets or providing advice on smarter choices. Implementation is devolved to local authorities or regional agencies.

Three specific pieces of legislation emerged from Stern, Eddington and the DaSTS exercise. Firstly, the Climate Change Act 2008, which established the 80% reduction target for CO_2 emissions by 2050, created a Committee on Climate Change to monitor and advise the Government on the levels of carbon budgets to be set and provides powers to establish trading schemes for the purpose of limiting greenhouse gas. Secondly, the Local Transport Act 2008 gives local authorities more powers to improve the quality of local bus services (Quality Contracts), propose their own arrangements for local transport governance to support more coherent planning and delivery of local transport, together with reforms to the existing legislation relating to local road-pricing schemes to allow more discretion on how these are implemented locally. Notably, the idea of a national road-pricing scheme was rejected by the Government in the face of media opposition and a national petition in 2007. Thirdly, the Planning Act 2008 is intended to speed up the process for approving major new infrastructure projects such as airports, roads, harbours, energy facilities such as nuclear power, and waste facilities. The Act creates a new body, the Infrastructure Planning Commission, to make decisions on major projects, based on new national policy statements and establishes a new Community Infrastructure Levy on developments to help finance infrastructure such as schools, hospitals and transport improvements.

5.7 The Coalition Government's Transport Policy

The Coalition Government, elected in 2010, has backtracked on some of these policies and raised doubts among transport campaigners and some professionals as to the Government's commitment to implement the main recommendations of Stern and Eddington. Specifically, the new administration has decided against an Infrastructure Planning Commission and instead will reserve powers with the Secretary of State for Transport on national strategic projects and devolve powers for regional infrastructure projects to local enterprise partnerships (LEPs), which bring together local authorities, business and other interests. At the same time the timetable for the production of local transport plans (LTP3) is being relaxed, which suggests that the new Government attaches less importance to LTPs or is waiting for the LEPs and local transport bodies (LTBs) to prepare their plans and priorities which can then be incorporated into LTP3. There are also plans to tone down the planning guidance for new development in PPG13 with a new National Planning Policy Framework that will make it easier for developers to build on green field sites rather than be channelled to brown field sites in urban areas. Concern has been raised by rural heritage organisations, planners and environmentalists that this could lead to more urban sprawl and car dependency, the opposite to what is intended in the DfT's DaSTS policy.

The Coalition Government's latest thinking on the future of transport is laid out in the White Paper on Local Transport published in January 2011, titled: *Creating Growth, Cutting Carbon: Making Sustainable Local Transport Happen*, which was published simultaneously with its bidding guidance on the new 'Local Sustainable Transport Fund' (DfT 2011). In the words of Norman Baker, the Under Secretary of State for Transport who launched the documents: 'This Government's vision is for a transport system that helps create growth in the economy, and tackles climate change by cutting our carbon emissions.' The White Paper and the LSTF – with a £560 million allocation (later increased to £600 million) – reaffirms the Coalition Government's commitment to the DaSTS agenda through investment in rail, low-carbon vehicles and public and sustainable transport, in its words: 'securing growth while cutting carbon'. In the medium term, the transport decarbonisation strategy centres around the progressive electrification of the passenger car fleet, supported by policies to increase generation capacity and decarbonise the grid. By prioritising spending on key rail projects, such as high-speed rail and rail electrification, the administration hopes that travellers will opt for the more sustainable modes instead of the plane and car. The Coalition Government has also made a commitment to continue the national concessionary fares scheme for elderly and disabled people inherited from the previous Labour Government, which provides free travel on off-peak bus services anywhere in England (Scotland, Wales and Northern Ireland have their own schemes).

There are also a couple of other items of interest in the White Paper that supports the green agenda – most notably the development of smart ticketing (smartcards or e-ticketing via smartphones) for public transport across most of the country by the end of 2014, and reviewing the way in which transport investment decisions are made to ensure that the carbon implications are fully recognised. The former is an ambitious goal that is broadly supported by transport authorities and aims to replicate the success of the Oyster Card in London in attracting new users to public transport. Since launching the White Paper, the DfT has announced it is replacing the current appraisal methodology for transport projects – the New Approach to Appraisal (NATA) – introduced by the Labour Government in 1998, with a new business case system that is more in line with Eddington's planning framework. The appraisal techniques applied in NATA will still be used but as part of a broader assessment framework and updating of appraisal methods. For instance, there will be higher values for carbon in line with values recommended by the Department of Energy and Climate Change and a social and distributional impacts analysis of schemes on users and non-users affected by projects.

Commenting on the changes in *Local Transport Today* (*LTT* 570), Peter Mackie, research professor at the Institute of Transport Studies, University of Leeds, was reported as saying that: 'The changes to the benefit-cost ratio, values of carbon, values of air quality and reporting of journey time changes at more disaggregate level are welcome and broadly what was expected following the NATA Review in 2009'.[3] The guidance on social and distributional analysis is a more substantial development, and it will be interesting to see how that requirement will be implemented in practice. Not everyone is as sanguine towards these changes, and in the same issue of *LTT* Professor Phil Goodwin (one of the authors of 'new realism') questions the usefulness of the changes, and whether it will change the dominant culture of transport appraisal in the UK. This is steeped in formal, quantitative methods which may not be any better than other models used in other countries that employ broader criteria influenced by political, strategic and social objectives.

What Goodwin is concerned about is the change of direction in appraisal based on pragmatism in securing funding rather than a principled approach that tries to determine the true worth of a scheme in economic, environmental and social terms. Goodwin's critique draws attention to the 'smoke and mirrors' surrounding the Coalition Government's transport policies. While the White Paper and the LSTF advocate green policies, the DfT has secured funding for several major road schemes across the country and proposed developing a high-speed rail network (HS2), which many campaigners object to on environmental grounds, including its carbon impact, and is nearly a hundred times more expensive than the LSTF. HS2 is the Coalition Government's flagship transport project, which they maintain is justified economically, with a high benefit-to-cost ratio. They claim it will lead to regeneration and create employment in the areas it serves in the midlands and north of England, divert traffic from domestic air travel with a positive carbon footprint, and will meet the capacity needs of growing demands on rail travel. Objectors believe that only the last argument is credible and point to the huge cost and environmental impact of the new line. They argue that the money would be better spent on an expanded LSTF, a national programme of rail electrification on all main routes, together with a coordinated strategy to improve access to all public transport services.

The HS2 project is consistent with the approach outlined in DaSTS, combining economic and sustainable transport goals, if one believes that these goals are reconcilable. HS2 is a triumph for those who see rail – and high-speed rail in particular – as the preferred mode for inter-city mobility. High-speed rail is the new 'motorways on steel' for inter-city travel.

The smarter choices agenda of constraining travel demand and substituting non-auto modes for car trips has been relegated to local action as part of the Coalition Government's 'localism' agenda.

5.8 Back to the Future: The Old Realities Reassert Themselves (but Not Quite Business as Usual)

Since the demise of the *New Deal for Transport* and following the DaSTS agenda, there is little talk about 'new realism'. This could be because it has become the dominant paradigm in transport planning and policy and therefore doesn't need to be articulated any more, or it could be that the concept has been re-engineered to suit the political, environmental and social preferences of different constituencies. For example, environmental groups and political parties all claim to pursue a green agenda and sustainable growth even though they have widely different objectives and policy remedies. They can't all be right! 'New realism' appears to have split into two camps. On the one side are sustainable transport 'purists', a coalition of green politicians, campaigners and environmental activists who promote radical policy prescriptions to decarbonise transport and create sustainable travel solutions, including coercive measures that go beyond smarter choices. This faction has used 'new realism' to create a discourse that is characterised by opponents as 'anti-car' and 'anti-motorist'. Even before concerns with climate change came to the fore, these purists were arguing against any new road building, as well as punitive measures to curtail car use on environmental grounds, to relieve congestion and preserve public transport as a viable alternative. During the 2000s the debate between environmentalists and the motoring lobby deteriorated into a slanging match between 'petrol heads' and 'eco-fascists'. Since then, the debate has calmed down somewhat and protagonists on both sides have developed more nuanced rhetoric to make their points. The transport campaigners have lobbied politicians, professionals and sections of the more serious media to advocate their position, and were successful in so far as the *New Deal for Transport* incorporated many of their ideas and values.

On the other side are transport 'pragmatists' who broadly agree with the DaSTs policy, employing a mixture of smarter choices, investment in rail and light rail schemes, promotion of public transport, cycling and walking, but accepting that some investment in roads is inevitable. This revisionist approach is supported by a broad coalition of traditional transport interest groups, including the motorist lobby, which had been over-shadowed and quiescent for much of the 1990s. The road lobby has since found its voice with the support of some media outlets and has pushed back many of the remedies proposed in the *New Deal*, such as national road pricing, and has waged a successful campaign against speed cameras. The 'war on motorists' was declared dead by the Coalition Government's Transport Minister on entering office, and there is a sense that the pendulum has swung back in favour of economic interests rather than environmental or social concerns, despite government support for sustainable transport. The transport pragmatists also find intellectual support in the 'new mobilities paradigm', which suggests that mobility in the broadest sense, rather than accessibility, is the key social process in contemporary society.

Ironically, the catalyst for this backlash may have been the Stern Review, which awakened institutions who have traditionally influenced transport policy that they need to take climate change seriously and respond to it. Indeed, in this context, the Eddington Study may be seen as an attempt to 'balance' Stern's prescription with an alternative narrative, a classic divide and conquer strategy. Stern, like the *New Deal* before it, challenged the hegemony of those who dominate transport decision making and threatened the power base of the DfT, the road lobby and business interests who saw that there was very little in it for them. In short, they needed to regain the policy initiative and in DaSTS and subsequent policy documents they have successfully redefined the terms of the debate to serve their interests. In this exercise they have successfully deployed third parties to argue the case for a more balanced approach to transport, such as the RAC Foundation, sympathetic academics and other opinion formers sceptical of the wilder excesses of the green transport agenda. This tactic mirrors that employed by campaigners in the run-up to Labour's election in 1997, except that in this case the tables were turned, and the target was New Labour's zeal for radical change that had to be curtailed.

The future never exactly repeats itself, and the 'predict and provide' model for road building is unlikely to come back in the near future, although it seems to have transposed itself into a viable model for the rail industry. Among the competitive transport lobby there is acceptance of the need to reduce the carbon footprint of transport, and they have been successful in conflating this with the problems of traffic congestion. The argument is succinctly summarised by the RAC Foundation in a number of reports it has commissioned (Bayliss 2009; Lucas & Jones 2009; RAC Foundation 2010). To paraphrase the RAC's position: 'relieving congestion would reduce carbon emissions because less fuel is wasted and it reduces travel time which in turn improves economic performance; traffic demand is forecast to increase so continuing investment in new road capacity to minimise congestion is required; and the way to reduce demand (and pay for the new roads) is to introduce road user charging starting with the national motorway network and trunk roads.'[4] As the RAC Foundation states in its submission to the Transport Select Committee's Inquiry into Transport and the Economy in 2010: 'Carbon is important but is one consideration amongst many. The objective of the formal appraisal is to put carbon evenhandedly alongside the other factors' (ibid., p. 7). The RAC Foundation strongly supports the Eddington Study recommendations: 'In the RAC

Foundation's view there is more that government could and should do in terms of adopting the recommendations of the Eddington Transport Study in the decisions it takes. We regret that neither the previous government nor the current one has published a National Policy Statement for the surface transport networks: that is an essential part of Eddington's process of implementing the principles of sound strategic transport planning' (ibid., p. 1). Regarding transport appraisal, the RAC Foundation offers the hypothesis that: 'for most transport projects the benefits from time savings (typically congestion reduction) and safety improvements are so much larger than the carbon benefits or disbenefits, that increasing the value of carbon would make little difference to the overall picture in most cases'. If true, the effect of the 2011 White Paper proposal to increase the price of carbon would seem to be what environmentalists refer to as 'greenwash', that is, a subterfuge to present green inaction as action. The Government appears to have accepted these arguments, and in the 2014 Autumn Statement on Public Expenditure the Chancellor of the Exchequer announced a major increase in funding for road schemes in the next parliament (2015–20).

The dilemma that confronts current transport policy and practice is that the longer we put off decisions on decarbonising transport, the more difficult it will be to achieve the reduction targets, as Stern points out. Policy makers know this, but short-term political necessities take priority over long-term actions. The politicians and decision makers are hoping that technology will ride to the rescue in the form of increased vehicle efficiency and carbon substitution, with a dollop of behaviour change thrown in (but not too much to upset the motoring constituency). It's the transport fantasy mentioned earlier, regurgitated in 'smoke and mirrors' White Papers.

But what happens if the greens are correct, and Stern's efficiency gains are not feasible? We could all suffer the consequences of climate change, oil depletion and other catastrophes. This is the doomsday ('Autogeddon') scenario. It's disheartening that the majority of the public who resist carbon-reduction strategies – and these are not just climate change deniers – consider the cures offered by the environmentalists to be worse than the disease. This is the central paradox of current transport policy: take meaningful sustainability actions and the reaction from the public, media and politicians will defeat it; take incremental steps to assuage the public and these may not be enough over the long term. We know we have a chronic problem but appear incapable of acting with enough vigour until it becomes acute, by which time it may be too late. There are enormous risks being taken with our transportation futures. Is this a pessimistic or realistic assessment of the current paradox? In truth, it probably depends more on one's belief system and values as much as any empirical analysis we care to undertake. Protagonists on both sides can marshal an impressive array of data and case-study evidence to support their positions. These are then used to support a discourse that legitimises the position adopted. The 'new realism' discourse dominant throughout the 2000s is still prevalent in professional circles but has lost some of its impact in the media, among politicians and the wider public. Discourses matter for setting the policy agenda and are discussed further in the following chapters, together with other political-economic influences on how power and decision making in transport is exercised and controlled.

Notes

1. Evidence to the Parliamentary Cycling Group by Transport Consultant, Lynn Sloman.
2. There is some question as to whether the shift in thinking has permeated more widely to the public and other professions beyond transport and, therefore, is this truly a paradigm shift? – see Vigar (2002) for a broader discussion. However, the evidence strongly supports the view that 'new realism' became the new conventional wisdom among transport policy makers and practitioners and in this sense demonstrates a paradigm shift.
3. Quoted in viewpoint article by Andrew Forster, *End of the road for NATA as Hammond revamps appraisal. Local Transport Today*, Issue 570, 6 May 2011.
4. This position is very similar to that expressed in the Urban Mobility Report by the Texas A&M Transportation Institute in the USA.

References

Bayliss, D. 2009, *Low Income Motoring in Great Britain*, RAC Foundation, London, UK.

Buchan, K. 2008, *A Low Carbon Policy for the UK*, Campaign for Better Transport, London, UK. Available from: http://www.bettertransport.org.uk/campaigns/research#10.> [accessed 31 March 2011].

Button, K.J. & Gillingwater, D. 1986, *Future Transport Policy*, Croom Helm, London, UK.

Cairns, S., Sloman, L., Newson, C., Anable, J., Kirkbride, A. & Goodwin, P. 2004, *Smarter Choices: Changing The Way We Travel*, Department for Transport, London, UK.

Cox, E. and Schmuecker, K. 2011, *On the Wrong Track: An Analysis of the Autumn Statement Announcements on Transport Infrastructure*, IPPR North, Newcastle.

Department for the Environment, Transport and Regions 1998, *New Deal for Transport: Better for Everyone*, White Paper, HMSO, London, UK.

Department of Transport 1977, Transport Policy, Cmnd 6836, HMSO, London.

DfT 1989, *Roads for Prosperity*, White Paper, HMSO, London, UK.

DfT 2007, *Towards a Sustainable Transport System: Supporting Economic Growth in a Low Carbon World*, HMSO, London, UK.

DfT 2008, *Delivering a Sustainable Transport System: Main Report*, HMSO, London, UK.

DfT 2009, *Delivering Sustainable Low Carbon Travel: An Essential Guide for Local Authorities*, HMSO, London, UK.

DfT 2011, *Creating Growth, Cutting Carbon: Making Sustainable Local Transport Happen*, HMSO, London, UK.

Docherty, I. and Shaw, J. (eds.) 2003, *A New Deal for Transport: Struggle with the Sustainable Transport Agenda*, Blackwell, Oxford.

Eddington, R. 2006, *The Eddington Transport Study: Transport's role in Sustaining the UK's Productivity and Competitiveness*, Department for Transport, HMSO, London, UK.

Goodwin, P., Hallett, S., Kenny, F. & Stokes, G. 1991, *Transport: The New Realism*, Report for the Rees Jeffreys Road Fund, Transport Studies Unit, University of Oxford.

Goodwin, P. 2002, 'Re-launching the 10 Year Plan for Transport. Fundamental Revision or Cosmetic Adjustment?' *Transport Planning Society, Annual Lecture, 2002*. Available from: http://www.tps.org.uk/main/library_2002/ [accessed 30 March 2011]

Headicar, P. 2009, *Transport Policy and Planning in Great Britain*, Routledge, London, UK.

Lucas, K. & Jones, P. 2009, *The Car in British Society*, RAC Foundation, London, UK.

Parr, B. 2008, 'What are the implications of the Government's response to the Eddington and Stern Reports for transport planners?' *Presentation to the Transport Planning Society*. Available from: http://www.tps.org.uk/main/library_2008/ [accessed 30 March 2011]

RAC Foundation 2010, *The Road Ahead: A Transport Policy for Difficult Times*, RAC Foundation, London, UK.

Sloman, L., Cairns, S., Newson, C., Anable, J., Pridmore, A. & Goodwin, P. 2010, *The Effects of Smarter Choice Programmes in The Sustainable Travel Towns*, Department for Transport, HMSO, London, UK.

Stern, N. 2006, *Stern Review: The Economics of Climate Change*, HMSO, London, UK.

TfL 2013, *The Mayor's Vision for Cycling in London*, Greater London Authority, London, UK.

Vigar, G. 2002, *The Politics of Mobility*, Spon Press, London, UK.

Part III
The Mobile Society
Political, Cultural and Social Dimensions of Travel

6 The Political Economy of Sustainable Transport

6.1 Sustainable Transport, Unsustainable Politics

Central to the sustainable transport policy debate is why it has failed to be implemented in little more than token measures if it commands such widespread support. Either the policy does not command as much support as its supporters assert, thus allowing it to be ignored, or the policy does not align with political-economic realities? Campaigners and activists make the mistake of assuming that policy equals action. Policy may indicate a particular preference and direction of travel, but it is not inviolate or an infallible position. Where policy and politics collide it is more likely to be implemented, but there are many situations where policy looks like it is the agreed solution but is never enacted.[1] The corollary is also problematic – that is, policy inertia or reluctance to amend a policy even when recognised as no longer working. In the sustainable transport debate, government policy and the transport profession is largely in tune with wanting to pursue a convivial transport system, but the realpolitik is that it does not command universal support among the public, local politicians and other interests who feel threatened by the policy, or see it as a 'wedge issue' that will open the door to more demands for further 'green transport' actions.

Transport policy studies have a rich history of investigating decision-making processes, borrowing theories and methods from political science to examine how power is exercised and by whom. These fall into two categories: pluralist theories explore how decisions are made through a process of 'disjointed incrementalism' (Lindblom 1959) or 'mixed scanning' (Etzioni 1968) of the information available, to reach a decision based on rational evaluation of the options (which, however, may be influenced by the views of opinion formers, special interests and lobbies); meanwhile game theory has been used to analyse how information is presented in such a way as to mobilise bias in favour of a preferred outcome or maintain the status quo by 'non-decision' making (Bachrach & Baratz 1962). Critiques of the 'predict and provide' approach to transport planning have shown how mixed scanning (the partial presentation of information) and bias is mobilised by lobbies, professionals and the media to influence politicians and policy makers to favour capital investment in road building, for example, rather than expenditure in revenue support for public transport.

In the 1970s, part of the revisionism of transport policy involved exposing the influence of special interest groups and their links to policy makers when considering specific transport schemes (Grant 1977; Hart 1977) and in national policy formulation (Hamer 1976; Taebel & Cornehls 1977). During this era, activists who opposed road building for environmental and aesthetic reasons, were a thorn in the side of the Department for Transport (DfT) at many public inquiries, but rarely prevailed.[2] The bias in the procedure of examining infrastructure proposals, especially when this emanates from the government, is deftly exposed in Tyme's treatise, *Motorways Versus Democracy*, which advocates the democratisation of decision making, especially at public enquiries, with information more freely available, and objectors provided with resources to evaluate the data and present their case (Tyme 1978). Needless to say, this hasn't happened but by the early 1990s the discourse on the benefits of road building had changed and the mobilisation of bias in favour of a 'new realism', especially public transport, was in the ascendency.

The differences in transport policies between countries, reflected in national political cultures, have also been subject to scrutiny. Dunn, for instance, in his comparative study of American and European transport policy, *Miles to Go*, identifies three political-economic cultures that have dominated transport policy discourses (Dunn 1980): firstly, a 'laissez faire' or deregulation transport culture, which Dunn associated with the USA political-economy of neo-liberal capitalism (and subsequently adopted by successive Conservative governments in the UK in the 1980s and early 1990s); secondly, a 'regulation' culture, which broadly follows a social-democratic political system practised in many European countries such as Germany and Italy, and which used to predominate in the UK until the 1980s; and thirdly an 'interventionist' left-leaning political-economic culture that favours ownership of national assets such as railways, as in France and Sweden. The reasons why different countries follow these political-economic cultures are complex and related to their history, but the important point is that transport policy is made within a political-economic cultural context. A radical policy shift such as occurred in the UK in the 1980s, when bus services were deregulated requires a cultural shift or strong political leadership, or both to be effective. The political culture sets the national agenda within which tactical decisions on specific schemes and policies are then formulated via the decision-making processes described earlier. Where the national policy has been in place for some time – the conventional wisdom – it is difficult to challenge the policy by bottom-up action alone. Ultimately, political leadership and power is required to change the policy from the top.

The idea that powerful institutions and lobbies influence the formulation of transport policy is not new, as experience from the 1970s demonstrates. In *The Politics of Mobility*, which covers the period from 1987 to 2001, Vigar employs sociological institutionalist methods that draw upon the latest sociological theories about social structure and power relations to analyse how these operate to dominate the policy discourse in such a way as to set the agenda and mobilise bias in favour of a preferred outcome (Vigar 2002). Where these interests align to protect a privileged position they exhibit unification of goal purpose and mobilise bias to support their position. How this bias is mobilised is explained by sociological institutionalism as the exercise of power and domination mediated through institutions (policy networks) and policy discourse. The collective phenomenology or interpretation of the issue that predominates is difficult to rebut or confront. Opponents of a specific policy, or who propose a different interpretation, face considerable problems in arguing their case against powerful interests and using language that is outside the dominant discourse.

Vigar's investigation provides some interesting insights to describe how the traditional transport policy networks and communities of practice have been able to exercise influence over transport policy and decision making despite the 'new realism' agenda advanced by a broad coalition of environmentalists and transport planners. Commenting on the difficulties that transport activists have in presenting their case for sustainable transport, Vigar notes that 'storylines associated with demand management, social justice and ecological conditions had only a minor influence on policy, shaping it rather than underpinning it' (ibid., p. 219). This was despite the full range of environmental and social issues becoming firmly embedded in transport policy discussions.

Vigar's analysis reaffirms the institutionalisation of decision making identified in earlier studies, albeit using the latest sociological methods to analyse how transport engineers and motoring organisations frame the policy discourse in quantitative and technical terms to advance their agenda. Even so, in a plural democracy alternative narratives and policy solutions can gain traction if they attract support from cultural communities that have influence. A specific example is the extension of local programmes of concessionary fares on buses for elderly and disabled people into a national scheme. This occurred in 2008, after Vigar was writing, and arose because of the coalescence of national politics and local policies in support of elderly and disabled peoples' mobility. A narrative justifying the development of a national scheme was created and legitimised by communities of interest from transport and lobbies for the elderly that subsequently became internalised in national policy discourse. Despite some opposition, the policy is difficult to challenge with powerful interests giving their full backing: this has stymied debate on whether the policy is the best way of supporting elderly and disabled travel needs.

A more radical analysis suggests that there is a 'fourth dimension of power', which gives the impression that power and decision making is being shared and is responsive, when in truth the institutional relationships remain the same (Lukes 1974). This radical view of how power is exercised – and manipulated in a conspiratorial manner – is difficult to prove or disprove and remains a theory, much like Marx's theory of power, which is mediated through the relations to the means of production.[3]

6.2 Central–Local Relations in Transport Policy

One of the fascinating developments in politics in the UK has been the devolution of power to governments in Scotland and Wales (Northern Ireland already had a system of devolved government). This has had some interesting impacts on transport policy, both positive and negative, from a sustainable transport perspective (Smyth 2003). For Scotland, which has achieved more powers and fiscal control over its economy, the result has been a substantial investment in new transport infrastructure, including a new road bridge over the Forth estuary (replacing an existing toll bridge with a non-tolled crossing), re-opening of once abandoned rail lines, rail electrification schemes, a light rail system in Edinburgh, together with enhancements to trunk roads including motorway extensions. This investment is the largest outside of London, much to the envy of other English regions, which don't enjoy the level of resources or local budgetary control that Scotland does. The Scottish Government has consistently defended its transport policies as being necessary to improve Scotland's economy and has not felt obliged to justify its policies to transport or environmental campaigners north of the border. Perhaps this is because the green lobby and activists are less organised in Scotland, or conversely the competitive transport lobby is better organised and the politicians are more in tune with their interests and public opinion. A similar situation exists in Northern Ireland.

Wales has also taken a slightly different transport policy route to England, even though it is as financially constrained as English local authorities and doesn't have the level of autonomy that Scotland has. Even so, the Welsh Assembly Government has adopted more sustainable transport measures: investing in public transport, walking and cycling ahead of roads, although this policy is weakening in the face of motorists' (and voters') complaints and the decline of bus ridership. Rail passenger numbers are holding up and the electrification of the rail network around Cardiff is a major boost to rail travel in south Wales, but in rural areas the bus network is sparse and accessibility problems persist. The Welsh Government has also taken some peculiar and controversial decisions, such as the policy of allowing free car parking at hospitals (outside urban centres), which is costing the health service money, and allocating a proportion of local transport funds to walking and cycling infrastructure, which is a blunt instrument in relation to local transport needs.

In England transport funding is being increasingly channelled through a variety of local bodies and quangos such as city mayors, local transport bodies (LTBs) and local enterprise partnerships (LEPs). A number of City Deals have been reached between the government and local cities over investment plans and priorities, and in the larger conurbations combined authorities are being formed to leverage funding and budgetary control over local expenditure. The Mayor of London was a new position created in 2000 with enhanced powers over the governance of Greater London, including transport. The first mayor, Ken Livingstone, used this to push through the Congestion Charge zone, which was implemented in 2003. Although opposed by many local interests and national politicians, the scheme is judged a success for combating traffic congestion in central London and generating revenues that are hypothecated to transport improvements, especially an expanded bus service. Even so, the second Mayor, Boris Johnston, elected in 2008, promised a referendum on an extension to the Congestion Charge zone in West London, which residents voted against, and was duly withdrawn in 2011. Mayors in other cities have since been elected but none have had quite the same impact as in London, in part because they don't command the same amount of power or resources, and because of ambivalence and even hostility from local politicians, who have made life difficult for some of them.[4]

The LTBs are made up of representatives of local authorities, LEPs and other interested parties, so are a mixture of elected and non-elected members. The purpose of the LTB is to evaluate schemes and prioritise investment in local transport. The LEP has a wider remit towards economic development but is also involved in transport scheme assessment and decision making. There are also various funds that are channelled through local authorities, so the governance arrangements for local transport are complex, sometimes confusing where there are overlapping areas of interest and geography, with the potential for conflicts over investment priorities. The Coalition Government introduced the LTB and LEP organisations to give more focus to economic development. At the same time a Local Sustainable Transport Fund (LSTF) was created for investment in smarter travel measures, recognising that these were likely to be given a lower priority by the LTBs and LEPs, which has proven to be the case. The LEP community of interest (shared values on the importance of economic development) does not align with the sustainability agenda of the local planners and the Government, hence another community of interest has persuaded the DfT to establish the LSTF. However, there is no doubt that the balance of power lies with the LEPs and that the LSTF is little more than a palliative measure.

The localisation of transport decision making through these new institutions is not quite what it seems, as ministers and the DfT retain considerable influence over what the funds can be spent on and where, especially for major scheme investments. The focus on investment inevitably favours road schemes followed by bus priority measures (rail investment is channelled through Network Rail, which has its own methods for determining investment priorities). Although these are meant to improve local accessibility and attract new development, they are often devoid of any wider consideration of the impact on the transport system, on trip generation and mobility in general, and ultimately congestion over the wider area. The cyclical nature of this decision-making process is depicted in Figure 6.1.

The cyclical process involves central and local institutions in setting the goals and objectives for transport investments, taking into account the needs of different constituencies. As described above, this involves a web of actors and institutions that shape the narrative and discourse within which problems are defined and resources allocated. The devolution of funding and powers to determine which schemes to prioritise makes this process even more convoluted. Conspiracy theorists or those who believe in the 'fourth dimension' of power will probably regard the localisation agenda as a classic 'divide and rule' tactic: while the locals are fighting between themselves over what schemes to fund, the real power-brokers in Whitehall and Westminster together with their allies in the City can get on with the task of making sure that transport policy goals focus on infrastructure, that is, capital expenditure, as transport's contribution to capital formation.[5]

The 'corporate' bias evident in transport policy is structured in such a way as to exclude potentially disruptive groups (Middlemass 1979). Thus, national decisions that are in the full glare of the media contrive to engage with environmentalists and activists – and may even be wary of legal actions to challenge a national policy decision; meanwhile, devolving policy to institutions that share a common goal deflects scrutiny and is easier for these local bodies to ignore pressure groups. The danger for central policy makers is that the local power-brokers will go 'off message' and adopt policies that are contrary to the national policy goal. This is what happened when the Mayor of London introduced the Congestion Charge, which temporarily caused central–local relations to deteriorate, as also happened a little later when the London Underground was divided into two operating companies as part of a private financing initiative (but subsequently returned to public ownership after they fell into financial difficulties). In the 1980s the Conservative governments wrestled control of many powers from local authorities that resisted the implementation of central policies and pursued their own local agenda.

According to Saunders the differences in policy goals reflect different interests and forces: 'for while social consumption policies are still by and large resolved in the competitive arena of democratic politics; social investment has been insulated by means of the corporate bias'

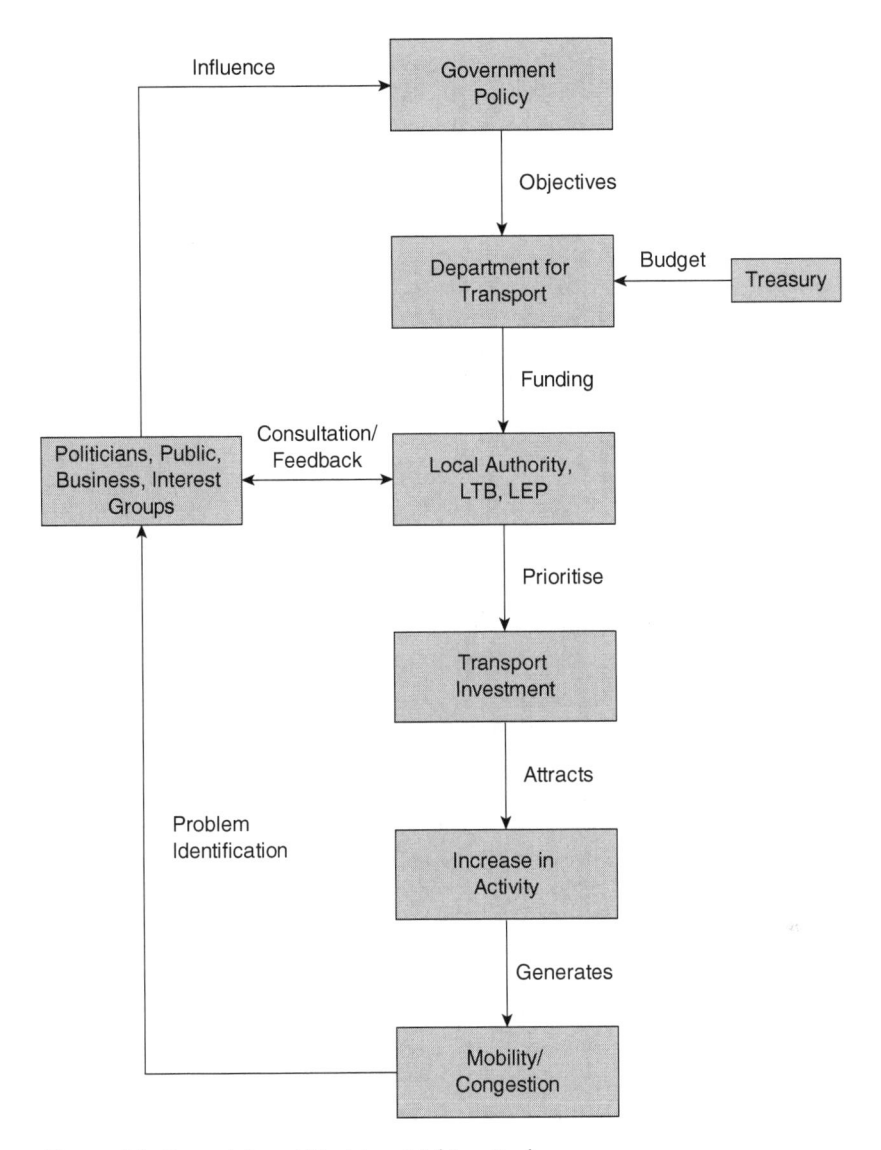

Figure 6.1 Central–Local Decision-Making Cycle.

(Saunders 1982, p. 60). Central policies are more likely to focus on social investment that functions primarily in the interest of capital whilst local policies concentrate on social consumption that benefits the local population. Together with the corporate bias that supports social investment over social consumption, this provides a powerful discourse that has been taken up by the LTBs and LEPs who do not have to respond to the local electorate. Further, the corporate bias and social investment narrative is legitimised by the neo-liberal free-market ideology that dominates political discourse in the UK (and many other liberal democracies following the capitalist economic model). The creation of bodies to channel investment through is part of the political tactic to by-pass opposition. This creates a rationality problem for the State, as evidenced in the rise of nationalist movements, who prefer local determination over control from the 'London government'.[6] The rationality problem is resolved by separating national and local policy making and legitimising the dual approach as described above (Saunders 1981). It is being resisted in Scotland (and to a lesser extent in Northern Ireland and Wales), and it will be interesting to see if transport policy divergence in devolved administrations continues in the future.[7]

It will be of particular interest to see if sustainable transport policies in Wales and Scotland progress better following devolution. If the narrative described above is correct, then 'smarter choices' and similar measures of social consumption (such as concessionary fares schemes) are unlikely to challenge social investment in capital infrastructure projects. As will be explored in the next chapter, the rationality of sustainable transport is up against some formidable opposition, not just the 'corporate bias' but the ethos of a competitive, consumer-oriented culture, that places a premium on personal mobility (as personal social investment or social capital) over collective forms of social consumption via public transport.

The situation in London could be regarded as an exception to this rule (see Chapter 5.2) and on the surface provides a counterfactual to the central–local relations model. This may look to be the case in transport terms, but seen in the context of capital formation, the public expenditure allocated to London is justified by the corporate interests as necessary to maintain London's pre-eminent position as a leading financial centre and world city. The transport investment and subsidies indirectly subsidise London businesses and contribute to its commercial success. The same arguments are not applied to other cities in the UK, which are perceived as being less important centres of capital formation, with lower profit potential, and therefore less worthy of expenditure on social consumption. Expenditure in the regions is more geared towards road and rail infrastructure investment, which can contribute directly to improving economic performance in priority to meeting social or environmental goals. This distinction is reflected in the political-economic arrangements in transport governance in the capital versus provincial cities.

6.3 Contested Policies, Unsustainable Mobility

The purpose of this chapter was to examine mobility in the context of the political economy of transport and urban development. Top-down analyses of policy making have demonstrated the influence of communities of interest in defining the policy discourse to suit their political agenda. The process is rarely rational, in the scientific sense, but an exercise laden with value judgements and technical analyses to justify the broader policy goals. It is not always successful and is open to challenge in a plural democracy, but the evidence suggests that economic interests and arguments outweigh social and environmental considerations. This partly explains why 'strong' (environmental and social) sustainable transport policies have not yet trumped 'weak' (economic) transport policies.

Planners need to understand decision-making processes that influence policies and how the discourse on transport and mobility is dominated by sectional interests, including corporate bias in the media and other institutions. Challenging powerful interests is always problematic, and especially so for a profession that tries to be non-political. The safe route is to react to current political trends rather than confront prejudices and bias. The transport profession does exert some influence on policy and can be said to exercise 'soft power'. Even so, the transport situation continues to deteriorate in the face of the trends identified in earlier chapters.

This is not to criticise transport planners for their technical capabilities, but to draw attention to their lack of ambition to consider radical proposals that would change the mobility landscape. To be fair, many of the solutions to transport problems lie outside of the domain of planners and engineers, who can only offer technical solutions to specific issues. In recent years the profession has attempted to highlight the need to change travel behaviour rather than rely on technical fixes; but these come into conflict with the mobility aspirations and auto-dominant lifestyles that the majority of households now consider normal. The dilemma facing the profession is that the sustainable transport system they envisage is not politically sustainable in a democratic culture such as that in the UK. Nobody has yet come up with a solution to this conundrum. In response, the profession has beat a retreat and engaged internally to promote a sustainable transport narrative that is widely accepted in theory but rarely put into practice beyond a few specific pilot projects. Meanwhile, as problems of travel congestion and pollution continue to deteriorate, so pressure will build up on the politicians and the planners to discover solutions. And as conditions get worse the politicians and the public may be open to more radical measures: indeed, it may take a crisis to convince all parties that radical action is needed.

Notes

1 A cynical view attributed to a senior civil service source regards policy as 'something you do when other means fail'.
2 The exception was the proposed ring of motorways around London, which was defeated by a broad coalition of local residents, businesses and environmentalists, which laid the foundation for similar protests around the country and

resulted in a re-think of transport policy towards a more balanced approach – the Age of Revisionism described in Chapter 5.
3 In Marxist theory power is exercised by control over the means of production and through alienation of the proletariat workforce. Power is controlled by the bourgeoisie upper class with support from the petty bourgeoisie middle class. Power relations can only change when the class structure is replaced by a new single class of communism.
4 In Autumn 2014 the Government proposed extending the London Mayor model to Manchester to create a northern 'powerhouse' as a counterweight to London's economic and cultural dominance. It remains to be seen, however, whether the London model and level of resources will be successfully transferable to other cities.
5 By definition capital formation is the process by which capitalism thrives and prospers. Capital investment from profits or public expenditure creates more opportunities for capital formation, which produce more profits and revenues for capital investment, and so on . . . .
6 The rationality problem of modern capitalist society is regarded by Habermas (1975) as a 'legitimation crisis', of how the State and capitalist interests justify the continued accumulation of profit, excessive executive pay and bonuses in priority and to social consumption.
7 Following the independence referendum in 2014 Scotland has been promised more powers, including control of transport expenditure.

References

Bachrach, P. & Baratz, M.S. 1962, 'The Two Faces of Power', *American Political Science Review*, 56, 4, pp. 947–952.
Dunn, J. 1980, *Miles to Go: European and American Transport Policies*, MIT Press, Boston, USA.
Etzioni, A. 1968, *The Active Society*, Free Press, New York, USA.
Habermas, J. 1975, *Legitimation Crisis*, trans. T McCarthy, Beacon Press, Boston, USA.
Hamer, M. 1976, *Getting Nowhere Fast*, Friends of the Earth, London, UK.
Hart, D. 1977, *Strategic Planning in London*, Saxon House, Farnborough, UK.
Grant, J. 1977, *The Politics of Urban Transport Planning*, Earth Resources Research, London, UK.
Lindblom, C. 1959, 'The Science of "Muddling Through"', *Public Admin Review*, 19, pp. 79–99.
Lukes, S. 1974, *Power: A Radical View*, Macmillan, London, UK.
Middlemass, K. 1979, *Politics in Industrial Society*, Andre Deutsch, London, UK.
Saunders, P. 1981, *Social Theory and the Urban Question*, Hutchinson, London, UK.
Saunders, P. 1982, 'Why Study Central–Local Relations?' *Local Government Studies*, 8, 2, pp. 55–66.
Smyth, A. 2003, 'Devolution and Sustainable Transport', in *A New Deal for Transport? Labour's Struggle with the Sustainable Transport Agenda*, eds. I. Docherty & J. Shaw, Blackwell, Oxford, pp. 30–50.
Taebel, D.A. & Cornehls, J.V. 1977, *The Political Economy of Urban Transport*, Kennikat Press, Port Washington, USA.
Tyme, J. 1978, *Motorways Versus Democracy*, Macmillan, London, UK.
Vigar, G. 2002, *The Politics of Mobility*, Spon Press, London, UK.

7 Cultural Influences on Transport Discourses

7.1 Sustainable Transport Discourse

The evidence points to two cultures in transport that dominate policy discourses. Firstly, there is the convivial sustainable transport narrative prominent among planners and environmentalists. Secondly, there is the competitive transport narrative that views transport as primarily an economic activity with users and providers adjusting their behaviour to market economic conditions. Despite the predominance of the sustainable transport discourse, and its adoption into government policy, it has not altered the competitive culture in society enough to change travel behaviour or car ubiquity. There has been some movement towards smarter choices travel behaviour, but the incremental changes accomplished so far are relatively minor and unlikely to decarbonise the transport system to the level required. Further, proponents of radical change also point to the other ills associated with car-based hypermobility, such as accidents, noise, severance and ugliness of streets littered with cars, not to mention the costs and congestion caused. So why is it that the sustainable transport discourse has not resulted in more effective action?

Discourse analysis, largely attributable to the philosopher Michael Foucault, examines how different ideas are expressed through policy language, giving meaning to these ideas, which is reflected in practice as well as policy (Banister et al. 2000). We saw in Chapter 5 that there are contested meanings in transport policy that have fluctuated in the decades since the Second World War. These policy discourses have involved elements of knowledge, methods and values that have coalesced around particular world views of how the transport system operates. They are broadly interpreted here as representing two value-oriented cultures, convivial versus competitive, which vie to dominate the policy discourse. The policy networks and communities of interest are able to exercise knowledge and power to dominate the debate and therefore shape the discourse, which in turn reinforces the policy prescription and values associated with it. Thus, as Banister et al. (2000) and Vigar (2002) have noted, the dominant influences in transport policy come from the technical, economic and management arena, which traditionally have been more conservative in their value orientation.

If policy discourses are instruments of knowledge and power, the question arises of how to change the power relationships and amend the policy discourse. The paradigm shift, for example, to 'new realism' – the dominant policy discourse through most of the 1990s and 2000s – has not materially changed travel behaviour or the political-economy of transport, which is still dominated by corporate interests. It appears that policy discourse operates at two levels. In the public realm and among professional circles, the social consumption narrative of 'new realism' predominates and produces policy prescriptions such as the smarter choices programme. Meanwhile a narrative of social investment of capital is still decided centrally by government and corporate interests, who are able to exercise more power and control over economic resources. This interpretation is a more radical view of how power is exercised and domination is accomplished. A neo-Marxist analysis would contend that the policy discourses are played out in the superstructure of social and political institutions whereas the real power is exercised by those in control of the capital and the means of production (national and multinational corporations and their acolytes in finance, government and other supra-national organisations). An alternative explanation is that the paradigm shift that has resulted in a scientific revolution (in knowledge) has not yet created a new ideology as part of the social revolution. Or to put it another way, the professional elites may be sold on 'new realism' but the masses have not yet bought into the idea. That may change, however, as the congestion crisis unfolds, and the public may be prepared to accept a cultural shift in their behaviour. This, it is contended, is a more likely outcome than the social revolution prescribed by Marxist theoreticians.

The sections below discuss the relationship between transport policy discourses and the culture of travel and mobility, especially the automobile. The counter-cultural influences of those advocating more convivial transport modes such as rail, buses or cycling have not coalesced into a broad movement sufficient to displace the cultural hegemony of the automobile. Hence the enthusiasm for trains or cycling remains a sub-cultural phenomenon. As discussed later cycling has elements of being a social movement, a cause celebre for environmentalists and sustainable transport activists, which has influenced government policy. Even so, to date it has not resulted in a cultural shift away from car travel. If anything, cycling is taking market share away from buses more than cars.

7.2 Automobile Culture

In a collection of essays on the cultural history of the automobile, Wollen poses a critical choice between 'Autopia', an enthusiastic embrace of the freedom and autonomy allegedly conferred by car ownership, and 'Autogeddon', an anxious acknowledgement of 'the automobile's dark side – car crashes, road rage, congestion, environmental damage, oil slicks, urban sprawl, car bombs and many other scourges' (Wollen & Kerr 2002). Car culture is the subject of numerous books, from cars in popular culture and the media through to cars as an icon of capitalism, the privatisation of social space, of cultural formation and transformation. A good synthesis is provided by Latham (2003). There is no doubt that cars are an important feature of western culture and by extension integral to the social structures of a consumer capitalist society. The signification of cars is seen in the vocabulary used in marketing the 'dream machines', which embody notions of style, freedom and control – values and norms widely held in western culture – and ownership of this resource conveys a feeling of power and domination. The portrayal of cars in advertising and popular culture goes beyond mere branding to instil a deeper psychological desire for a lifestyle of privilege and freedom. To be without a car is to be a 'loser' rather than a 'winner'.

According to Gartman, the automobile as an object of consumption, carrying meanings and identities, has evolved through three stages during the 20th century, each characterised by a peculiar cultural logic (Gartman 1994, 2004). Firstly, in the age of class distinction the car served as a status symbol. It marked out differences between classes, while simultaneously misrecognising and legitimating their origins. Secondly, in the age of mass individuality the car was a reified consumer commodity. It served to obscure qualitative class differences underneath the illusion of mass individuality, in which status was reflected in the quantity of desired automotive traits that could be afforded. Thirdly, in the age of sub-cultural difference the car expressed the different identities of lifestyle groups in a levelled and pluralised consumer culture, as theorised by postmodernism (for example the use of sport utility vehicles or 'Chelsea tractors' by urban middle class households juxtaposed with the popularity of small, fuel-efficient cars among reluctant drivers with a green conscience). The extension of the cultural logic of each of these automotive ages ultimately contradicted its configuration, and pushed the car forward to the next age.

As part of the mobilities paradigm Urry has studied what he calls the system of automobilia or 'car system', which he contends is an important element in 'globalization' (Urry 2004). He deploys the notion of systems as self-reproducing or autopoietic. This notion is used to understand the origins of the 20th-century car system and how it has come to dominate transport systems across the globe. His arguments parallel observations about the relationship between auto ownership and consumer capitalism, which is now expanding in developing countries. Urry considers whether and how the 20th-century car system may be transcended and whether such a new system could emerge to create a new post-car system that would have great implications for urban life, for mobility and for limiting projected climate change. He identifies elements in information culture, counter culture and social enterprises as perhaps laying the seeds for a non-car system.[1] Like other commentators on car culture, Urry provides a critique of the influence of cars at different levels in our society but fails to offer a convincing alternative that will appeal to the consumers who by their own volition, not through 'false consciousness' or exploitation, have adopted auto-consumer lifestyles. One interpretation of auto culture is that auto-mobility has replaced religion as the 'opium of the masses'.

Auto production and cars are often held up as archetypal features of industrial capitalism and its transformation from the early laissez-faire phase into contemporary (late) capitalism associated with social democracy and market regulation. Social scientists have even coined a term from transport – *Fordism* – after Henry Ford, to describe the mass production system he introduced for auto manufacture based on the principles of Taylorism or scientific management. Ford's achievement was to produce cars cheaply enough to be affordable to the growing middle classes in post-First World War America. Subsequently, other auto manufacturers, most notably General Motors, contributed towards the development of car culture in the USA and were influential in transportation policy formulation in national politics as well as in local governments. Case studies of US cities have shown how GM and other auto interests deliberately undermined local street car networks to promote their auto products (Taebel & Cornehls 1977). In some cases this even led to buying out streetcar networks and replacing them with buses. Los Angeles is often cited as an example of this, hastening the decline of mass transit and substitution by private car mode, stimulating the auto induced urban sprawl it is today. There was also support from other quarters which saw the new auto orthodoxy as the future and purposefully set out to design cities for auto travel rather than transit. Robert Moses, New York City 'transportation commissioner' in the 1930s to the 1960s, was an enthusiast for highways and famously opposed the building of a mass transit connection to the city's Idlewild Airport (now called JFK Airport) on Long Island.

The relationship between transport businesses and society has changed radically in the last 50 years. For instance, commuter rail and intercity rail in the USA are now dominated by public-owned transportation authorities, as are local bus and metro services. In recent years there has been a revival in urban/suburban rail travel in the USA supported by federal and local funding. Indeed, compared with Europe the USA now has a more regulated and publicly funded transport system across all modes. Cars and planes may be privately operated, but they drive and land on mostly publicly owned infrastructure. Mobility has been crucial to US culture and economic development, and auto-mobility has assumed a national status akin to the National Health Service in the UK. It is a 'third rail' issue in

American politics (touch it at your peril!). Hence the reason why the federal government and states intervene to hold down gasoline prices, build more infrastructure and even set up insurance commissioners to ensure that motorists achieve a 'fair deal' to support their way of life. One of the interesting features of American transportation is how support for public transport such as metro schemes and commuter rail, costing billions of dollars, incurs little opposition from the motoring organisations or politicians of all parties. The reasons are a combination of mobility-related factors: firstly, the transit schemes are sold as a means of reducing traffic congestion through modal shift and, therefore, benefit motorists who remain in their cars; secondly, the money invested is part of the overall transport expenditure and is justified as providing balance, so long as it doesn't take tax dollars away from road improvements; and thirdly, most Americans recognise that poor people and those dependent on transit services need adequate mobility to get around. Thus, so long as transit investment doesn't threaten the auto's dominance it will be supported. And in some cities, such as New York, Washington, DC and San Francisco, the important role of transit is acknowledged as part of the urban transport system and given preference over auto modes.

Exploring more than a century of transportation culture, Brian Ladd sees no end to the car conundrum (Ladd 2009). Private vehicles can take a person almost anywhere, and the advertisements promise endless freedom, but there's also 'the failure of drivers' experience on clogged highways to measure up to their fantasies'. Can something we are completely dependent on ever be truly liberating? With oil supplies questionable, congestion newly gripping India and China, and few solutions to choked roads here at home, the car is in a precarious spot. But as Ladd points out, so far the car's doomsayers have been wrong every time. A more light-hearted look at the psychology of car culture is provided by Tom Vanderbilt in his book, *Traffic: Why We Drive The Way We Do? (And What it Says About Us)* (Vanderbilt 2009), which provides some fascinating insights into how different cultures react to traffic issues, and how we can learn from these to improve driving techniques, make better use of the road system through technology, share road space between different users and reduce accidents. As the title indicates, Vanderbilt's focus is on the driver and the driver's experience of traffic, and he deliberately avoids talking about the negative environmental consequences of the motor car, because he believes that (quoting from elsewhere) 'it will be easier to remove the internal combustion engine from the car than it will be to remove the driver'. This view is widely held in automotive industry circles, and by some governments, who are keen to push electric and hybrid vehicles as a substitute technology that minimise the car's impact on the environment.

Environmental campaigners often rile against cars and car culture because of its association with industrial capitalism, big business and its influence on society. 'What is good for GM is good for America' was possibly true in the 1950s but has lost most of its significance in the 21st century post-industrial landscape, especially as in 2009 the company went bankrupt and had to be rescued by the US Government. The leftish journalist and environmental campaigner, George Monbiot, has commented on the extreme libertarianism of the auto-lobby in the UK, accusing it of being part of a political ideology to promote individualism above society (Monbiot 2005). 'The more you drive', he opines, 'the more bloody-minded and individualistic you become. The car is slowly turning us, like the Americans and the Australians, into a nation that recognises only the freedom to act, and not the freedom from the consequences of other people's actions'. Monbiot believes that the rise of libertarianism is traceable back to Prime Minister Thatcher's transport policies, citing her belief in 'the great car-owning democracy', and her comment that, 'a man who, beyond the age of 26, finds himself on a bus can count himself as a failure'. According to Monbiot, Thatcher's road-building programme was an exercise in both civil and social engineering: 'Economics are the method', she told us, 'the object is to change the soul'.

Monbiot is not the only one to make the connection between automobility and neo-liberal ideology, which places more emphasis on individualism than social solidarity, but it could be that he is attacking the symptom rather than the cause. Which came first, libertarianism or the automobile? History will show that libertarianism and individualism pre-date the motor car, and societies that control freedom of movement often follow authoritarian ideologies, such as Stalin and Mussolini, which seem a long way from the liberal socialism with which Monbiot empathises. Mussolini may have got the trains to run on time but only as part of a fascist state. Monbiot's rant is entertaining journalism, and could be dismissed as such, except that it strikes a chord with fellow environmentalists and is representative of a particular transport ideology that is an undercurrent in contemporary transport planning.

Associating car use with neo-liberal ideology and a selfish culture of individualism is simplistic. Given the numbers of adult car licence holders (65% of adults), a great many of these must be supporters of Labour, the Liberal Democrats and other parties, rather than the Conservatives. In most elections, including the one held in 2010 that led to a coalition government of Conservatives and Liberal Democrats, transport policy hardly featured in the campaign. Voters were more interested in issues such as the economy, health and education. Since then the new government has introduced some motorist-friendly policies but continued to support rail and bus services (with some cutbacks to the latter). Some green activists like to play the confrontation game of pitching motorists against eco-friendly others, but this type of childish finger-pointing does not help to understand why the car is so popular and ubiquitous among all sections of society.

Presenting the car and car users as anti-social and environmental luddites is not helpful; neither is it correct. Many car users are likely to support environment-friendly policies. What has to be recognised is that while their choice of car mode is self-serving, and may even be selfish from an environmentalist perspective, it is a rational move in the type of society we have created in which competition and consumerism render them powerless. Car ownership may not be sustainable for the environment but is one of the few tools that empower people in a competitive market society; for some – perhaps a majority – it is a means to economic sustainability in an uncertain world: a survival technique in the neo-liberal market-dominated society.

In the USA the influence of the car on creating monotonous clusters of local communities is well known. In his book, *The Geography of Nowhere: The Rise and Decline of America's Man-Made Landscape*, Kunstler explores the effects of urban sprawl, civic planning and the automobile on American society (Kunstler 1994). The book is an attempt to discover how and why suburbia has ceased to be a credible human habitat, and what society might do about it. 'The future will require us to build better places,' Kunstler says, 'or the future will belong to other people in other societies', which is a warning that uninteresting places do not attract innovators or provide a creative environment for innovation. He observes how US cities are often designed along similar principles, with strip malls spread along suburban highways, with the same box stores and fast food shops. Similar trends, if not quite extreme, can be seen in UK cities. We may not have strip malls but out-of-town shopping malls populated by the same national chain stores are now commonplace, as are suburban supermarkets.[2] High streets, once occupied by a variety of independent traders selling a range of goods, are 'dead zones' dominated by fast food restaurants, betting shops and charity stores. Perhaps we should update Kunstler's description to call it the 'geography of everywhere' rather than the 'geography of nowhere'. There is little doubt that the demise of traditional shopping centres is a by-product of the convergence of consumer-capitalism and mass car ownership.

A similar critique of transport trends in the UK is made by John Adams, who has warned about the dangers of over-reliance on auto-mobility for a long time. For example, in a lecture to the Royal Society of Arts in London in 2001, titled 'The Social Consequences of Hypermobility' (ibid.), he catalogues a list of bad consequences in a hypermobile society dominated by auto and air travel, ranging from pollution and deteriorating environments to worsening community relations brought about by mobility apartheid and anti-social travel behaviours rather than a culture of conviviality. This view, from one of Britain's leading transport academics, is widely shared among transport professionals and intellectuals but less likely to be voiced by politicians and policy makers. It is an uncomfortable truth that mobility is a mainstay of consumer capitalism that creates problems as well as solutions. Adams seems nostalgic for some pre-mass auto society; perhaps he fondly remembers his youthful days when children played in the street unthreatened by traffic. Regrettable it may be, but the auto genie was let out of the bottle decades ago and no matter how much we may wish to recapture the pre-auto days, they have long gone, and the majority don't see the car as the problem even when offered a more environmentally friendly and convivial alternative.

There has been a reaction against the strip-mall type of sprawl in the USA, which is reflected in professional practice as well as the vision of community leaders (Schilleman, Gough & Hardy 2013). Rather than see streets as thoroughfares for traffic, the new urbanism perspective sees them as centres for activities – for shopping, employment and recreation – which need to be attractive settings for these purposes. This has given rise to context-sensitive design, transit-oriented development, pedestrian-friendly environments and 'liveable streets', where space is shared between a number of different uses and transportation modes. The street environment – and by proxy the transportation modes that use it – are designed to promote the economic and social wellbeing of the neighbourhood. In transport speak, this means being a trip attractor rather than a link on the network to somewhere else. Not all streets can play this role, but the idea is to create pleasant environments for all users, whether on foot, bicycle or automobile, and design the use of road space in the context of its primary use as residential street, retail (high street), local distributor road or urban parkway. A similar theme has been evident in the Netherlands and other European countries since the 1980s. The UK has experimented with shared-space schemes that incorporate good design into the street landscape. This is part of an attempt to accommodate different road users while simultaneously revitalising the attractiveness of central places that have traditionally been important activity centres. As a further bonus, attractive streets and neighbourhoods boost property values, which benefits property owners as well as local government finances. It's a win–win situation apart from through traffic, which may get delayed by such schemes. This can be mitigated by a suitable local by-pass or one-way street arrangement, especially if these also employ good design principles.

A study by the RAC Foundation, *The Car in British Society*, found that the car is now the dominant mode of travel in most people's daily lives, and is seen as a major asset by most households (Lucas & Jones 2009). While average annual car mileage per car seems to be levelling off, these are still above the targets aimed for in the Government's sustainable transport strategy and have the potential to undermine achieving a low-carbon economy. The report concludes that for most of UK society car use is now the norm, with 77% of households owning a car. This is particularly the case for groups that have traditionally not had access to a car, such as lower-income households, older people and women. Interestingly, the relationship between household income and car ownership is weakening, as lower-income households are acquiring cars. This suggests that the type of area where people live and their level of access to local services and public transport is becoming a stronger predictor of people's car use than the traditional indicator of household income. Thus the role of place – especially high-quality, high-density urban development – and the different opportunities that it offers in providing viable alternatives to the car, will be an important consideration in any future policy measures for car use restraint. Despite some successes with voluntary policies to reduce people's car use through place-based smarter choices measures, central and local policy has largely been unable to affect drivers' choices to use their cars for most journeys.[3]

The needs and circumstances of the driving population vary enormously, in terms of their socio-demographic characteristics, social and psychological drivers and motivations, their economic and physical circumstances and their roles and responsibilities. This means that some people are more resistant to change than others and some more vulnerable. For some the loss of freedom and personal control is a big factor; for others it is the perceived lack of availability of viable public transport alternatives for some or all of their journeys. The report draws some interesting conclusions highly pertinent to the propositions in this book:

1. Most adjustments made by travellers have been marginal in nature and there is a general lack of understanding of the likely consequences, both for the economy and society, of major reductions in car use, beyond those which can be achieved by voluntary means *within a stable environment* (my emphasis).
2. Detailed empirical research is needed in order to fully examine the nature and extent of the 'costs of adjustment', particularly where economic and political pressures result in households having to cut back their car use, beyond which they would voluntarily. This should seek to identify the kinds of measures that could be taken, both by the public and private sectors, to reduce any undue burden and/or social exclusion arising from economic or political pressures to reduce car use.

This is recognition of the hardships that may be inflicted on households through coercive measures such as road-user charging. This would especially impact low-income households' access to employment and other activities. A study of the role of the car in low-income households conducted by the National Centre for Social Research describes how the car plays an important role in supporting access to key services, social networks and life opportunities, and any increase in motoring costs or income reduction could threaten the wellbeing of these households (Taylor et al. 2010). The study did not go on to recommend how these could be mitigated, but this is an issue that will have to be addressed in future as congestion and mobility constraints become more critical.

7.3 Gender and Mobility

The benefits conferred by car ownership are evident in the changes seen in the position of men and women, benefitting men first in the 1960s and 1970s, followed by women in the 1970s and onwards. The 1950s, 1960s and 1970s are often held up as decades when upward social mobility was a positive feature of British society. Social mobility refers to the ability of people from low-income, low-skill backgrounds to advance up the social and income scale through achievement in education or work-based training. In a meritocratic system people advance on merit rather than through personal connections or nepotism perpetuated by the class system. While a laudable aim, a true meritocratic society has never been accomplished, and elitism is still a feature of British society, as evidenced in education, the professions and politics. Nevertheless, the post-war era was more open and meritocratic than the pre-war years, and significant progress was made in creating opportunities whereby people from lower-class backgrounds could move up the social scale.

This era of social mobility correlates with the rise of car ownership among those on or below average incomes. Is this coincidental, or is there a process at work here that extended the horizons of the lower classes socially and geographically? This is a question that seems to have escaped social scientists and transport researchers but is, I believe, important for our understanding of the role of the car in weakening working class allegiance and promoting a more individualistic outlook as Monbiot and Adams have observed. Consider, for example, the situation of the average (male) worker in the 1950s. Most likely he was employed in a factory manufacturing products. His choice of job, housing location and means of transport were limited and most likely prescribed by the social circumstances he was born into. Social class and knowing one's place was still a dominant theme in British culture. Consequently, aspirations among the lower classes were low.

By the 1960s this began to unravel and accelerated a trend begun in the 1950s where a more hedonistic and free-wheeling culture challenged the cultural hegemony of the middle and upper classes. Younger workers, in particular, who had the skills and disposable income to indulge in auto ownership found that this empowered them in the employment market as well as enhanced their status among their peers. A skilled worker who could travel by car was less constrained in his work location. Some also saw this as an opportunity to set themselves up as freelance businesses (for example, electricians, plumbers and other skilled craft trades) and with a car or van they could sell their services over a wide area (trading up from the motorbikes that were popular among young men).[4] With these changes came a wider choice for those workers with the entrepreneurial zeal and acumen to take a risk and look beyond the traditional workplace to other occupations and locations. This would not be possible without motor transport. In time this footloose mentality caught on among lots of other workers and also among employers. The traditional industrial factory or inner-city location was no longer as accessible or flexible to meet new consumer goods production. New industrial estates in edge-of-town locations were not only cheaper but were more attractive to a workforce no longer tied to public transport.

These changes were gradual and not uniform across the country. They were influenced by the decline of manufacturing employment and traditional industrial trades, and the growth of secondary and tertiary services that were themselves less tied to traditional sites. Historian Eric Hobsbawm identified the 1970s as the time when working class culture was losing its central role in society, and when left-wing parties could no longer appeal only to this class (Hobsbawm 1978). This had a significant impact on the Labour Party and its leaders, including Neil Kinnock (in the 1980s) and Tony Blair (in the 1990s), subsequently broadened the appeal of Labour through the New Labour project, which advocated a 'third way' in politics that would appeal to middle class liberals and leftists as well as its traditional core voters. New Labour distanced itself from 'Old Labour' and its roots in the trade union movement, militancy and working class culture. These major upheavals in party politics and social culture were occurring during an era when auto ownership was expanding the horizons – socially and spatially – of low- and middle-income households. No simple cause and effect is claimed, but the correlation would seem to be more than just coincidental.

Through the 1960s and 1970s the main beneficiaries of this newfound mobility were men, especially men in skilled occupations. Men were more likely to hold a driving licence and were the primary users of the car to get to work. Even so, the household began to benefit from the car's availability outside of business hours, and through the 1970s women's car licence ownership increased, as did the number of women owning their own cars. This trend continued through the 1980s and 1990s to such an extent that women's licence holding almost matches that of men today, and the multi-car household with adults controlling their own vehicle is attained by about one-quarter of all households in the UK.[5]

The rise of car ownership and the demise of public transport in the UK are not coincidental. The rise in incomes in the post-war economy brought car ownership within the reach of millions of consumers, including those on moderate and low incomes; at the same time, the re-engineering of the economy away from centralised manufacturing units to dispersed employment and retail sites encouraged car use for personal mobility.

Thus, car ownership was not just a consumer fad in response to advertising or cultural trends but a lifestyle choice in response to changes in employment patterns and even social relations within the household.

These changes mirror those in the USA, although they occurred a decade or two later in the UK, and demonstrate that the spread of auto ownership among all classes is a universal phenomenon that is evident throughout the developed world, and starting to take off in developing countries as well. In the specific context of gender and the automobile, an interesting perspective is provided by Margaret Walsh (Walsh 2004). She provides a feminist perspective on the growth of automobile use among women, which can be traced back to the 1920s, when the era of materialism and consumerism began. During the inter-war years men had priority over the use of the 'family' car, but the post-war boom in auto ownership included a rapid take-up by women. Walsh identifies the suburbanisation of US cities as a major factor in encouraging car use by women: life in the suburbs was miserable without the means of accessing more distant facilities. By 1960 15% of households owned two or more cars and this rose to 28% in 1970 (this level was only attained in the UK three decades later).

Walsh asks where the two sexes fit into this new level of mobility. In the 1950s the car was predominantly used by men to travel to work. For female suburbanites, who were less likely to be in employment, the car was a means to attain upward mobility and independence. The car became a second home. Eventually as women's employment expanded in the 1960s and beyond, the car was used as much for travel to work as shopping or child-related activities. Yet as Walsh notes there is more to gender auto-mobility in the post-war years than putting more women behind the wheel on a regular basis. Women view cars differently from men, even if they use them to the same level, and mass auto use is also commonplace among older teenagers – male and female – which has influenced their perceptions of transportation and suburban lifestyles. For both sexes, of all ages, the car changed the way of life for all members of the household. By the 21st century, the two sexes have become more alike in their access and use of cars, which Walsh attributes to women gaining more equality than any changes in automobile technology. Women's driving patterns and use of cars in the USA is similar to men and there is greater diversity among women drivers than between the sexes. Walsh attributes women's increased participation in the labour force as the impetus for their greater familiarity with and usage of automobiles. Walsh contends that by the 1990s, feminine cultural mores became more central, if not dominant, which may explain why auto companies are targeting women more in their adverts and in the features offered.

A similar conceptualisation of auto-mobility has been expressed by Joel Garreau in his book, *Edge City*, which describes post-war US urban and demographic patterns (Garreau 1992). He observed that the doubling of cars in the USA between 1970 and 1987 resulted not only from women's greater involvement in the work force, but also from their demands to work in locations that were convenient to their homes and chosen mode of transport, the automobile. It has become an axiom that as women took to the car in increasing numbers society and work has become more shaped around the vehicle. Garreau argues that the edge city has become the standard form of urban growth worldwide, representing a 20th-century urban form unlike that of the 19th-century central downtown, and would not be possible without the automobile.

Access to a car enables personal mobility and independence, but paradoxically it has contributed to more complex lifestyles for women, who have to juggle work and domestic arrangements. For women with child-caring responsibilities, the car is the vehicle through which they manage their personal space, a second household, and this is most easily accomplished in low-density suburban areas where the convenience of auto access is manifest. Other feminist writers on auto-culture have also noted the loosening of gender differences (Scharff 1991), and it is hard to disagree with Walsh's conclusion that 'By taking to the wheel more often they have contributed to the ever-changing face of the world's dominant motorised society' (ibid., p. 10).

The influence of women on auto-culture identified in the USA may not be as pronounced in the UK or other countries, but many of the trends are similar and, if correct, this has important consequences for how we tackle the challenge of reducing our dependence on cars.[6] Kaufmann (2002) provides evidence of how the car has enabled women with child-caring responsibilities to juggle the complex work–home balance, devising a timetable for the whole family that is often complicated and predicated on the use of a car. Congestion introduces unpredictability that has to be factored into the timetable of activities.

The two main features of post-war car ownership are the creation of lifestyles linked to auto use and the growing complexity of trip patterns that reflect these lifestyles. People have bought into these lifestyles for positive reasons to do with choice, income, life-cycle stage, or the household economy, to use a shorthand description. At the same time, they have adopted patterns of car use in reaction to the way that the materialistic and consumer market-oriented society has developed. To be without a car is to be disadvantaged except for in a few central city locations. To be competitive in consumer capitalism demands a high level of mobility. Women possibly feel this more than men. Car access, for many, is felt to be a matter of survival in the (sub)urban jungle, enhanced by feelings of security and comfort. Any measures that undermine this are likely to be viewed as threats and fiercely resisted. It also raises an interesting question, to paraphrase Kaufmann, of whether women's motility differs from men's motility, and if so, what this means for a sustainable mobility system.

7.4 The Culture of Mobility

Is it possible to envisage a society and a transport system in which personal car use is the exception rather than the norm? Researchers such as Gartman and Urry suggest that the cultural differentiation associated with car ownership may be on the wane. To use postmodernist vernacular, the car is no longer 'cool' or the icon it once was, especially among younger people. If as speculated in Chapter 3 we are witnessing a 'peak car' effect, the next generation may adopt more sustainable travel behaviours that are less automobile-centric. The active travel discourse, for example, that promotes more healthy lifestyles, is gaining traction among the public, evident in the growing popularity of cycling and walking. Are we therefore on the cusp of a cultural shift whereby the next generation may choose to fulfil their mobility needs along another axis on the meta-mobility spectrum?

There is evidence that younger people are more interested in cyber-mobility than auto-mobility as a cultural medium for networking and social interaction (Metz 2014). Communicating by social media opens up the possibility of participating in aspatial communities of interest without the need for physical interaction or spatial movement. Some commentators have speculated that cyber-mobility will reduce the need for travel, although as previously noted the evidence for this is mixed. There is little doubt, however, that mobile communications and social media are transforming how personal networking takes place, as well as how business is conducted. We can observe these changes and measure their impacts through the number of users and amount of traffic on social media sites, the internet, etc., without fully understanding yet the implications for our transport systems and mobility. From a cultural perspective the car, as a mass-market product, is losing some of its status as a cultural symbol, apart from perhaps the most iconic and expensive vehicles that advertise an elite lifestyle. For many consumers the car has become an artefact of modern life – like the washing machine and microwave oven – a necessary addition to the household economy, albeit one that is the most expensive item to own after property. The car is unique, and still desirable, but is losing some of its appeal among the younger generation and may no longer be regarded as essential for a mobile lifestyle.[7]

New mobile cultures may be emerging, therefore, that conflate virtual and spatial mobility in different meta-mobility configurations. These are part of a qualitative revolution in how information is accessed, shared and acted upon to create more personal virtual geographies of the world we inhabit. Our 'global network village' stretches our mental maps of space and place, to distant corners of the world and cultures, which we can peer into in real time via social media. Our horizons are limited only be the extent of our networks and the amount of time we are prepared to invest in maintaining them. The internet and its web-based off-springs have not just changed the business model but altered mind-sets towards people, places and activities.

Traditional discourses that were created in the modernist era of the 1960s and 1970s resonate less in a postmodernist multicultural society. These cultural developments together with the internet and other social trends are changing peoples' outlooks, and this in turn is changing their attitudes and behaviour towards mobility and transport. This theme is explored further in the next chapter, which examines the sociology of mobility.

Before then, one particular trend in travel and transport that symbolises a new motility discourse is worthy of attention: namely, mobility diversity. Examples include the use of premium travel services and travel exceptionalism, such as to exotic destinations. In both cases it represents a new form of mobility diversity that aims to dissociate the travel experience from mass transit or tourism. This can be observed in a number of different contexts: for example in business travel on trains and planes, which offer premium economy, business- and first-class compartments. These compartments are often under-utilised even though the economy-class seating areas are full, reflecting a yield management model that aims to maximise revenues rather than passengers. Travel companies price their tickets to manage demand and travellers will often adjust their travel times and routes to take advantage of premium service where this is only marginally more expensive than standard fares. Travel elitism is also evident in the lexicon of travel status, where economy or standard categories are referred to condescendingly as 'cattle class' compared with more privileged seats.

Within the leisure market the trend towards more unusual and exotic destinations is another manifestation of this mobility diversity. It reflects a cultural desire to experience places and cultures 'far from the madding crowd', made possible by these places being more accessible than hitherto. This is evident in, for example, the 'gap year' phenomenon among western youth – a break between graduation from university and starting on the career path. Backpacking through the jungles of Amazonia, the African Bush or the sites of Asia has become almost a rite of passage for many twenty-somethings. Doing something different and unique is a trait that is expected in younger people, and the cultural experience they gain is hopefully of benefit to them and the communities they visit. A similar adventurous spirit is evident among older generations. Mid-life crises can be assuaged by treks through the Himalayas or across the Antarctic ice sheet; luxury cruises target the elderly and those seeking a different type of package holiday experience. The traditional package holiday to a foreign resort in, say, Spain or Mexico is still popular among the masses, but the more discerning traveller will seek out the speciality cruise, expedition or bespoke tour. The tourist gaze into local cultures is a feature of contemporary leisure travel.[8]

For everyday travel, such as the commute into work or the school run, this diversity takes on a number of different forms. The car becomes a shield against the outside world, an extension of the home or office environment. The smartphone provides a distraction or perhaps source of entertainment on the train or bus, avoiding the need to interact with others.

The personal spaces we erect while in transit allow us to create our own individual mobile habitat, to be anonymous among the ubiquity we share with strangers. It is ironic that mobility and transport, which is designed to bring people together, has morphed into devices to keep us apart.

These examples suggest that the differentiation in automobile culture is migrating to other travel situations for business and leisure purposes. We may be travelling less by car but satisfying our mobility through other means and modes that reflect our travel status. Mobility and transport is more than just a means of getting from one place to another. It's a social leveller and differentiator, a cultural force for good and bad. The competitive and convivial transport discourses are being reproduced in new mobility domains or classes as explored in the next chapter.

Notes

1. Sociologist Manuel Castells has made a similar observation, arguing that an information age could lead to more leisure time and a decrease in consumption, which is contradictory to the current forces of consumer capitalism.
2. The term 'cloned towns' has been coined to reflect this monotonous style of development in the UK.
3. The RAC report notes that 'the achieved reductions will need to be significantly greater than the 11% reductions that have already been witnessed through best practice travel planning initiatives in urban areas'.
4. Many workers owned motorbikes or scooters, which provided enhanced mobility, but these have obvious limitations in carrying passengers or equipment.
5. Women's car use and licence ownership is less overall than men but converging among younger cohorts.
6. In their analysis of the peak car phenomenon (Chapter 5), Le Vine and Jones (2012) note that women drive about one-third fewer miles than men, even though women's car ownership is approaching that of men's. Women, therefore, could be said to be less dependent on cars than men, but if their use increases towards men's, which some predict, then the impact on congestion and CO_2 emissions would offset gains made elsewhere.
7. Auto manufacturers have sensed this trend and offer 'infotainment' services as part of the in-car equipment, including access to social media and the internet. Concern has been raised that these services can distract the driver while driving, even when hands-free, resulting in dangerous driver behaviour.
8. This tourist gaze is the modern equivalent of wanderlust, travelling in style to view other places and cultures: that is, a contrived form of exploration, as opposed to cultural engagement associated with travel as an adventure into the unknown or serendipity.

References

Banister, C., Turner, J., Richardson, T. & Young, S. 2000, *Unravelling the Transport Web: Delivering the New Transport Realism in a Complex Policy Environment,* Report for the Rees Jeffreys Road Fund, University of Manchester, School of Planning and Landscape, UK.

Garreau, J. 1992, *Edge City: Life on the New Frontier*, Knopf Doubleday, New York, USA.

Gartman, D. 1994, *Auto-Opium: A Social History of American Automobile Design*, Taylor & Francis, New York, USA.

Gartman, D. 2004, 'Three Ages of the Automobile. The Cultural Logics of the Car', *Theory, Culture & Society*, 21, 4-5, pp. 169-195.

Hobsbawm, E. 1978, 'The Forward March of Labour Halted?' *Marxism Today*, September, pp. 279-286.

Kaufmann, V. 2002, *Re-thinking Mobility*, Ashgate, Aldershot, UK.

Kunstler, J.H. 1994, *The Geography of Nowhere: The Rise and Decline of America's Man-Made Landscapes*, Simon & Schuster, New York, USA.

Ladd, B. 2009, *Autophobia: Love and Hate in the Automotive Age*, University of Chicago Press, Chicago, USA.

Latham, R. 2003, 'Autopia or Autogeddon? Recent Books on "Car Culture"', *Iowa Journal of Cultural Studies*, 3, Fall, pp. 172-180.

Le Vine, S. & Jones, P. 2012, *On the Move: Making Sense of Car and Train Travel Trends in Britain*, RAC Foundation, London, UK.

Lucas, K. & Jones, P. 2009, *The Car in British Society*, RAC Foundation, London, UK.

Metz, D. 2014, *Peak Car: The Future of Travel*, Landor, London, UK.

Monbiot, G. 2005, 'They Call Themselves Libertarians; I Think They're Antisocial Bastards', *The Guardian*, 20 December. Available from http://www.theguardian.com/uk/2005/dec/20/politics.publicservices [accessed 2 January 2015].

Scharff, V. 1991, *Taking the Wheel: Women and the Coming of the Motor Age*, Free Press, New York, USA.

Schilleman, B., Gough, J. & Hardy, D. 2013, *Sustainable Transportation: State of the Practice Review*, ITE Sustainability Task Force, Institute of Transportation Engineers, Washington, DC, USA.

Taebel, D.A. & Cornehls, J.V. 1977, *The Political Economy of Urban Transport*, Kennikat Press, Port Washington, USA.

Taylor, J., Barnard, M., Neil, H. & Creegan, C. 2010, *The Travel Choices and Needs of Low Income Households: The Role of the Car*, Department for Transport, HMSO, London, UK.

Urry, J. 2004, 'The "System" of Auto-mobility', *Theory, Culture & Society*, 21, 4-5, pp. 25-39.

Vanderbilt, T. 2009, *Traffic: Why We Drive The Way We Do? (And What it Says About Us)*, Vintage Books, New York, USA.

Vigar, G. 2002, *The Politics of Mobility*, Spon Press, London, UK.

Walsh, M. 2004, 'Gender and the Automobile in the United States', *Automobile in American Life and Society*, Science & Technologies Studies Program, University of Michigan–Dearborn, 2004. Available from: http://www.autolife.umd.umich.edu/ [accessed 5 April 2011].

Wollen, P. & Kerr, J. (eds.) 2002, *Autopia: Cars and Culture*, Reaktion, London, UK.

8 The Sociology of Mobility

8.1 The Mobile Society

Another way of looking at transport and mobility is to consider the spatial transformation that has accompanied the de-industrialisation and urban decentralisation of post-war industrial societies, which according to Axhausen has led to two broad interpretations of the processes at work: 'One side argues that the capitalist elite offered the suburbanites a Faustian deal, which they were duped into accepting – trading the material comfort of oversized houses and car dependency for the loss of localised solidarity and a healthy environment; the other side sees the process as the liberation from localised ill-health and limited social and economic horizons, which was generously and sensibly supported by democratically desired public policies, such as tax-supported incentives for home acquisition, tax-deductible commuting costs, efficient funding and execution of road construction' (Axhausen 2005, p. 93).

Axhausen's two interpretations capture the essence of the differences between the convivial and competitive transport ideologies. Subsequently social scientists have become more interested in how spatial transformation and transport development has affected social processes. This has led to the emergence of a 'mobilities' paradigm as a sociological insight into the realm of transport and mobility – see Box 8.1. The main protagonist of 'mobilities' theory is Professor John Urry, who in his book *Mobilities* describes a number of mobility systems and how these are at the centre of many policies and peoples' lifestyles (Urry 2007). The mobilities paradigm has upset some in the transport profession because it appears to downplay the role of transport, positioning spatial movement alongside other forms of mobility. There may also be a dislike for describing mobility in sociological terms that transport practitioners are unfamiliar with, and they may feel threatened that their subject area is being invaded by other disciplines that have a different perspective on transport issues. There is no doubt that the new mobilities paradigm is very different from traditional transport theory and does not concern itself with explanations of movement patterns or network analysis. Rather, the focus is on understanding mobility from a social sciences perspective and in the context of major changes in mobility – in all its forms – in the late 20th century and early 21st century. Urry and his followers contend that these have huge implications for society and how we study it, and require new 'mobile rules' of sociological methods (Kaufmann 2002; Sheller & Urry 2006; Urry 2000). Urry uses the concept of 'motility' (after Kaufmann 2002), defined as 'the way in which an individual appropriates what is possible in the domain of mobility and puts this potential to use for his or her activities',[1] as central to 'mobilities' theory, and is essential to the meaning of mobility domains as described later.

Box 8.1 The 'Mobilities' Paradigm

The 'mobilities' paradigm views mobility as a primary activity of existence and a vector of social status. Thus mobility is imbued with social capital, and a person's ability to use or 'capitalise' on this resource is dependent upon their physical, economic and social circumstances as well as their psychological motivations and desires for travel. The mobilities methodology focuses on mobility and fixity rather than social classification as determinants of human action and how social institutions operate. Thus, the fluidity of the social system is reflected in the social and spatial mobility it offers.

A fluid society may offer more opportunities for independence – social and spatial – but this should not be confused with notions of openness or freedom, as individualism may result in greater exploitation or ubiquity, such as car dependency. In contrast, collectivism, which is often associated with less dynamic or 'fixed' societies, may be more cohesive despite the lack of opportunities. While these concepts may not be mainstream to transport professionals, they are working themselves into transport publications (see, for example, Banister 2005). There is also a *Mobilities* journal dedicated to publishing research in this topic, including transport. It seems likely that these concepts will become more prevalent in debates about transport futures.

According to Kaufmann, the key question is how motility is acquired and transformed into mobility, in other words, from aspiration and potential into observable travel. As Kaufmann says, 'the degree of congruence between motility and mobility indicates the degree of fluidity of mobility practices' (ibid., p. 45). Convergence between these two concepts indicates a degree of fluidity and control over transport resources and a person's ability to satisfy their motility goals. In contrast, a large degree of separation between motility and mobility indicates fixity in transport arrangements that may constitute a latent demand, unsatisfied need and mobility hardship. The key construct of Kaufmann's theory is that in earlier times, such as the first half of the 20th century when cities were primarily defined by the extent of their public transport networks, motility and mobility were convergent; but in today's society motility expectations have risen and are more difficult to match other than through auto-mobility. With increasing congestion and cost, this situation is bound to get worse. Kaufmann develops his mobility theory into sociology of experience to analyse the implications of motility and mobility divergence. For example, are people more free when they are more mobile? (Or is the convergence of motility and mobility stronger among the most mobile people?) Do people seek maximum speed in their mobility? Is it more difficult to transform certain types of motility into mobility? (For example, travel for disabled people).[2] As mobility practices get less fluid, the calls for radical action will increase.

Transportation scientists have yet to fully digest the implications of the new mobilities paradigm, but there are those like Urry who suggest that it is mobilities' 'turn' to offer a new paradigm for an integrated theory of spatial mobility and sociology. The question for transport planners is whether they continue to pursue their own paradigms, adopt the new mobilities agenda, or come to some accommodation between the two. This is not simply an academic question or a turf war between different disciplines; it is central to how our transport systems and mobility will be understood and delivered in the future (Greico & MacDonald 2007). In contrast to the transport paradigms, the mobilities paradigm is not based on technical analysis and policy prescriptions, but seeks to explore how the new mobility exercised by the masses – in geographic space and cyberspace – is changing the landscape for travel, and how this affects our social and economic institutions and vice versa (Jensen 2009). It is a much more fundamental critique of how society is being re-engineered to meet mobility goals, and how these in turn reinforce the demand for more mobility. The mobilities paradigm employs a range of positivist and deductive methods to analyse the role of mobility in society, including the interface between transport systems and social systems. It's a broad canvas and clearly goes beyond the realm of transportation science. Because it ventures into territories unfamiliar to transport planners it presents a challenge to understanding the implications for transport planning and transportation systems development. In the context of creating a sustainable mobility system, the mobilities paradigm is integral to our understanding of the relationship between meta-mobility and sustainable transport practices.

The 'mobilities' paradigm should not be confused with the New Mobility agenda developed in the USA to identify the next generation of sustainable urban transport systems. This is an example of the conventional wisdom approach to urban transportation problems that focuses on 'new fuel and vehicle technologies; new information technologies; flexible and differentiated transportation modes, services and products; innovative land use and urban design; and new business models' (Zielinski 2006). The New Mobility agenda in the USA could be characterised as a re-engineering of the 'predict and provide' model updated to take advantage of the latest technology and intelligent transportation systems.

The mobilities paradigm builds upon a long tradition of sociological inquiries into urban planning and human geography that stretches back to the late-19th century/early-20th century in the writings of German philosopher and sociologist, Max Weber (Weber 1921/1986), together with one of the founders of the Town and Country Planning movement, Patrick Geddes (Geddes 1915). In the 1920s and 1930s the Chicago School (University of Chicago) was the first major institution specialising in urban sociology. The Chicago School had an enormous influence in the emerging fields of urban social ecology, city growth and structure, and social theories of urban space (*Urbanism as a Way of Life*, Wirth 1938). It also influenced urban economics including how accessibility influences land values (bid-rent theory) and city zonal structures.

By the 1970s more critical theories of the relations between capitalism and urbanism began to emerge through the works of Harvey and Lefebvre, who take a neo-Marxian position in arguing that capitalism controls space to ensure its own reproduction (Harvey 1973; Lefebvre 1991). Harvey analyses core issues in city planning and policy – including transport costs – examining the relationship between social justice and space. How, for example, do policies on transport and mobility reinforce existing distributions of income? Lefebvre wrote several influential works on cities, urbanism and space, including *The Production of Space* (1974), in which he contends that there are different modes of production of space (i.e. spatialisation), from natural space ('absolute space') to more complex spatialities whose significance is socially produced (i.e. social space). Lefebvre's thesis is that space is a social product, or a complex social construction (based on values, and the social production of meanings), which affects spatial practices and perceptions. This argument shifts the research perspective from space to processes of its production, including the political character of the processes of production of space. As a Marxist theorist, Lefebvre claims that this social production of urban space is fundamental to the reproduction of society, hence of capitalism itself. The social production of space is commanded by a hegemonic class as a tool to reproduce its dominance: '(Social) space is a (social) product . . . the space thus produced also serves as a tool of thought and of action . . . in addition to being a means of production it is also a means of control, and hence of domination, of power' (ibid., p. 26).

Harvey and Lefebvre are generally credited with creating a 'revolutionary geography', one that transcends the structural limitations of existing approaches to space, which focus on the physical realm and quantitative analysis. The relevance to urban transport and mobility is how mobility is not just a manifestation of physical movement but a social process that shapes our perception of space, how space is managed and reproduced. We may feel that we have freedom of movement but in reality our mobility is conditioned by the social spaces created in the city. This radical interpretation is not accepted by all urban sociologists and has been critiqued and modified by, among others, Castells and Giddens.

Castells was a key developer of the variety of Marxist urban sociology that emphasises the role of social movements in the conflictive transformation of the city, (cf. post-industrial society). He introduced the concept of 'collective consumption' (such as public transport) comprehending a wide range of social struggles – displaced from the economic stratum to the political stratum via state intervention. In the early 1980s, he concentrated upon the role of new technologies in the restructuring of an economy. The *Information Age* trilogy is his best-known work, in which he states: 'Our societies are increasingly structured around the bipolar opposition of the Net and the Self' (Castells 1996, 1997, 1998). The 'Net' denotes the network organisations replacing vertically integrated hierarchies as the dominant form of social organization; the 'Self' denotes the practices a person uses in reaffirming social identity and meaning in a continually changing cultural landscape. From a mobility perspective, the transportation network and internet provides the infrastructure that enables communication and travel, and the way these are used defines our mobile selves. Another way of interpreting this is as mobility diversity (described in Chapter 7), for example how we travel and to which destinations. Unlike Lefebvre, Castells takes a human-oriented approach to the impact of technology on society and concedes that economic structures are not deterministic but can be used to benefit people if they have the resources and wherewithal to know how to use it to their advantage.

Neo-Marxists acknowledge that class relations and power distribution have changed since the 19th century when Marx formulated his theory of capitalism, but still analyse power relations in terms of who controls the economic base, and regard policies developed in the superstructure of social and political institutions as superficial. For neo-Marxists, economic power resides in the multinational corporations that control world trade, aided and abetted by financial institutions – global and national – and defended by nation states that support a capitalist economic model. It is more complex than this, and among socialists there are differences of opinion and emphasis as to whether capitalism will ever be replaced by communism as Marx predicted. There are those who view capitalism as a regenerative economic system (by creative destruction) that has learned to adapt to technology and social movements (Schumpeter 1942/1994). Hence, references to post-industrial capitalism, consumer capitalism, info-capitalism and postmodern capitalism point to the latest stage of capitalism development. Only the term 'late-stage capitalism' suggests a final episode, but this is by no means universal even among Marxist theoreticians. Capitalism has demonstrated its ability to adapt to technology and social movements.

Max Weber was one of the first to broaden out Marx's theories to allow a different social stratification that was not simply determined by its relation to capital but by other influences such as status and party affiliation (Weber 1964). Thus, a more flexible social structure is possible, with individuals' allegiances and outlook influenced by factors such as charisma, religion, race and gender as well as their wealth. Later authors such as Giddens have developed this approach further by insisting that the process of structuration – by which social structures are created – is not fixed but is continuously evolving (Giddens 1984). Gidden's theory of structuration, which underpins Vigar's sociological institutional study of the *Politics of Mobility* (see Chapter 6.1), is interesting to transport because it includes the possibility that space and time–space relations (accessibility) can influence social structure. If correct, this implies that mobility and accessibility opportunities may be complicit in structuration (mediated through the way that transport systems affect life chances and social mobility). For example, in 19th-century Britain the working class did not venture far from their place of work, worked long hours, and their horizons were generally limited to their locales. These 'rules' affected their actions, which determined their social structure, and the structure was upheld as long as it was reproduced in action. Hitherto social structures or 'models of society' were taken to be beyond the realm of human control. By contrast, in 21st-century Britain time and space rules are very different, with structures that enable different types of action such as complex trips by car, train and low-budget airlines within a different time–space horizon that previous generations would not comprehend.

Giddens identifies three types of structure in social systems: 'signification', 'legitimation' and 'domination'. Signification produces meaning through organised webs of language; legitimation produces a moral order via naturalisation in societal norms, values and standards; and domination produces (and is an exercise of) power, originating from the control of resources. To understand how they work together, consider how the signification of a concept such as 'smarter choices' in transport policy speech, borrows from and contributes to legitimisation (e.g. sustainable travel discourse) and coordinates forms of domination (i.e. smarter travel options), from which it in turn gains further force. To be effective and widely adopted the behaviour needs to be justified in these three structures. To date, smarter travel policies have not achieved the level of domination that advocates would wish despite support from legitimation sources (politicians, the media) and signification to issues such as climate change, carbon emissions and congestion reduction. This is probably because it is not in a position to exercise power and control resources to alter people's behaviour, specifically their use of cars, or challenge the power of corporate interests like the auto industry and the oil companies.

Another example is the referenda on establishing congestion charging zones, widely supported by the transport profession and policy makers, but voted down by local people – as happened in Edinburgh, Manchester and West London. In these cases, the proponents may have won the argument (signification), but were unable to legitimise the change among the local population who do not share the same values. Consequently, the opponents were able to question the legitimacy of the policy and dominate the policy discourse. This is how the process works in a democratic society. It's possible that unpopular policies can be forced through without each of the social structures being in alignment, but when this happens there is always the threat of reversal once power changes.

Giddens stresses the importance of power, which is the means to the end, and hence is directly involved in the actions of every person. Power, the transformative capacity of people to change the social and material world, is closely shaped by knowledge and space–time. Transportation systems have fundamentally altered our perceptions of space–time over the centuries, especially the automobile and airplanes, as has mobile communications, and this enhanced mobility has given people more power (social capital) over their lives. Consequently, policies that attempt to change mobility arrangements will be scrutinised closely by those affected in terms of their power to control their personal mobility. The demise of the *New Deal for Transport* highlights the limitations of the environmental lobby in the face of growing media scepticism and opposition from motorists. Many constituencies, including transport professionals, opposed the transport reforms introduced by the Conservatives, but the revenge sought by those under the cloak of New Labour and the *New Deal* failed to understand how the transport landscape had changed by the mid-1990s and specifically the dominant role that auto-mobility now played in the lives of all classes, including those on low incomes. There were significant changes in urban land use and the morphology of cities, and these simultaneously reinforced car-oriented lifestyles. A similar trend is evident in aviation, where long-distance travel on budget airlines has created mass tourism to overseas destinations. As Urry and others point out, mobility is more than movement; it is a social process through which individuals exercise power (domination, social capital), legitimised by social norms (such as car culture, overseas tourism) and given significance by the organised webs of language (like car adverts and exotic foreign destinations through the media).[3]

8.2 Mobility Domains

The mobilities paradigm places mobility at the centre of our understanding of behaviour and social action. In this schema fixity and fluidity are key determinants in how mobile or dynamic the society is, and the mobility of people within that society. Mobilities challenges many assumptions in traditional sociology, especially those around social classification and the relations between social structure and action. It does not provide a unified theory of social mobility; rather it offers some new methods for sociological analysis and sociological insights into travel behaviour that link behaviour to social structure and social action. People are not just agents able to determine their own mobility but constrained by mobility resources available to them, which are governed by social institutions and processes beyond their control. People with more resources to empower their mobility potential, that is, motility, are more fluid, have greater choices and generally have more control over their lifestyle and life chances. In contrast, people with access to fewer mobility opportunities because of income, disability or domestic constraints, are more fixed and motility poor.

In *Mobile Lives*, Elliott and Urry refer to the power that stems from mobility as 'network capital'. People with very high levels of network capital experience high levels of geographic mobility and can influence the movement of others (Elliott & Urry 2010, p. 11). Network capital is largely subjectless (not a tangible commodity), communications-driven and information-based, in contrast to economic or cultural capital, which is, for the most part, built up by individuals.[4] In *The Rise of the Network Society*, Castells describes how social and information networks can give an edge to one's status and fluidity in contemporary urban society (Castells 1996). The network defines the morphology or structure within which economic and social relations take place, ranging from informal social media networks to formal institutions such as the European Union. The implication is that networks have superseded class relations as cultural drivers that shape social relationships. Networks can be virtual, but also spatial, such that mobility and network capital are intertwined. As stated by Elliott and Urry, mobility on its own does nothing but is important as the means of acquiring network capital (ibid., p. 59). Network capital is facilitated by high levels of personal mobility (for work and consumption purposes). Competition and commercial culture rely on high levels of mobility and networking for production, distribution and consumption. To be a successful player in this system requires access to mobility resources and, therefore, the transport system is a key resource in how network capital is acquired and used.

Network capital is central to the mobilities paradigm because it is the means by which motility is realised. Elliott and Urry compare their formulation to Marx's focus on social relations of capitalist production (and not only on the forces of production per se). Their reasoning is that 'it is necessary to examine the social relations that the means of mobility afford and not only the changing form taken by the forces of mobility. Network capital is the capacity to engender and sustain social relations with those people who are not necessarily proximate' such that 'Those social groups high in network capital enjoy significant advantages in making and remaking their social connections, the emotional, financial and practical benefits being over and above, and non-reducible to, the benefits people derived from economic and cultural capital' (ibid., p. 59). They contend that a more equal society requires redistribution of network capital from the haves to the have-nots and give an example of network capital inequalities in relation to car crashes, which kill and injure over tens of thousands of people each year (mostly in developing countries). Most of the victims do not own a car and there is, thus, weak network capital for those without access to a car. As the authors point out there are huge inequalities between car owners/users and cyclists and pedestrians (ibid., p. 63).

The nearest approximation to network capital in transport planning is the concept of accessibility, the measure of proximity in space–time. A denser network of roads or public transport means greater connection opportunity and a facility at the centre of a network has the greatest access potential. As described in Chapter 2, accessibility potential varies by individual, who has a unique space–time prism, but it is possible to identify mobility groupings or domains in the mobility/network capital continuum.

This is illustrated in Figure 8.1, adopting the concepts of network capital and mobility as defined by Elliott and Urry and by Kaufmann. Network capital is the broader socio-geographic definition of power to realise one's motility, while mobility is defined by the amount of fluidity or fixity an individual can exercise. The mobility domains are depicted in relation to the two vectors of network capital and mobility. Four mobility domains are defined by the level of convergence between the amount of network capital (motility) and level of mobility. For illustrative purposes the domains are shown as discrete, whereas in reality there is more of a continuum from those with low access to network resources and fixed mobility to those with a high level of network capital and mobility. Four domains are identified, which is consistent with research on driver market segments (Bayliss 2009; Stradling & Anable 2008). The chart also shows movement between the domains, such that movement to a higher domain of network capital and mobility represents a shift towards higher motility and vice versa. Another feature is that movement between the domains is possible for short periods or specific types of travel, for example travelling in premium seats on an international flight compared with the normal everyday standard class journey into work. Similarly, while on holiday many tourists like to explore and be 'mobile independents' or upgrade to the 'mobile elite'.

The Sociology of Mobility 131

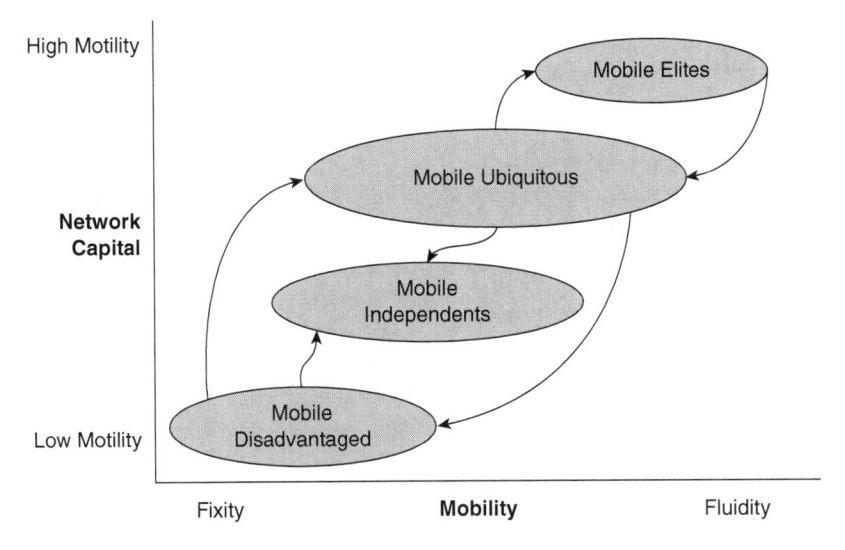

Figure 8.1 Mobility Domains.

The largest mobility domain is referred to as the 'mobile ubiquitous' and comprises an estimated 28.5 million UK adults in 2009 (57% of total adults). Their ubiquity derives from their auto-mobility practices (the auto-bourgeoisie), which is pervasive across the country, and includes a number of low-income households who may be car-dependent in the sense that they feel obliged to run a car even though they may have difficulty affording it. It is difficult to estimate the number of car-dependents but research for the RAC Foundation in 2009 (Bayliss 2009) estimated that 38% of the lowest income quintile of households owned one car (approximately 4.5 million adults). There is no way of knowing how many of these are reluctant car owners. It is also difficult to estimate those reliant on the primary car driver (spouses, children). There are around 48 million adults (over the age of 19) in the UK and 65% of these have a driving licence (around 31 million). An estimated 6.5 million adults live in households that don't have cars, either 'mobile independents' or 'mobility disadvantaged' domains.

'Mobile elites' incur the fewest constraints and have the highest capabilities. This domain includes the celebrities and cultural high-flyers who lead fluid lifestyles, travelling extensively as part of their work or lifestyle, with travel privileges such as business class, prestigious hotels and such like.

The 'mobile independent' domain, as the name implies, comprises people who chose to live lifestyles that are not constrained by their access to network capital, and may enjoy a level of mobility equivalent to those with 'mobile ubiquity'. These include people who may be transitioning through a particular life-cycle stage where auto ownership is not deemed necessary or too expensive (for example students) or they have made a positive choice to live a car-free lifestyle.

Finally, the 'mobile disadvantaged' are the most constrained of all the mobility domains having the fewest choices on where they travel and when. This is the group that is sometimes referred to as the socially excluded (it should be noted, however, that not all people in this domain are mobility deprived, and likewise there are people in 'mobile ubiquity' households who could fall into the category of socially excluded).

Research on responses to questions about attitudes to car use and the environment has shown how complex an area this is, with many factors influencing attitudes and behaviour (Lyons et al. 2008). Nevertheless, these can be synthesised into four groups (Stradling & Anable 2008):

1. Die-hard drivers like driving and would use the bus only if they had to.
2. Car complacents are less attached to their cars, but currently see no reason to change.
3. Malcontented motorists find driving stressful, would like to reduce their car use, but cannot see how.
4. Aspiring environmentalists are actively trying to reduce their car use and already use other modes where possible.

The first three categories fall into the 'mobile ubiquitous' domain, which shows that this is a broad church of car users who feel compelled to conform to the dominant mode of transport even though they may have reservations. The fourth category is consistent with the 'mobile independent' domain.

Segmentation studies have divided non-car users into three types:

1. Car sceptics are travel aware, environmentally aware and manage without a car (preferring bicycles, walking or public transport) – mobile independents.
2. Reluctant riders tend to be older and less well off, dependent on public transport and, where possible, travelling as passengers in others' cars – a mixture of mobile disadvantaged and mobile independents.
3. Car aspirers, including the unemployed in lower-income groups, environmentally unaware, need better access than that provided by public transport and for this and other reasons aspire to car ownership – mobile disadvantaged.

Stradling and Anable refer to research in Scotland that found that these groups each comprise about 8% of the adult population (ibid., p. 186), meaning that 76% of the population belong to the 'mobile ubiquitous' or 'mobile elite' domains, and the car aspirers and reluctant riders would like to join them if they could. This leaves the 'mobile independents' with around 12% of the adult population. This may be a higher proportion in cities but it indicates the magnitude of the challenge for those advocating a change in travel habits towards more active lifestyles that emphasise walking and cycling modes. The point is that mobility as network capital is critical to contemporary lifestyles and the majority associate this with auto-mobility despite the efforts of planners, the Government and others to send out a different message.

8.3 Transport Radicalism and Social Movements

In their book, *Mobile Lives*, Elliott and Urry argue that the contradiction in capitalist societies is not so much that of class conflict resulting from the growth of the revolutionary proletariat, but from how 20th-century capitalist relations of production have undermined the very forces of future capitalist production. In particular, the high-carbon economy/society of the last century and the concomitant congestion is the emergent contradiction that 20th-century capitalism unleashed (ibid., p. 132). The thesis holds that mobility systems and mobile lives will lead to the downfall and destruction of the capitalist economy and usher in a new form of society that will need to manage and control mobility more sustainably. This could be achieved through a socialist/collectivist model of social relations based on equality and limits to growth, or a commercial/consumerist model based on market forces and prices to determine the allocation of resources.[5]

The theory is supported by other radical interpretations of the social forces at work in the contemporary city. For example, in *Rebel Cities*, Harvey describes social movements that challenge the implicit social order and the hypermobility of consumer-capitalist culture (Harvey 2012). Harvey's book is a tribute to Lefebvre's *The Right to the City* published in 1968, and reaffirms Lefebvre's radicalism that the strength and power of the dominant (capitalist) practices must be eradicated through a broad revolutionary movement. In Harvey's words 'The whole capitalist system of perpetual accumulation, along with its associated structures of exploitative class and state power, has to be overthrown and replaced. Claiming the right to the city is a way-station on the road to that goal' (ibid., p. xviii). Harvey claims that these social movements are re-setting the agenda for a different conceptualisation of urbanisation and how cities are organised.

The protest movements have emerged in response to mainstream political parties moving to the centre. Some political parties like the Greens have been created to fill the void, but have so far failed to make a political breakthrough and remain on the fringe of mainstream politics. The protest movements aim to influence the debate and discourse around a specific theme or in some cases a broad anti-capitalist or environmentalist agenda. In the transport arena there are several lobbies and interest groups that aim to influence government policy and understanding of transport issues. Among the more established groups are the Campaign for Better Transport (formerly Transport 2000), Friends of the Earth and Sustrans, which campaign for more sustainable transport solutions such as public transport and cycling in priority to road infrastructure. On the other side are motoring organisation like the Automobile Association and the Royal Automobile Club who, as their titles imply, support pro-car friendly policies. There are also professional lobbies including the Chartered Institute for Logistics and Transport, the Chartered Institution of Highways and Transportation and the Transport Planning Society, which are more neutral in their evaluation of transport policies but tend to be influenced by the current political landscape. In their own way all these groups have exerted some influence over government policy, and indeed government and local authorities often consult with these organisations on various proposals. These lobbies, in a sense, have gone native and more often than not cooperate with the government rather than be conflicted.

Apart from these established organisations there are guerrilla groups that form to oppose/advocate specific schemes or policies, such as opposing a new road, taking action to highlight climate change targeted at transport companies (such as blockading oil refineries or petrol stations), and mass cycle rides to promote better cycling provision. The rise of the cycling lobby is interesting because it combines elements of a broad coalition of cyclists in favour of better cycling infrastructure (see Chapter 5) with an assertive (some would say aggressive) cycling sub-cult that associates cycling with an anti-car, new urban mobility culture, that is, a social movement as much as a cycling lobby – see Box 8.2.

Box 8.2 Cycling as a Social Movement

Cycling has risen up the UK transport agenda in response to successful lobbying for more cycle provision, an active travel programme promoting more healthier lifestyles, and experience from the Netherlands and other European countries, where cycling accounts for as much as one-third of local travel. The Government has responded with a range of measures and increased funding, with Transport for London taking a lead in developing new design standards for cycling infrastructure.

Even so, a more assertive sub-cult of cyclists has emerged – mainly in London – who are aggressive in claiming the streets for cyclists, and cycle assertively – sometime recklessly – putting themselves and other road users in danger. These self-styled 'cyclenistas' are in the vanguard of a radical transport social movement that aims to take back the streets for sustainable transport even if it puts them into

> conflict with traffic. The cyclenistas have organised mass bike rides to promote their cause and disrupt traffic. So far, their impact is confined to London, but they have sympathisers across the UK and within the transport profession. Their radical agenda to transform the UK into 'a Holland' is unlikely to be heeded by the politicians or the public.
>
> Cycling is popular as a leisure activity but outside of London and a few provincial towns it remains a minority mode of transport, with fewer than 2% of all trips, although this may increase as cycle-friendly policies are rolled out. Cycling as a social movement seems a passing phase that attracts the 'mobile independents' but is unlikely to threaten the dominance of cars, rail or buses used by the other mobile domains.

I do not share Harvey's prognosis or his belief in the power of social movements to overthrow capitalism. Rather, history suggests that social movements can shake up and modify capitalist practices but rarely threaten the very existence of the capitalist system. In this sense, I lean more toward the 'creative destruction' view of capitalist reinvention as opposed to its demise and replacement with a communitarian system. This appears to be the view of other analysts of contemporary society, including the sociologists of mobility. Harvey and his fellow neo-Marxists are in the minority, which does not mean they are wrong, but their interpretation of urban social movements and spatial organisation finds few followers outside the radical fringe of academia and politics.

Nevertheless, Harvey has at least drawn attention to the interface between spatial and social organisation, most visible in the city. Harvey is correct to assert that urbanisation is fundamentally a capitalist process of accumulation and reinvestment of surplus value, something that transport planners rarely appreciate. Urbanisation, including transport systems development, is therefore a class-based phenomenon of some sort, since surpluses have to be extracted from somewhere and somebody, with control over the use of the surpluses typically lying in the hands of a few. As Harvey states, 'capitalism is perpetually producing the surplus product that urbanisation requires' and 'The reverse also holds. Capitalism needs urbanisation to absorb the surplus products it perpetually produces. In this way an inner connection emerges between the development of capitalism and urbanisation' (ibid., p. 5).

Transport systems and mobility play a crucial role in facilitating the expansion of urban areas and the production and distribution of surplus value. This includes the exploitation of resources such as labour to produce the surplus value. In the chapter on 'The Urban Roots of Capitalist Crises', Harvey describes how mobility, once a liberating force in social mobility, has become a means of exploitation in increasing competition among the workforce as well as in the consumption of goods. Many people in the transport profession have a simplistic view of transport systems as modes for spatial movement, separating these into private and public modes, personal and collective domains and, as previously noted, believing a simple narrative of public transport 'good', car 'bad' dichotomy. As Harvey's critique points out, capitalism does not care if the exploitation is by any specific mode of transport; what is important is that the transport systems provide the requisite level of mobility to allow the surplus value to be created. This is the essence of the urban capitalist transport system. Transport infrastructure is one of the main methods of recycling surplus value that in turn produces created places that have inflated land values through which rents can be appropriated. (For example, schemes like Crossrail in London serve corporate interests in increasing land values and at the same time increasing competition among the workforce by extending the commuter hinterland, all subsidised by the state.)[6] Thus, transport and mobility is not just a derived demand but integral to the processes of capital accumulation and the production of surplus value (profit).

Harvey believes that ultimately this exploitation via mobility and other social processes will lead to a crisis of capitalism. My view is that the demand for ever-increasing mobility will create a congestion crisis that will undermine the efficiency of the capitalist economic model and the ability of people and businesses to function effectively, which will require a political response to be resolved. This will be played out within the democratic institutions of the capitalist nations (or a solution imposed in more authoritarian states), and a restructuring of the political-economy, but I doubt this will lead to the overthrow of the capitalist system.

8.4 Future Scenarios for the Mobile Society

The congestion crisis will affect the mobility domains in different ways. The 'mobile independents' may welcome the opportunity this might bring, especially those who support more radical sustainable transport policies and the possibility of creating collectivist transport out of 'Autogeddon'. This wishful thinking is unlikely to prevail. The 'mobile elites' as always will have the resources to protect their privileged position, so the domains who will suffer most are the 'mobile disadvantaged' and 'mobile ubiquitous' groups. Revolutionaries like to think that those at the bottom will gain most from any denouement but history suggests that vulnerable people remain vulnerable whoever is in charge. Since the demise of the proletariat/bourgeoisie class distinction a more appropriate 'precariat' label has been devised that describes a precarious group of people who are least able to protect themselves from external forces. In mobility terms, they lack network capital, and have few resources to protect themselves when circumstances change.

The largest group impacted are the 'mobile ubiquitous', and most political action will be expended in addressing their concerns. This is the domain of people who live mobile lives vested in car use, rail commuting, frequent flying and use of the latest mobile technologies to support their lifestyles. They seek to capture as much network capital as their mobility resources allow. This is the domain that will be most impacted by the congestion crisis, and rather than seek to overthrow the capitalist transport system they are more likely to try and preserve those elements that enable them to continue their mobile lives. Reforming the transport system is more likely to appeal to this domain than revolution. For these reasons, this domain is the one that a sustainable mobility settlement is primarily aimed at, with indirect benefits for the 'mobile disadvantaged' and the 'mobile independents'. The 'mobile elite' may endure some loss of privileges from the new mobility settlement, but this will be the price of reformation rather than revolution.

As part of their examination of mobile lives and the mobilities paradigm, Elliott and Urry outline four possible scenarios for future society, which they refer to as Corbusier, Schumacher, Hobbesian and Orwellian. Briefly, these are described as follows: Corbusier society is characterised by hypermobility and technology that substitutes cyber-mobility for spatial mobility, and produces a low-carbon technical fix to energy use; alternatively, Schumacher society could be organised around local sustainability as advocated by environmentalists, a 'small-is-beautiful' philosophy and eco-communalism; in contrast, the Hobbesian scenario depicts countries seeking to compete more aggressively to capture resources to maintain their high-energy lifestyles in a kind of 'regional warlordism', which may descend into a fortress economy with regional blocs defending their resources and society becoming much harsher and more barbaric; or, finally, an Orwellian society controlled by digital networks that monitor and control movement and the production of goods and services so as to sustain the economy.

None of these are attractive propositions for future society and imply that changes to the social democratic system of government that has dominated advanced societies since the industrial revolution will be required. Unlike Harvey's prediction of a social revolution leading to communism, these scenarios describe to varying degrees modified versions of democratic capitalism, or managed forms of capitalism in some cases. Only the Schumacher scenario comes close to the Marxist definition of 'primitive communism' (that is, a return to a pre-feudal political economy). These are big questions about how society may be organised in 2050, when issues of climate change, fossil fuel depletion, population explosion and environmental destruction will, it is forecast, be critical.

From a mobilities/transportation perspective only two of these scenarios seem likely, at least in the developed economies, namely the Corbusier and Orwellian scenarios, or perhaps a mixture of the two. The Schumacher vision may prevail in some cultures that can exist sustainably without trading much with other countries, for example, South Pacific Islands or New Zealand. This scenario is consistent with the convivial transport arrangement, especially if combined with some elements of the Corbusier model. The Hobbesian scenario of regional conflict to capture key resources may prevail in countries with large reserves of natural resources such as the Middle East or Russia, that don't have a strong tradition of democracy and instead have strong nationalism or religious values. Another factor that has to be considered is the political-economic traditions of each culture and society. In some cultures – China, for example – introducing a new model for society may be easier than elsewhere. China already has elements of an Orwellian state with structures for surveillance and monitoring people's movement, and the Chinese Communist Party may lean toward this model in preference to the Corbusier system of accommodating hypermobility. In western liberal democracies, the Corbusier model is more likely to be adopted, if only by default, as the one most acceptable to the electorate. Some outliers of Schumacher local sustainability may occur and co-exist with the Corbusier–Orwellian states.

These scenarios are conjectures of what might happen, deduced from analyses of current trends and projections that may not turn out the way the authors believe. The impact of new technologies and innovation, for example, are difficult to predict, and there could be cultural shifts that move behaviours voluntarily towards conviviality. The signs, however, point towards a deepening congestion crisis, brought on by population growth and rising mobility expectations, which will undermine the competitive transport system and by extension the consumer-capitalist economy. Something will have to change. If the current mix of 'new realism' policies cannot deliver a sustainable transport solution then more radical actions and policies will be needed. A social revolution ushering in a communitarian society seems improbable, at least in mature democracies, so the alternative scenarios described by Elliott and Urry appear more credible. Of these, the combination of Corbusier and Orwell is consistent with technology and social trends in developed countries and is capable of delivering a balanced sustainable mobility system.

8.5 The Social and Political Implications of Mobility

The dialectic of post-war transport developments described by Axhausen – either a liberation movement or Faustian deal – is the thesis and antithesis of a mobile society. The liberation afforded by auto-mobility produces a reaction in increased congestion, which negates the earlier benefits. This is the paradox of mobility: the action of mass personal mobility – liberation via social consumption – causes congestion and a dysfunctional transport system. This in turn prompts further action to improve the reliability of travel through more spending on infrastructure (social investment) and expanding cities (the Faustian legacy). In the short term people and businesses can only react by adjusting their travel times or destinations: in the medium and long term they may relocate to optimise their accessibility by the preferred mode (conserving their network capital). A ratchet mechanism is established whereby each attempt to meet mobility demands creates more congestion, further sprawl and longer travel times, eventually resulting in unsustainable mobility (social consumption exceeding social investment).

How the social system will respond to manage the mobility crisis is speculated by sociologists and urban theorists. Harvey offers the prospect of a social revolution brought about by radical urban social movements in response to urban crises such as rising congestion and costs. The internal contradiction of mobility and congestion affecting capitalism is a theme developed by Elliott and Urry, who describe four possible scenarios for the organisation of society to manage the mobility crisis, not a revolution as such, but a radical reform nonetheless. How realistic are these future visions for society? The vision proffered in this book is the combination of technology and control in a hybrid Orwellian–Corbusier model. This scenario provides the social structure for the mobility management regime described in the next chapter. Less radical prognosis for changing travel behaviour through persuasive methods appear weak in comparison.

The ability of people to respond to and empower their mobility is determined by how they acquire network capital and their flexibility to use this in the urban milieu. The axiom of network capital assigns people to mobility domains related to their mobile fixity/fluidity. These mobility domains indicate the degree of convergence between mobility and motility, the greater the convergence the more power and control people have over their mobile lives. Thus mobile elites have access to mobile resources and the flexibility to use these. In contrast, the mobile disadvantaged have limited choices in their access to mobile resources and are more fixed (constrained) in their mobility. In between are the mobile independents and the mobile ubiquitous, the latter forming the largest group. Their mobile lives, dominated by auto-mobility, are out of kilter with sustainable mobility practices, and until they can be brought into some kind of balance congestion and mobility problems will get worse until they become intolerable and threaten lifestyles as well as the stability of the urban economy. We need a more convivial transport arrangement that creates the conditions to enable sustainable mobility for all.

Notes

1 Not to be confused with motility in natural sciences, which refers to the ability to move spontaneously and actively, consuming energy in the process. Examples include moving food through the gut (peristalsis) or sperm moving towards an egg.
2 Conceptually motility relates to how mobility is accomplished, reflecting travel status and capability, and not just the frequency and speed of travel. The sociology of travel experience explores the use of language to authenticate travel status and behaviour.

3 In *Re-thinking Mobility*, Kaufmann identifies mobility potential – i.e. motility – as the key to understanding individual actions. Mobility practices become standardised or ubiquitous around certain norms that people feel comfortable conforming to, such as car travel or rail commuting. With increasing connectivity and reversibility (flexibility) forms of mobility and ubiquity are established. Motility also represents the social capital of mobility and, therefore, a motivator influencing travel behaviour.
4 Network capital can also be regarded as a component of social capital (acquired through work, politics, religion or professional association) whose significance has grown with the ascendency of mobility.
5 There is a middle course of 'managed capitalism', advocated by liberals and social democrats as a means to control the excesses of capitalist accumulation and balance social consumption and investment. The interventionist political-economic cultures of countries such as Sweden, Germany and Japan are presented as examples of how managed capitalism can work. Critics, however, point out that these countries only adopt a managed approach once capitalism has succeeded in producing a wealthy society, or is implemented in mono-cultural societies with a strong national identity that puts the national interest before personal interest, such as Singapore. It requires strong political action to counter economic forces that are pushing for neo-liberal policies and 'monopoly capitalism' practices. It is also worth noting that the managed capitalist societies mentioned suffer from congestion like other countries, and while they may find it easier to implement collective measures these may only be temporary solutions.
6 This does not mean that schemes like Crossrail do not offer value for money, and may deliver greater mobility benefits compared with other schemes. But the distribution of those benefits and who gains most is an important question that is often overlooked or subsumed in the agglomeration effects of major projects.

References

Axhausen, K.W. 2005, 'Social Networks and Travel: Some Hypotheses', in *Social Dimensions of Sustainable Travel*, eds. K.P. Donaghy, S. Poppelreuter & G. Rudinger, Ashgate, Farnham, pp. 90–99.

Bayliss, D. 2009, *Low Income Motoring in Great Britain*, RAC Foundation, London, UK.

Castells, M. 1996 (second edition, 2000), *The Rise of the Network Society. The Information Age: Economy, Society and Culture, Vol. I*, Blackwell, Cambridge, MA; Oxford, UK.

Castells, M. 1997 (second edition, 2004), *The Power of Identity, The Information Age: Economy, Society and Culture, Vol. II*, Blackwell, Cambridge, MA; Oxford, UK.

Castells, M. 1998 (second edition, 2000), *End of Millennium, The Information Age: Economy, Society and Culture, Vol. III*, Blackwell, Cambridge, MA; Oxford, UK.

Elliott, A. & Urry, J. 2010, *Mobile Lives*, Routledge, London, UK.

Geddes, P. 1915, *Cities in Evolution*, Williams & Norgate, London, UK.

Giddens, A. 1984, *The Constitution of Society: Outline of the Theory of Structuration*, University of California Press, Berkeley, USA.

Greico, M. and MacDonald, K. (eds.) 2007, 'Accessibility, Mobility and Connectivity: The Changing Frontiers of Everyday Routine', *Special Issue of Mobilities*, 2, 1, pp. 1–14.

Harvey, D. 1973, *Social Justice and the City*, Johns Hopkins University Press, Baltimore, USA.
Harvey, D. 2012, *Rebel Cities*, Verso, London, UK.
Jensen, O.B. 2009, 'Flows of Meaning, Cultures of Movement: Urban Mobility as Meaningful Everyday Life Practice', *Mobilities*, 4, 1, pp. 139–158.
Kaufmann, V. 2002, *Re-thinking Mobility*, Ashgate, Aldershot, UK.
Lefebvre, H. 1991, *The Production of Space*, Blackwell, London, UK. (First published in 1974).
Lyons, G., Goodwin, P., Hanly, M., Dudley, G., Chatterjee, K., Anable, J., Wiltshire, P. & Susilo, Y. 2008, *Public Attitudes to Transport: Knowledge Review of Existing Evidence*, Final Report to the Department for Transport, Centre for Transport and Society, University for the West of England, Bristol, UK.
Schumpeter, J.A. 1942/1994, *Capitalism, Socialism and Democracy*, Routledge, London, UK.
Sheller, M. & Urry, J. 2006, 'The New Mobilities Paradigm', *Environment and Planning A*, 38, 2, pp. 207–226.
Stradling, S. & Anable, J. 2008, 'Individual Transport Patterns', in *Transport Geographies: Mobilities, Flows and Spaces*, eds. R. Knowles, J. Shaw & I. Docherty, Blackwell, Oxford, UK.
Urry, J. 2000, *Sociology Beyond Societies: Mobilities for the Twenty First Century*, Routledge, London, UK.
Urry, J. 2007, *Mobilities*, Polity, Cambridge, UK.
Weber, M. 1921/1986, *The City*, Free Press, Illinois, USA.
Weber, M. 1964, *The Theory of Social and Economic Organization*, ed. T. Parsons, The Free Press, New York, USA.
Wirth, L. 1938, 'Urbanism as a Way of Life', *American Journal of Sociology*, 44, pp. 1–24.
Zielinski, S. 2006, 'New Mobility: The Next Generation of Urban Sustainable Transportation', *The Bridge*, National Academy of Engineering, 36, 4, pp. 33–38.

Part IV
Mobility Management
From Gridlock to
Sustainable Mobility

9 Mobility Management

9.1 Concept of Operations

This section examines the third proposition of the book (summarised in Box 1.1, Chapter 1) that sustainable mobility will be accomplished through a mobility management regime comprising regulation and control of mobility demand together with pricing mechanisms to incentivise adherence to the new regulatory framework. This regime follows from analysis of the two other propositions throughout this book, namely:

- Unfettered mobility and congestion are locked into a downward spiral that threatens peoples' lifestyles and their ability to function effectively in the urban milieu.
- The urban economy will suffer as congestion increases and will reach a tipping point at which inefficiencies threaten gridlock in the transport systems and wider society; at this point the electorate and business interests will demand more radical solutions than have hitherto been contemplated.
- The solution will need to be fair, equitable and affordable and capable of being sustainable to the economy, society and the environment, that is, a sustainable mobility system.
- Transport technology has the capability to mitigate the environmental impact of auto-mobility and enhance the travel experience across all modes, but it cannot on its own produce a solution to congestion. What technology can offer is the ability to manage and control mobility more effectively and efficiently through the application of location aware technologies allied to logistics and pricing systems.

It is contended that pricing mechanisms on their own will be unacceptable as an arbiter to match demand to the available supply; therefore, mobility by surface mechanical modes will be rationed through regulation of movement adjusted to the capacities of the transport systems.[1] The trade-off is between mobility freedom and equal access to transport resources at affordable prices. As described below, utilisation within the annual personal allowance of 'mobility miles' will incur no penalties but there would be restrictions on access, with steep penalties for excessive use of transport resources beyond the per capita annual allocation.[2]

Congestion and associated ills represent a market failure to balance demand and supply. A chronic weakness of any open transport system is that demand cannot be rationed efficiently and relies, therefore, on congestion as the means of controlling the throughput on the network. This is especially problematic on roads and trains, and to a lesser extent on bus systems. Congestion pricing to allocate demand more efficiently (and provide revenue to add to supply) is technically feasible but politically difficult except in specific locations such as city centres. Tolls on bridges and roads provide the equivalent of fares on public transport, but their imposition is selective and opposed in many countries. Pricing has to be part of the solution alongside other considerations such as equity and environmental justice. The other potential solution, to increase supply to meet projected demand, is not feasible on cost or environmental grounds, as evidence demonstrates.

A better alternative is a policy of mobility rationing based on an annual allowance of mobility miles per adult capita. We already have the technology and logistics know-how to make this a feasible proposition across the passenger and freight transport sectors. This concept is referred to as 'mobility management', and the method of implementation as 'travel demand logistics management' (TDLM).

9.2 Travel Demand Logistics Management

TDLM is proposed as the method to accomplish sustainable mobility management. The method involves applying the principles and practices of logistics to managing the demand for travel to the capacity of the transport system. It inverses supply chain logistics, which seeks to optimise the delivery and distribution of goods through the transport system, by limiting throughput to the system capacity. There are a number of key elements that are briefly outlined below (note that these are intended to be introduced over a period of years):

1. thorough inventory of transport system resources, capacity and throughputs under different conditions;
2. monitoring and management of flows in real time;
3. modelling and optimisation of transport networks and services to maximise use of capacity;
4. planning and scheduling of system interruptions and downtime for maintenance and other activities; this includes adding redundancy into the throughput calculations to account for perturbations such as bad weather and unforeseen events such as accidents;

5   advance notification of journeys so these can be assigned to the transport network (some spare capacity will be built in to accommodate last minute trips, charged at a premium rate);
6   journey planning independently or via mobility managers; instantaneous communications and feedback to smartphones and other devices; and
7   real-time communication and tracking of all vehicles and journeys on public transport and vehicles via vehicle-to-vehicle, vehicle-to-instrumented highway and vehicle-to-person telematics.

Many of these features are already available and used in logistics and intelligent transport systems. TDLM takes it to another level and integrates the logistics management concept with the system capacity. The key conceptual difference with how present transport systems work is that currently we have unconstrained demand that we estimate from survey data or crowd-sourcing techniques, whereas TDLM constrains demand to the capacity of the system. Demand that exceeds capacity will be redirected to another route, time or mode. Not all trips will be met under this regime, which is where the mobility managers and pricing component comes in. There are some disadvantages with this solution but on balance the efficiencies gained will outweigh the inconvenience caused to a minority of travellers. There is no perfect solution to resolving the mobility crisis, only second-best solutions, and mobility management is the least worst of all options. Over time users will get used to the new TDLM regime and make their trip reservations in a similar manner to other services. Block bookings can be made but only for specific periods, after which the user must reapply. The TDLM will incentivise people to make the most sustainable journeys, as these will encounter fewer restrictions.

At present even when we have accurate data we can only use this to forecast demand for strategic planning purposes such as adding more infrastructure. By knowing the capacity of different systems we can assign demand efficiently and guarantee the user the journey time and quality journey they expect. Simulation models can be used to optimise flows under different conditions. Only journeys that cross a cordon boundary will be registered. It is possible that intra-zonal trips may exceed capacity, in which case special measures may be required. However, in most cases capacity will only be reached with a mix of inter-zonal and intra-zonal trips, so cross-boundary movements can be managed effectively.

Modelling these movements is complex. However, advances in scheduling software and computing capabilities will make management of these movements feasible. Mobility management and TDLM are core features of the manifesto for mobility outlined in the next chapter. Before then, however, the role of congestion pricing, smarter choices and infrastructure investment is defined. These measures will not be successful on their own but can be effective as part of the mobility management solution proposed here.

9.3 Congestion Pricing: Monetising Mobility

The mobility management scenario outlined above is technically feasible but faces opposition from those who would object to the type of controls described. Some would see this as too much interference in freedom of movement, an infringement of civil liberties and a contravention of data privacy laws. Politically it may be a hard sell as well. So what is the alternative to mobility management?

Transport economists have for a long time advocated a pricing solution to manage traffic demand, and a road-pricing theory based on the 'social marginal cost' of travel has been around since the 1950s (Beckmann 2013). The social marginal cost is the cost imposed on other road users by the addition of one's vehicle. In free-flow conditions there is no impact, so the cost is zero, but as congestion builds up and traffic slows the delay in travel time is a cost imposed on all road users. This cost should be reflected in the charge to use the road. It would discourage those users with a lower utility value for travel, for example discretionary travellers, as opposed to those whose journeys are essential. In theory, road charges could be adjusted to reflect peak and off-peak travel and thereby achieve a more efficient use of the road space. Since the theory was first developed it has been extended to include other external costs imposed on non-road users, such as the effects of noise and greenhouse gases, as well as wider network effects. It is generally recognised that it would be impractical to apply separate charges for each road at different times of the day, so an area-wide charging zone such as those in Central London, Oslo, Stockholm and Singapore are seen as the most practicable solution. An alternative approach is to impose tolls at certain key sections of road, such as a bridge or tunnel, which is more targeted and offers an unavoidable method of collecting the charges.

With modern technology it is possible to pay toll charges electronically and do away with toll booths; this is the direction that most toll roads are moving towards. The electronic tags that communicate between the vehicle and the toll transponder could be integrated with global positioning systems (GPS) or other location-tracking systems (in smartphones for instance or the car's satnav device) so that, in theory, road charges could be applied more discretely rather than area wide. The technology is advancing to enable this, and in future this could become an option, perhaps in combination with the trip reservation system mentioned earlier. An example is the vehicle miles of travel (VMT) fee concept that was piloted among a select group of motorists in Oregon in 2006–2007. VMT fees are distance-based fees levied on a vehicle user, as opposed to tolls, which are facility-specific and not necessarily levied strictly on a per-mile basis. The VMT fee is charged in exchange for fuel taxes or vehicle tax. The concept is applied through the use of an on-board device, equipped with GPS or other technology, to capture the distance driven by a vehicle and relate that to a method of charging, which could range from manual cash payment to automatic deduction from a prepaid customer account. It has since been modified and tested in twelve cities across the USA, and demonstrates the feasibility of distance-based congestion pricing, which can be varied by time of day and even the types of road used (Hanley & Kuhl 2011).

In practice, road-user charging faces opposition from motorists, motoring organisations, sections of the media and politicians ideologically opposed to such charges. Referenda held in Edinburgh, Manchester and London (on the western extension to the charging zone) all voted against these schemes, and an on-line national petition (on the Downing Street website in 2007) against road-user charging was signed by nearly two million people. There are also economic distribution effects that are not fully understood and could have significant impacts on social groups as well as the wider economy. The debate over how to charge motorists for the direct and indirect costs of car use is therefore highly political: individual motorists view the charge as a tax on their mobility, while small businesses and other lobbies worry that the charges will add costs to their business. On the other side, transport economists, environmentalists, liberal-green politicians and large swathes of the transport profession see road-user charges as a rational mechanism to manage congestion and make sure that motorists pay the full price for their road use.[3]

In 2011 taxes on fuel and vehicles raised about £24 billion more than is spent on road building and maintenance, and this surplus is treated as general government revenue rather than being hypothecated to transport (Department for Transport (DfT) 2012). However, if the indirect costs of transport are taken into account, including traffic congestion, which is estimated to cost business £8 billion per annum (Confederation of British Industry (CBI) 2012),[4] and other environmental costs, the surplus is much less and may even be in deficit. Estimates on the costs of congestion vary and there is no definitive data produced by the DfT or other body, unlike the position in the USA where an annual Urban Mobility Report produced by the Texas A&M Transportation Institute is widely accepted as a good indicator of the state of congestion in 101 US cities (see Chapter 3). The 2012 report, for instance, calculates that in 2011 congestion caused urban Americans to travel 5.5 billion hours more, and purchase an extra 2.9 billion gallons of fuel, with a total congestion cost of $121 billion.[5]

The CBI has proposed a variation of road-user charging based on a 'regulated asset base' (RAB) model, in which an independent, price-setting regulator oversees investment from private operators for stable, capped returns (CBI 2012). The returns would be fees paid for each vehicle that uses a road managed by a private operator, with the fees being exchanged for the vehicle tax currently levied on all motor vehicles. In time tolls could replace the vehicle tax to raise additional investment for transport.

The RAB model is widely used in the utilities industry, such as water companies, and is proposed by the CBI as a means to increase investment in road infrastructure. The reallocation of vehicle tax to road operators would reduce the surplus revenues to government, but would be tax neutral on the individual motorist.

The CBI proposal is in response to the Coalition Government's plan – *Action for Roads* (DfT 2013) – that would transform the Highways Agency, which manages the strategic road network, into a publicly owned company with six year funding certainty for capital projects and maintenance. This is along the lines of how Network Rail is constituted, with the ability to raise funds in the private market. The CBI believes that there is a shortfall of around £10 billion in funding for Highways Agency projects and therefore advocates the RAB model as a solution to bridge the gap. The Government, however, has opted to increase the funds for road investment and maintenance directly from government expenditure rather than adopt the RAB model, fearing that this would provide them with less control over transport expenditure and would be politically unpopular with motorists. The DfT will specify the Road Investment Strategy from 2015 to 2020, implemented through a new Highways England agency. The DfT is not ruling out alternative arrangements for funding and managing the strategic road network in England but it looks as though the RAB model is a step too far politically.

The CBI approach offers a painless way (to the motorist) to increase funding for road schemes through charges directly related to road use. However, the bluntness of the charges defeats the object of making the motorist aware of the costs they are imposing on others and thereby to change their travel behaviour. In the CBI approach, levying a charge against vehicle tax would be a means to fund more road infrastructure, whereas the original proponents see the charges acting as a constraint on demand to bring it more into line with supply. The RAB model could be more acceptable to the motorist but is unlikely to resolve congestion problems even with extra investment in roads. The 'predict and provide' paradigm, implicit in the CBI model, has been shown not to be an effective long-term solution.

Action for Roads represents a defeat for the supporters of the 'new realism' paradigm, and a step back towards the 'predict and provide' model of previous eras. This was predicted in Chapter 5 and is entirely consistent with the political economy of transport as practiced in the UK. It represents an attempt to monetise the cost of mobility and congestion as part of the appraisal of the costs and benefits of transport schemes. Some motorists may be prepared to pay road-user fees in order to have a better quality of journey, but the evidence suggests they are a minority and most likely from the higher income cohort. The evidence from the M6 Toll Road in the West Midlands is cited as an example of the resistance of motorists to tolls where an alternative exists; and in the USA, where toll roads are more commonplace, they are not always successful. For example, the tolled express lanes alongside State Route 91 in Southern California were taken back into public ownership following failure of the operator to cover its construction and operating costs (variable pricing was applied in the peak and off-peak hours and despite significant congestion on the non-toll highway not enough drivers were persuaded to pay a toll for a quicker journey).

The lesson seems to be that where motorists have an alternative route they will use this in order to avoid paying a toll, despite the savings in journey time. The reasons are complex but include inertia (familiarity with an existing route), cost ('can't pay') and objections to paying any more for their travel ('won't pay'). Calculating the costs and benefits of mobility is fraught with difficulties. Apart from the complex economics involved, policy makers have to grapple with the politics of mobility. Reducing congestion to a problem that can be solved by transport economics is naïve, and as a one-dimensional solution is unlikely to succeed. This is because different groups are likely to be affected disproportionately. There are plenty of publications on the technology available for road-user charging, on scheme designs, and on the benefits in terms of congestion relief and revenues raised, but relatively few analyses of the winners and losers. These may be difficult to identify, but the lack of studies into the distribution effects of road-user charging seems odd given the importance attached to it by the transport profession. Perhaps it's because they suspect the results will be seized upon by opponents who will focus on the losers rather than the winners?

Nonetheless, the equity effects of road pricing have been researched in a few studies, which are briefly reviewed below. In the US context Levinson asks whether road-pricing strategies are regressive or progressive (Levinson 2010). As he notes, the theoretical literature is mixed, as is the empirical literature. Levinson synthesises the literature to date on both the theory of equity, as applied to road pricing, and the findings of empirical and simulation studies of the effects of particular implementations of road pricing, and suggested remedies for real or perceived inequities. He concludes that while there are certainly potential issues with equity associated with road pricing, those issues can be addressed with an intelligent mechanism design that provides the right incentives to travellers and uses the raised revenues in a way to achieve desired equitable ends. These include cutting other taxes and investing in infrastructure and services. Litman reaches a similar conclusion and argues that transportation equity can also by accomplished through subsidies to public transport and traffic management measures that benefit non-auto users (Litman 2002). Other studies are not so positive, and a US Government Accountability Office (GAO) inquiry into traffic congestion and road pricing in fourteen federally funded schemes found that equity income impacts have not always been evaluated (GAO 2012). Potential concerns include income equity (whether low-income drivers are disproportionately affected by congestion pricing) and geographic equity (whether one geographic area is more negatively affected than another, such as when traffic diversion occurs). It adds that concerns about equity may grow as pricing projects become more widespread and equity concerns may become more acute where sponsors are using pricing not only to manage congestion, but also to raise revenue to build new projects. Raising revenue can be at odds with managing congestion (such as increasing vehicle throughput) if higher tolls can produce more revenue from fewer paying vehicles. The report notes that congestion pricing in the USA is in its relative infancy, with about 400 miles of priced lanes in operation, although its popularity is growing. It concludes that congestion pricing's impact on traveller behaviour and equity has yet to be fully explored.

In the UK context, a couple of studies into the equity impacts of road pricing have been conducted by motoring organisations, independent researchers and the DfT. These demonstrate the technical feasibility of congestion pricing together with the (expected?) benefits it would bring to (most?) motorists. The position is summarised in a report prepared by the RAC Foundation, *The Acceptability of Road Pricing* (Walker 2011). This contends that despite opposition from some quarters, including the public and sections of the media, road pricing is acceptable to motorists so long as four conditions are met:

1 it is equitable and those disadvantaged by the scheme are compensated in other ways;
2 it is revenue-neutral, or revenues are reinvested in transport;
3 it does not have a high cost overhead – most studies suggest that this should not be more than 5% of the revenue raised; and
4 people who are likely to be affected have confidence that road pricing works, demonstrated in pilot projects.

The RAC Foundation believes that equity concerns have been exaggerated and point to experience in London and Stockholm, where initial objections and scepticism were overcome once the schemes had time to bed-in (although the withdrawal of the western extension of the London congestion zone following local opposition undermines this conclusion). If the congestion pricing is revenue-neutral, then on balance it should be equitable. However, the report acknowledges that there will be winners and losers and it is difficult to identify who these are and what adjustments they may need to make to overcome travel difficulties (such as moving job or house). Road pricing may be regressive, since lower-income groups tend to pay a larger share of their income on transport than do the wealthy; but this is not automatically unfair, and the choice is often between regressive alternatives, not between a regressive and a progressive choice.

As Schweitzer and Taylor point out, the question should be: 'Are congestion tolls fairer than other means of transportation finance?' They affirm that 'we should not subsidise all drivers (and charge all consumers) to help the small number of poor travellers who use congested freeways in the peak hours and peak directions. Rather we should help those who are less fortunate, and see to it that the rest of us pay our own way on the roads' (Schweitzer & Taylor 2008, 2010). A lot depends on how the revenue raised is spent, especially if it is hypothecated to public transport improvements, as happened in London. The RAC report concludes that 'road pricing in reality would appear to be less unfair than is generally assumed, and should not be opposed on grounds of equity. And in one sense we would all be winners because congestion and pollution would be reduced' (ibid., p. 23). This view seems to prevail among the transport profession in general.

In a sister report, *Roads and Reality: Motoring Towards 2050*, the RAC Foundation has laid out how a system of national road charging on the strategic road network could be implemented (Banks, Bayliss & Glaister 2007). In this case the authors are less concerned about equity and more interested in how road-user charging can raise revenues for improving the road network: 'The Government should not use the possible future introduction of road pricing as an excuse for not improving the strategic road network. More effort needs to be made to mitigate some of the adverse environmental effects of road improvements, for instance more tunnelling and quieter road surfaces. The study clearly shows that road improvements will be essential with or without road pricing' (ibid., p. 71). A national lorry charging scheme is also proposed prior to implementing one for general traffic, and this is likely to receive fewer objections (and more support) from motorists. The European Union (EU) has already proposed such a scheme and some EU countries, including Germany, have been piloting a variety of lorry-charging technologies.[6]

Finally, the lack of knowledge and data on the social and distributional impacts of road pricing is revealed in a report prepared by the Centre for Transport and Society, University of the West of England, for the Department for Transport (Parkhurst et al. 2006). The report includes a comprehensive literature review and analysis of the empirical evidence derived from road-pricing implementations across the globe. The research covered a broad range of topics and investigated the impacts along nine key themes, including income, age, gender, ethnicity, household type, disability, scheme design and boundary changes, spatial issues and transport modes. The authors comment that 'It is important to emphasise that the evidence base on social and distributional impacts is extremely limited, *and little literature exists of which social and distributional impacts are the primary focus of research* [my emphasis] . . . Nevertheless, the emerging body of research on existing (or near market) road pricing schemes does provide some valuable guidance on the interrelationships between type of scheme and social and distributional impacts, together with implications of road pricing at different life stages, and consultation and public acceptability' (ibid., p. 6). The report concludes that proposals for new road pricing schemes need to involve consideration of equity issues from the earliest stage. This 'equity proofing' process will need to be based on the systematic gathering of clear evidence across all important segments of society, defined in terms of social group, economic status, demographic and ethnicity criteria.

Since these reports were produced, road pricing has moved down the policy agenda and is no longer the hot topic it was in the period 2005–2010. The equity issues and the political difficulty of proposing a scheme that is fair and effective has proved too problematic for political parties to grapple with while in government. Yet the feeling remains that at some stage in the future road pricing will become important as road congestion increases. The equity and distributional issues will then have to be confronted. As argued in this book, pricing alone is unlikely to provide the answer, and to address equity concerns other means of mobility management will need to be deployed alongside pricing mechanisms.

9.4 Limitations of Smarter Choices Travel Programmes

The 'new realism' paradigm has provided the justification for the development of 'smarter choices' programmes described in Chapter 5. The expectation is that these measures will improve use of non-auto modes and lead to longer-term changes in people's travel behaviour that favours active travel rather than the use of cars. The evidence to date, however, is somewhat disappointing. This is not to say that these programmes are not worthwhile: they can produce many benefits locally, and may also provide a testing ground for mobile technologies that inform travellers of travel choices.

Advocates of smarter choices also point to changes in travel behaviour among younger cohorts of the population with respect to car ownership and use, especially the peak car effect in London and other cities, where good alternative travel options are available. The evidence on this is mixed and the jury is still out on whether this represents a fundamental realignment of urban travel behaviour or a temporary blip in auto-mobility growth. The consensus is that persuasive measures that form the core of smarter choices can make a small difference locally, but in the bigger national picture are unlikely to resolve the problems of congestion or reduce carbon emissions to the desired level on their own. They can make a small tactical contribution but otherwise are insufficient to be strategically significant.

The conclusion therefore is that smarter choices need more coercive measures such as parking restrictions, parking place levies and congestion-charging policies to be effective in changing travel behaviour. As discussed earlier, these coercive measures are difficult to sell to a sceptical public and politically are perceived as a losing policy among voters. Smarter choices also run into cultural barriers related to travel behaviour. The premise behind them is that people have choices in how they travel. Objectively this may be the case, but the dominant mobility discourse (discussed in Chapter 7) presents a powerful narrative that affects perceptions of travel choice. This cognitive dissonance among many car users acts as a powerful antithesis to the 'smarter choices' thesis. Either it is changed by force (coercive measures) or changing circumstances.

There is also a theoretical problem in that by being selective smarter choices may target those more vulnerable and with lower mobility (network capital), while leaving others to pursue unsustainable mobility lifestyles. Thus, inadvertently, smarter choices may promote inequality and environmental injustice.[7] There are no sanctions in the current programme to curtail 'bad' behaviour. Naked self-interest may, therefore, trump attempts at collective consumption. Consequently, smarter choices are a weak response to meeting the requirements for a sustainable mobility system.

9.5 The Role of Infrastructure Investment

Part of the rationale behind road pricing is to secure funds for further capital investment in roads and associated infrastructure. Indeed, proponents of this approach believe that this policy is saleable to the motoring public so long as improvements in the road system can be guaranteed. It requires a commitment from government to ring-fence (hypothecate) car taxes (direct and indirect) for road expenditure and, as described in the discussion of congestion pricing, a number of methods have been put forward to accomplish this. It is hoped that improving road infrastructure will alleviate congestion enough to avoid the need to implement excessive congestion charges, suppressing demand sufficiently not to alienate the majority of motorists. This is a political trade-off as well as an economic solution.

The problem with this approach is that it will not make a lot of difference to the total stock of road miles and requires a huge commitment to road investment, which the country cannot afford. Unlike the earlier era of infrastructure investment (circa 1950–1970) when car ownership and use was still at modest levels, the current situation is very different and auto-mobility across the road network is already at saturation levels, or approaching it, in many areas. Building more roads or widening existing ones may provide some short-term relief but will not provide a long-term solution in the face of population growth and rising mobility aspirations from the public and business. The 'predict and provide' model has been shown not to work and transport theories such as the Downs–Thomson paradox explain why. Even if the funds were available in the quantities that organisations such as the

CBI and RAC Foundation suggest, this would only add 1 or 2% to the total stock of road lane miles.[8] This is not to say that some new infrastructure is not needed or desirable, but to put it into context the proposition that we can build our way out of the pending congestion crisis is simply not credible. It may work if implemented alongside congestion pricing that reduced demand, but as already noted this would impact enough motorists to render it near politically impossible to implement.

A similar conclusion can be made with respect to rail and other segregated forms of public transport – metros, light rail and bus rapid transit systems. These can be even more costly than road schemes. They may be justified as part of a balanced approach to local transport, especially if they encourage mode switching, but in many cases they are justified in terms of relieving overcrowding on existing or adjacent corridors. While this may be warranted, it does raise a question as to whether a 'predict and provide' approach for public transport is defensible if it is not correct for road schemes. In short, can we ever add to the public transport stock sufficiently to meet rising demands, and is it cost-effective? To take two examples: cross-London rail links and the High Speed Two (HS2) rail project connecting London with Birmingham, Leeds and Manchester. Both are massive projects costing tens of billions of pounds, but how effective will they be in tackling congestion and at what price vis-à-vis other schemes that may offer better value for money or more effective local solutions? How many more Crossrail schemes, for example, can we afford? By extending the commuter rail hinterland are we just stoking up demand that means that trains are always crowded? And by improving public transport accessibility in London, is this contributing to increasing land values, higher density residential accommodation, and rocketing rents and property prices? What price transport improvements, and who pays? The work of scholars such as Harvey, Lefebvre, Castells and Urry, who study mobility in the context of the urban economy and capitalism, seem particularly relevant to this discussion.

9.6 Mobility Management: A New Paradigm for Sustainable Transport

We are confronted with a dilemma in tackling congestion: road pricing is politically difficult (in a democracy), 'smarter choices' programmes are not robust enough to challenge the dominant culture of auto-mobility, and infrastructure investment is too costly (financially and in environmental impact). We also face international pressures to maintain a competitive economy and meet climate change obligations under various treaties and protocols. So what is the solution? And how do we reconcile the conflicts in delivering a sustainable mobility system that balances economic, social and environmental goals?

The solution proposed here is a new mobility management approach that constrains demand to the capacity of the transport systems. This should be accomplished in a more equitable way than road-pricing solutions alone and can be organised to deliver a sustainable meta-mobility system. Mobility management incorporates elements of congestion pricing, 'smarter choices' and new infrastructure, but in a more comprehensive strategy that enables doing more with less, that is, making sure we optimise transport resources alongside investments in additional capacity.

Mobility management will encourage mode shift to more sustainable transport modes, boost local public transport, especially bus services, and act as a catalyst for new innovative services such as demand-responsive transport, car sharing and other schemes. It will balance social consumption and social investment in transport, shifting expenditure into revenue rather than capital investment. It will need to build upon a new compact with the public and business that recognises the need to intensify transport and use it more efficiently and effectively in tackling CO_2 emissions, lower energy utilisation and environmental sustainability. This makes sense for the economy, which will otherwise choke under the weight of congestion and become gridlocked. This will also benefit disadvantaged groups, who will gain from the new settlement, with better and more affordable public transport services.

All of these gains will be made with one major compromise to freedom of mobility by mechanised modes. It is not a perfect solution, but it is technically feasible and a fairer strategy to managing our congested cities and delivering sustainable mobility for the future. The policy may be contested by those attached to existing prescriptions, but as these fail to deliver and are shown to be wanting, alternative remedies will be sought. By 2035 the mobility crisis will justify the deployment of more radical solutions, as hypothesised in the Preamble (see page xvii). Mobility management does not require a social revolution and is consistent with technology and cultural trends leading towards the Corbusier–Orwellian society. This may not be the most desirable outcome, but the alternatives of descent into chaotic gridlock or a social revolution are even worse to contemplate.

Notes

1 Air travel and sea ferries are excluded from this regime due to their specialist service and ability to ration movement by price effectively, and because they already fall under regulatory regimes that license the number of air and sea movements.
2 Mobility miles is similar to the concept of personal carbon allowances and trading that have been developed by the Carbon Trust and others (and supported in the Stern Report). The difference is that mobility miles are more broadly aimed at managing travel demand and are simpler to apply than CO_2 credits. Nevertheless, mobility miles quotas could incorporate some of the methods and targets proposed in personal carbon allowances. Further information is available

158   *Mobility Management*

    in The Carbon Trust *Personal Carbon Allowances White Paper* (2011) http://www.carbontrust.com/resources/reports/footprinting/personal-carbon-allowances-white-paper [accessed 22 January 2014]. See also Hillman and Fawcett (2004).
3 This position is consistent with neo-classical economics and pricing theory that has been discredited by the banking crisis and economic crash of 2008, which was supposed to be regulated by free-market competition, but turned out to be a classic bubble spurred on by greed and 'irrational exuberance'. Market failures and connivance between companies to manipulate prices have also been observed in other industries such as energy. The faith of transport economists in market mechanism to deliver an efficient transport system is challenged by recent experience and there is widespread scepticism that market solutions exist for public services like transport, without damaging the consumer, the economy or both. It is also ironic that supporters of road pricing include environmentalists and those on the progressive left of politics who normally oppose neo-liberal free-market policies.
4 This estimate is derived from the Eddington Report 2006, and quoted in *Bold Thinking: A Model to Fund Our Future Roads* (CBI 2012).
5 See Chapter 3 for further information. The US Federal Highway Administration, Office of Transportation Management (HOTM) collects data from nineteen urban areas to demonstrate the ability to develop performance measures from ITS data. The report is available quarterly and provides congestion trend data. A congestion trends report is also developed each fiscal year that explains congestion trends for that year.
6 EU countries also implement vignette schemes whereby motorists and truckers pay a fee to use motorways and major trunk roads. The vignette is purchased annually or for shorter periods and may apply to specific areas. It was first introduced in Switzerland to ensure that foreign traffic crossing the country paid a contribution towards road maintenance, but it has since been applied more widely to generate revenue for road infrastructure and is the model for the RAC Foundation scheme proposed for the UK.
7 It may also be the case that showing people travel alternatives may lower their journey cost, which has a direct benefit. However, these are considered as secondary to environmental and transport objectives in most schemes.
8 In the 2014 Autumn Statement on Public Expenditure, the Government proposed a three-fold increase in road investment, in expanding smarter motorways, dualling trunk roads and by-passes over the period 2015–2020, which represents a return to the competitive policy position ('predict and provide') of earlier decades. Like these earlier programmes, the policy is based on the mistaken belief that there is a supply-side solution to traffic congestion, and will likewise fail to provide a long-term solution, although they reap a short-term political benefit.

References

Banks, N., Bayliss, D. & Glaister, S. 2007, *Roads and Reality: Motoring Towards 2050*, RAC Foundation (in association with Arup), London, UK.
Beckmann, M.J. 2013, 'Traffic Congestion and What to Do About It', *Transport-Metrica B: Transport Dynamics*, 1, 1, pp. 103–109.
CBI 2012, *Bold Thinking: A Model to Fund Our Future Roads*, CBI, London, UK.
DfT 2012, *Transport Statistics Great Britain 2012*, HMSO, London, UK.
DfT 2013, *Action for Roads: A Network for the 21st Century*, HMSO, London, UK.

GAO 2012, *Traffic Congestion: Road Pricing Can Help Reduce Congestion, But Equity Concerns May Grow*, GAO-12-119, Washington, DC, USA.
Hanley, P.F. & Kuhl, J.G. 2011, 'National Evaluation of Mileage-Based Charges for Drivers', *Transportation Research Record: Journal of the Transportation Research Board*, Washington, DC, pp. 10–18.
Hillman, M. and Fawcett, T. (2004). *How We Can Save the Planet*, Penguin, London, UK.
Levinson, D. 2010, 'Equity Effects of Road Pricing: A Review', *Transport Reviews*, 30, 1, pp. 33–57.
Litman, T. 2002, 'Evaluating Transportation Equity', *World Transport Policy & Practice*, 8, 2, pp. 50–65.
Parkhurst, G., Dudley, G., Lyons, G., Avineri, E., Chatterjee, K. & Holley, D. 2006, *Understanding the Social and Distributional Impacts of Road Pricing. Report Two: Rapid Evidence Assessment, Final Report*, Centre for Transport & Society, University of the West of England, Bristol, UK.
Schweitzer, L. & Taylor, B.D. 2008, 'Just Pricing: The Distributional Effects of Congestion Pricing and Sales Taxes', *Transportation*, 35, pp. 797–812.
Schweitzer, L. & Taylor, B.D. 2010, 'Just Road Pricing', *ACCESS* (Magazine of the University of California Transportation Center), 36, pp. 2–7.
Walker, J. 2011, *The Acceptability of Road Pricing*, RAC Foundation, London, UK.

10 Manifesto for Sustainable Mobility

10.1 Prospectus

The manifesto described in this section is not a perfect solution and is arrived at reluctantly only because the other policy solutions on offer are considered unworkable and even worse than mobility management. The prognosis is that we need a sustainable mobility solution, and this can only be delivered by managing travel demand to the capacity of the transport system. The premise is that this is not only fairer but will enable the development of sustainable mobility practices, thus being supportive of environmental goals as well as being more politically viable as a working solution that the majority, especially the mobile ubiquity class, can sign up to. Sustainable mobility will utilise the latest information and communication technologies to manage travel demands and assign journeys to the transport systems (supply) in the most optimal manner. The travel demand logistics management (TDLM) system will come to dominate transport planning.

In order for TDLM to work effectively, the objectives and outcomes of such a regime need to be spelled out in sufficient detail to address the social and spatial requirements of users, whether individuals or businesses. The manifesto described below sets out the principles and philosophy for a sustainable mobility system, the concept of operations for mobility management and the method of implementation with TDLM. It puts forward a practical programme to implement the vision of transport and mobility by 2035 outlined in the Preamble. This approach is consistent with the Corbusier–Orwellian social system described in Chapter 8, which is considered the most likely model for future governance within a capitalist political-economy. While this may not be very appealing it is the trend in many societies. In the UK, for instance, the steady move toward the 'surveillance state' has been observed, with closed-circuit television (CCTV) cameras omnipresent in town centres and on major roads. This surveillance extends to monitoring internet communications, and British society, in common with other democracies, has become more paranoid towards anti-social behaviour (criminal or otherwise) and more risk-averse to issues ranging from health and safety to child protection, which justifies more background checks, monitoring and surveillance.[1] In some respects we have already gone beyond what Orwell envisaged, and our technical capabilities to design and control urban environments would be admired by Le Corbusier. Transport systems display similar transformations. CCTV is common on buses and trains. Insurance companies offer 'black box' monitoring devices to motorists who wish to reduce their insurance costs (akin to the tachographs used in heavy goods vehicles). These may become compulsory in the future. Booking a train journey on-line requires registering your personal details, which can then be mined for marketing purposes. Mobile telephones are already location-aware, allowing users to be tracked.

The nations in which the Corbusier–Orwellian model is most likely to take off are mono-cultural states where authoritarian regimes are in control (even when legitimised by elections). Countries such as Singapore, China, Vietnam, Japan, South Korea, Russia and some Middle Eastern nations come to mind. These countries embrace advanced technology and are adept at using this to control social institutions, including traffic management, urban planning and state surveillance. These illiberal regimes have few qualms about restricting personal freedoms for the common good, as the dominant party sees it. As they confront the mobility crisis with more controls over movement they will be a test bed for the types of mobility restrictions and technologies described in this book. Their goal is to maintain and advance their economic interest and compete effectively in the global market. As transport and mobility is a key factor in securing their competitive advantage, they will do what it takes, within reason, to cajole their populations to accept changes in behaviour that meet this goal. The policy discourse is determined by the ruling elites, who then impose it on a compliant population.

As the benefits of mobility management become evident in terms of managing congestion and gaining competitive advantage, democratic countries will respond by implementing similar measures. Thus, the colonial model, whereby the developed world taught the poorer nations how to develop their economies, will be transposed into the emerging nations showing the advanced economies how to use appropriate technology and other methods to manage mobility and congestion effectively. The democratic nations will want to develop policies that reflect their cultural history and political-economy. The manifesto outlined below is an attempt to create a mobility management policy that balances the need to be sustainable – economically, socially and environmentally – with political democracy. If successful, it could become a paradigm for other countries.

10.2 Programme

Key Objectives

- Enhance journey time reliability and prediction by limiting congestion.
- Reduce carbon emissions and other greenhouse gases produced by transport to the targets agreed in the Kyoto Protocol and subsequent international agreements.
- Support economic development by maintaining the mobility of people and goods.
- Provide a multimodal sustainable mobility system that is fair, equitable and affordable, and consistent with the principles of a competitive market economy.
- Significantly reduce vehicle collisions and injuries on local roads and eliminate accidents on the automated highways (trunk roads and motorways).
- Improve the safety and travel experience of cyclists, walkers and those with special needs.
- Make all transport systems fully accessible and easy to use for disabled travellers with customer support available throughout the journey experience.

Implementation

- Utilise intelligent transport systems and location-aware technologies to monitor and control vehicle movements.
- Adopt mobile technologies and apps to communicate between the user, the vehicle and the provider to schedule and route trips according to booking and reservation rules determined for different modes and geographic areas.
- Establish mobility managers to manage the travel demands and logistics for all users (passengers and freight).
- Create a national budget of mobility miles that would be allocated to each adult (over 16) that could be spent on different modes according to agreed formulae, for instance: 1 mobility mile = 1 car mile, 4 bus miles, 5 commuter rail miles, 10 inter-city rail miles, etc. Mobility miles could be bought and sold in the market place. Thus, someone who travels sustainably would be rewarded by being able to sell their surplus miles for cash. People who wish to travel more than their annual allocation would need to buy additional miles or incur severe financial penalties for going over their limit. Key workers would be given special exemptions but would still need to register their mileage and trip movements.
- Regulate and control private and public transport services via a trip reservation system. Public transport fares, routes and timetables would

be planned and coordinated in an integrated manner with multimodal ticketing and timetable coordination. Monitoring of service demand would enable fine-tuning of services. Money saved on not having to invest in costly infrastructure projects could be redirected to investing in front-line services.

- Each trip would be registered with the user's smartphone – console device – which all adults would carry. Failure to register a trip in a car, bus, train or other mechanised mode would result in a fine or other sanction, and possible denial of service. For example, two people travelling by car would have their presence automatically registered in the communications between their console and the in-car telematics unit, and their mobility miles would be shared accordingly (1 car mile = 0.5 mobility miles x 2). This would encourage car sharing. Disabled people and others with mobility problems could be given an added allocation, which could be spent on taxis or other shared transport services. Travel by walking or cycling would not incur any such restrictions.

- All trips outside of the origin travel zone, except for walking and cycling, would need to be registered (i.e. pre-booked). Failure to do so would result in severe penalties and possible loss of travel privileges. Travel across a travel zone boundary would be registered at one of the cordon points. This would be necessary in order to allow the mobility managers to coordinate the trips to the capacity of the roads and public transport systems. Travel zones would vary in size depending on urban, suburban or rural area. For example, a rural travel zone could cover a county or part of a county, whereas in higher-density areas the zone would be smaller. The zones would be fine-tuned to travel patterns and adjusted annually (or more frequently under extraordinary circumstances).

- Transport models would be developed to forecast and plan movements hourly and daily, and simulate travel to optimise use of the transport capacity under different scenarios. Trips would be booked by discrete time slot. If a slot is not available the next nearest one would be offered either side of the desired travel time. Alternate travel by public transport or other modes would also be offered. Long-distance trips crossing multiple zones would be coordinated by regional mobility managers. Trips on trains, metro and commuter buses would be booked in a similar fashion. All passengers would be guaranteed a seat apart from on the London Underground, urban metro, and some inner-city rail services. Commuter rail would be pre-booked with only a few standing places allowed. Failure to pre-book would mean working from home or making alternate travel arrangements, such as home delivery of products or services. Mobility managers would be used by firms and special event organisers to manage their customers' travel needs.

- Auto-travel on the motorways and major trunk roads would be semi-automated. Once the car joins the motorway the car's telematics would take over and be guided by the instrumented highway infrastructure and global positioning systems (GPS) equipment. The driver could then relax and do other things such as check their emails or watch television. When their exit is reached the driver would be notified and instructed when to leave the convoy. This system would mean that more traffic could be accommodated on the motorways and collisions would be avoided. Breakdowns are rare with the electric-hybrid vehicles that would replace the old internal combustion engine vehicles.
- The car telematics would also assist the driver on local roads. A variety of warning devices and controls would be installed in the vehicle as standard and the number of accidents and injuries would be cut dramatically. Traffic and travel speeds would be monitored continuously and motorists could opt for route guidance to avoid possible bottlenecks or roadworks. Car speeds would be limited to the posted speed limit on all roads. Although congestion would be reduced substantially it would not be entirely eliminated and delays could still arise from vehicle breakdowns or roadworks, but as the latter would be planned in advance the mobility managers could direct traffic and plan the day's traffic to take this into account. The system is not perfect, but it would work a lot better than at present.

Positive Outcomes

- Better management of transport systems, with reduced congestion, increased reliability and predictability of journey times.
- Delivers sustainable mobility: smarter choices and carbon emissions targets in line with climate change obligations.
- Improved performance and productivity for business and the economy.
- Development of new, innovative transport techniques, vehicle technologies and business opportunities in mobility management and logistics sectors.
- Creates a new market for 'mobility miles' that brokers mobility between travellers ('shareholders') through the price mechanism.
- More comfortable journey experience for all travellers, including those with special needs, with guaranteed levels of service such as a reserved seat on most public transport systems and a guaranteed 'ride home' if something goes wrong.
- Consumer-friendly public transport with regulated fares to ensure that the passenger gets a fair deal.
- Improved safety of all travellers with fewer accidents and injuries.
- Promotes active travel with health benefits, as more people find walking and cycling attractive.

Mobility Restrictions

- Travel choice restrictions would have an impact on some people – would require more journey planning and discourage last-minute trips.
- Monitoring of personal movements would result in some loss of individual liberty; all adults would be required to carry a console device in order to use mechanical modes.
- Potential re-direction to routes and services against user wishes.
- Some people living in deep rural areas may be disadvantaged, as might some business travellers, but the majority of users would benefit. Compensation mechanisms could be put in place for those disadvantaged disproportionately.

Affordability

- By 2035 – the timeline for this policy to be fully implemented – the Government will have to devise new methods for taxing electric/hybrid vehicles. There are a number of options, including raising the annual vehicle tax, charging road users directly via tolls or other method, increasing other taxes such as income tax or VAT on electricity, or a combination of these. The mobility management policy does not change this requirement and provides some additional revenue options, such as charging a fee when booking trips that cross cordon boundaries (with premium pricing at peak periods) or a fee on each mobility mile used (these fees could be incremented so that the first 1000 miles are free but then increase in multiples of a thousand miles). This would encourage more frugal use of motor vehicles.
- The revenue raised could be similar to current amounts and therefore be neutral overall. The motorist would not be any worse off than at present and may be better off if they use their mobility miles wisely and efficiently. As the aim is to reduce congestion to manageable levels – say 20% below current annual passenger-kilometres – the likelihood is that the Government would lose up to 20% of its revenues through this policy. However, there would be economic gains to motorists and business through improved journey times.
- At the same time, less capital expenditure is required on road infrastructure and the savings made could offset lower road-user fees.
- Because the road space is rationed through the reservation system, some car drivers would be persuaded to use alternate modes and specifically public transport. The buses and trains would gain passengers and therefore increase their revenues and productivity. Thus, lower subsidies would be required to support bus and rail services.
- Mobility managers would be financed from fees paid by customers (employers and individuals) and may also gain income from acting as brokers for the sale and purchase of mobility miles.

- Public transport fares and service levels would be regulated and designed to attract passengers, especially those switching from cars. Costs would be covered by a combination of fares and revenue support from public expenditure.
- Electricity prices for charging cars would also be regulated, with special tariffs for off-peak charging. Communal charging points in car parks and other public places would be installed and maintained by public and private sector organisations, who would re-coup the cost from a fee recharged from the power companies.
- All transactions would be made and paid for via the latest smartphone apps, which in the decades to come will be more advanced and smarter than today's devices, operating on 5G or higher high-speed networks. Prices and other market information would be transparent and the consumer would have greater awareness of mobility options and access to mobility managers who could arrange their travel needs if required.

Timescale

These measures would be deployed incrementally, with a target start date of 2015 and full implementation by 2035. The following timeline and work programme is proposed:

Phase Alpha: 2015–2020. Research and development and testing of the various technologies and components listed in the programme. This would involve collaboration between public and private sector organisations with protocols and perhaps legislation required to enforce the mobility management policy. The government would establish a Mobility Management Institute (MMI) to guide the policy development and a TDLM Academy to train technicians, managers and policy makers in the methods and techniques of mobility management. The public would be educated in the policy goals and implementation through a series of initiatives, ranging from social media to commercial advertising, incorporation in driving tests, and through the gradual deployment of the technologies and techniques. Production of sustainable mobility targets, including annual mobility miles per capita, miles per mode and prices.

Phase Beta: 2020–2025. Roll out different elements of the programme in a series of pilot demonstration projects in different parts of the country. These would be fine-tuned and enhanced following feedback from users and evidence obtained from monitoring the services. Businesses would be signed up to deliver specific elements of the programme such as mobility managers, and encouraged to compete to supply the equipment and services required. By the end of this phase a national plan to deploy all the elements of the work programme would be finalised by the MMI. Update national sustainable mobility plan, targets and prices.

Phase Gamma: 2025–2030. Full national deployment of the mobility management programme with published plans and targets. Continue to research and develop new technologies and techniques to deliver the programme elements more efficiently and effectively. The MMI would monitor the programme deployment and produce an annual audit that would adjust the targets for the next year in line with the overall goals. The TDLM Academy would continue to train people in the knowledge and skills required in TDLM.

Phase Omega: 2030–2035. By this phase the programme and technologies should have matured and be fully integrated into the social and business life of the country. The annual audit and monitoring would continue and targets would be adjusted accordingly. New technologies and techniques would be deployed as needed. The MMI and TDLM Academy would continue to function. At the end of this phase the success of the mobility management policy should be scrutinised in terms of meeting national goals and international agreements. If these were being met the policy could continue, or be superseded by a more appropriate strategy to meet the country's mobility and transport needs looking forward to 2050. If mobility management were successful then the targets to cut carbon emissions in transport would be on track to be met, as would the goals to limit congestion, and perhaps by then we could relax some of the mobility restrictions or think more expansively about the type of transport systems we want for the future.

10.3 Concluding Remarks

The programme outlined above is a speculation on the future arrangements for transport planning and delivery. The prognosis will not be comfortable reading for those who believe we can carry on as usual with some minor tweaking of current policies, such as mainstreaming 'smarter choices' travel measures or investment in more transport infrastructure. Undoubtedly such measures would help ameliorate the pressures on the transport network, but most people in the transport sector, including policy makers, have not grasped the ramifications of growing mobility and how this is fuelling gridlock throughout our transport services. Conventional supply-side and demand-management measures are not enough. We are in denial about the pending congestion crisis, just as there are those who are in denial about the long-term effects of climate change caused by burning fossil fuels. The congestion crisis is forecast to reach a tipping point before global warming becomes critical and, like climate change, congestion is a global phenomenon. Indeed, the congestion crisis may manifest itself first in emerging economies before it becomes critical in developed countries. In short, we face a chronic situation that is no longer resolvable by traditional remedies and policy creep toward more sustainable practices. A quantum shift in thinking and praxis is required.

Perhaps the biggest challenge is creating a new policy discourse that can overcome the current impasses between the convivial and competition discourses: we need to re-think mobility not as a standalone transport issue but as a central facet of social structure and how an advanced society works. Transport professionals have been critical of the travelling publics' attitude towards sustainable transport policies and their reluctance to change behaviour in response to smarter choices programmes, but perhaps the planners and policy makers should reflect on their own position and attitudes towards sustainable transport, or more pertinently sustainable mobility, and consider whether their diagnosis and remedies, which are almost entirely transport-specific, are relevant to peoples' mobile lives in contemporary society. Mobility has become a means of acquiring network (social) capital and is a vector of personal power and control in a society driven by competitive forces. Is it any wonder that people vote against measures that are likely to disempower them?

It is likely that car manufacturers will develop fuel-efficient, ultra-low-emission vehicles by 2035 powered by electric propulsion or hybrid technologies that meet CO_2 emission targets. In this case one of the major objections to car use will disappear. The focus, therefore, should switch to how to reduce congestion while maintaining mobility that is sustainable environmentally, socially and economically. The meta-mobility system described herein is predicated on the need to balance these requirements and to do so in a fair and equitable manner.

Free-market solutions are unlikely to find favour with the public and, ironically, with corporate interest including business and finance, which will resist solutions that threaten their domination of the capitalist economy. Road pricing could undermine the economic geography of the UK and cause major disruption to retail, distribution and industry. This may not all be bad, but tackling congestion through regressive road pricing would affect many communities and businesses adversely. One only has to look the broad opposition to tolls on roads such as the A14 in Cambridgeshire to understand that this policy is never going to gain any political traction. Even the CBI's modest proposal to use a regulated asset base model to pay for new road infrastructure was rejected by a Conservative-led coalition government. In Scotland the Government has removed tolls on the new Forth Bridge and the Welsh Assembly Government wants to do the same on the Severn Bridge. Tolls on the Humber Bridge have been halved and proved popular with motorists and businesses.

Finally, the mobility management measures proposed together with the TDLM methods are consistent with the political-economy of democratic capitalism. As explored in Part 3, mobility is not simply about getting from one place to another but is a social process that together with the deployment of transport resources is exploited by the capitalist system to create the surplus value that is then reinvested in more capital formation. It may be obvious to make the point, but de facto transport services and policy discourses reflect the needs of the dominant political-economic system, which is democratic capitalism. This book does not challenge this ideology, because it seems unlikely that a social revolution will overturn capitalism any time soon. Some transport activists and campaigners would like to see a different social system, but in the absence of any evidence that this is going to happen we are left with the more limited choice of making the system work better and in a fairer manner than it currently operates. Reverting to some arcane economic ideal such as road pricing is just diverting our energies away from exploring real-world solutions that are doable. The mobility management/TDLM regime is put forward in this spirit.

Note

1 It is ironic that the risk-aversion does not extend to carrying children in cars, which is one of the most dangerous activities to subject a child to, in terms of potential injuries and death.

Index

accessibility 20, 27–33, 139; bus services 72; DaSTS 83; local transport plans 45; manifesto for sustainable mobility 162; network capital 130; *New Deal for Transport* 75; structuration theory 127; US *Urban Mobility Report* 50
accidents 4, 77, 105, 130, 162, 164
Action for Roads (2013) 150
active traffic management (ATM) 22, 57
active travel 13n1, 118, 133, 164
Adams, John 111–112, 114
air transport: aviation lobby 13n5; budget airlines 128; business travel 119; carbon emissions 79, 81; regulation 157n1; trends 40–41
airport charges 8
Amsterdam 34n5
Anable, J. 132
Antwerp 50
ATM *see* active traffic management
austerity 68
Australia 25
autogas xiv
automated vehicle location (AVL) 57, 63
Automobile Association 134
auto-mobility 4, 20, 61, 124, 128, 138; accessibility 31; culture of 5, 106–114, 120; dominance of 45; environmental impact of 145; global trends 36; mobile ubiquitous group 139; network capital 133; transport intensity 26; United States 46, 50; *see also* cars

AVL *see* automated vehicle location
Axhausen, K.W. 122, 138

Baeton, G. 11
Baker, Norman 85
Banister, D. 24, 26, 80, 105
behavioural change 82, 89, 103, 133, 139, 168
Belgium 24, 50
bias 95–96, 97, 100, 101–102, 103
biofuels 82
Birmingham 18, 74, 156
Black, W.R. 22–23
Blair, Tony 115
Brazil xviii, 36
BRICS countries xviii, 36, 81
Brundtland Report (1987) 20, 21
Brussels 50
Buchan, K. 79, 80, 82
Buchanan, Colin 3, 33, 66
bus transport xvi, 12; Age of Austerity 68; Age of New Realism 68; allocation of demand 146; deregulation 67, 69, 96; elderly and disabled passengers 32; investment in 100, 156; London 71, 72; manifesto for sustainable mobility 163; mobility management 157; mobility miles xvii; *New Deal for Transport* 76; post-modern urban design 33; Quality Contracts 72; Quality Partnerships 71, 76; scheduling 64; smarter choices measures 78, 79–80; trends 40–41; Wales 98

business travel 119, 131, 165
businesses 11, 12, 166

Campaign for Better Transport (CBT) 79, 80, 82, 134
Canada 25
Canberra 18
capacity 37, 38, 65, 146
capitalism xviii, 6, 7–8, 13n2, 104n5, 104n6, 117, 139; capitalist elite 122; car culture 107, 108, 109–110, 111; Castells on 120n1; democratic 168–169; future scenarios 137; Los Angeles 19; 'managed' 140n5; neo-Marxist perspectives 125, 126–127; network capital 129–130; relations of production 133; social movements as resistance against 133–135; urban capitalist transport system 135–136
carbon emissions 3, 6, 15; car sharing 62; manifesto for sustainable mobility 162, 164, 167; mobility management 157; RAC Foundation 88, 89; reduction targets 21, 24–26, 38, 42, 77, 79, 80–84, 89, 162, 168; technology 64; 'tragedy of the highways' 11; trends 44; US *Urban Mobility Report* 46, 47, 50; *see also* greenhouse gases
cars 3–4, 12, 17; accessibility 28–30; automobile culture 5, 106–114, 120; car clubs xvii, 62, 64, 78; car sharing xvii, xviii, 61–62, 78, 157, 163; carbon emissions 44; commuting 74; cultural shift 118; dependence on 31; Downs-Thomson paradox 8–9; driverless 60, 62; emerging economies 42, 81; gender issues 115, 116–117, 120n5, 120n6; hypermobility 105; in-car infotainment services 120n7; intelligent transport systems 57–58; journey speeds 9–10; low-emission vehicles 168; mobility domains 131–132; mobility gap 13; mobility miles xvii; network capital 130; new realism 74; 'peak car' travel hypothesis 42–44, 68, 120n6, 154; 'road trips' 52n1; smarter choices measures 78–79, 154–155; social and employment-related changes 114–116; social exclusion 28; Thompson's typology of cities 17–18; *Traffic in Towns* report 3; trends 36, 37, 40–41; *see also* auto-mobility; electric vehicles; roads

Castells, Manuel 120n1, 126, 129, 156
CBI *see* Confederation of British Industry
CBT *see* Campaign for Better Transport
central business districts 10, 18
central-local relations 98–102
Chartered Institute of Logistics and Transport (CILT) 37–39, 43, 45, 134
Chartered Institution of Highways and Transportation 134
Chicago School 125
child-care 117
China xviii, 24, 36, 42, 109, 138, 161
CILT *see* Chartered Institute of Logistics and Transport
cities xvi, 10–11, 15–17; accessibility 27; capitalist 7–8; central business districts 10; CILT report 37; edge cities 20, 117; global trends 37; neo-Marxist perspective 125; social movements 133–135; Thompson's typology 17–18; United States 111; urban capitalist transport system 135–136
City Deals 99
class 107, 114, 115, 126, 133, 136
climate change 3, 5, 11, 21, 34, 41, 89, 167; Age of New Realism 68; Europe 51; forecast rise 6; future scenarios 137; rising sea levels 12; 'tragedy of the highways' 11; UK policy 77, 80–84; ultra-low emissions vehicles 60; *see also* carbon emissions
Climate Change Act (2008) 21, 77, 79, 80, 84
CNG *see* compressed natural gas

172 *Index*

Coalition Government 52n3, 68, 78, 84–87, 99, 110, 150, 168
collective consumption 126, 155
collectivism 123
communities of interest 20, 69, 97, 99, 105
commuting xv–xvi, 9, 10, 17, 28–30, 74; CILT report 37, 39; US *Urban Mobility Report* 46, 49
company cars 43
competitive transport 5, 6, 70, 88, 138; Age of Austerity 68; Age of Contestability 67; Age of Road Infrastructure 66; discourse of 105, 120, 168; Scotland 98
compressed natural gas (CNG) xiv
concessionary fares 32, 85, 97, 102
Confederation of British Industry (CBI) 149–150, 155–156, 168
congestion xviii, 3, 4, 6, 20, 34, 103, 139; central business districts 10; CILT report 37, 39; city expansion 8; downward spiral of 145; Level of Service standard 21–22; limits to economic growth 50–51; Los Angeles 19; manifesto for sustainable mobility 162, 164, 165, 167; as market failure 146; paradox of mobility 8–9, 138; RAC Foundation 88; rationing by xvii; technology 65; United States 109; unpredictability 117; urban capitalist transport system 136; US *Urban Mobility Report* 46–50
congestion pricing 5, 9, 146, 148–154; Mayor of London role 99, 100; mobility management 157; referenda on 11, 128, 149; *see also* road pricing
Conservatives 67, 69, 74–75, 96, 100, 110, 128, 168
convivial transport 4–5, 6, 11, 33, 61, 70, 95; Age of New Realism 68; Age of Transport Revisionism 67; counter-cultural influences 106; discourse of 105, 120, 168; Schumacher society 138; sustainable mobility 139

Corbusier society 137, 138, 139, 157, 160–161
corporate bias 100, 101–102, 103, 106
costs 4, 33; of congestion 48, 49, 149; motoring 113; public transport 62; social marginal cost 148; Stern Review 81
Crossrail 136, 140n6, 156
culture of mobility 118–120
cyber-mobility 20, 118, 137
cyberspace 27, 32–33, 36–37, 124
'cyclenistas' 134–135
cycling xvii, 12, 17, 19; active travel discourse 118, 133; Age of New Realism 68; Age of Transport Revisionism 67; carbon reduction 38; convivial transport 5; London 10, 73; manifesto for sustainable mobility 162, 163, 164; National Cycling Strategy 76; Netherlands 34n5; post-modern urban design 33; realists 87; segmentation studies 132; smarter choices measures 78, 79–80; social movements 134–135; sub-cultural enthusiasm for 106; transport intensity 26; Wales 98–99

Dallas 18
Darlington 78
DaSTS *see Delivering a Sustainable Transport System*
deaths 3, 36, 130
decision making 95–98, 99–100, 101, 103
delays 12, 47, 48, 49
Delivering a Sustainable Transport System (DaSTS) 83–84, 85, 87, 88
demand 42, 43, 63, 65, 146; local transport plans 45; London 50–51; new realism 74; travel demand logistics management 146–147, 160, 166–167, 168–169
demographics 43, 44
Denmark 34n5
density 15–16, 19–20, 26
Denver 18
Department for Transport (DfT) 28, 43, 73, 96

deregulation 67, 69, 70, 71, 96
developing countries 12–13, 21; car ownership 81; global trends 42; greenhouse gas emissions 25; mass mobility 36; megacities 16; STPM 23; *Transport Outlook 2011* report 40; *see also* emerging economies
devolution 98
disabled passengers xvii, 30, 31–32, 85, 97, 162, 163
disadvantage, mobile 131, 132, 136, 137, 139
discourses 90, 105–106, 168–169
diversity 16, 17, 119, 126
domination 127–128
Downs, A. 9, 19
Downs-Thomson paradox 8–9, 155
driverless cars 60, 62
Dunn, J. 96
Durham 18

economic development xviii, 7, 10–11, 70, 99; Age of Austerity 68; greenhouse gas emissions 25; manifesto for sustainable mobility 162; United States 108
economic growth 34, 39, 85; congestion limits to 50–51; Eddington Transport Study 82; International Transport Forum 39–40; *New Deal for Transport* 76; Stern Review 81
economic interests 102, 103
Eddington Transport Study (2006) 82–84, 88–89, 158n4
edge cities 20, 117
Edinburgh 11, 18, 128, 149
elderly passengers 31–32, 85, 97
electric vehicles xiv, 44–45, 60–61, 79, 85, 109, 164, 165, 166, 168
elites, mobile 130, 131, 132, 136, 137, 139
elitism 114, 119
Elliott, A. 129–130, 133, 137, 138, 139
emerging economies 36, 42, 81, 161, 167; *see also* developing countries
employment xvi, 17, 29–30, 113, 114–116

entropy 16
environmentalists 39, 45, 87, 89, 97, 100; Age of Austerity 68; car culture 109–111; drivers 132; electric vehicles 61; road-user charging 149; Schumacher society 137; social movements 133; US *Urban Mobility Report* 50
equity 26–27, 70, 151–154, 162, 168
Europe 50–51, 96, 112
European Union (EU) 21, 25, 58–59, 129, 153, 158n6

fares xvi, 8; concessionary 32, 85, 97, 102; manifesto for sustainable mobility 164, 166
feminist perspective 116, 117
Ford 60, 108
Fordism 108
fossil fuels 20, 21, 40, 137, 167
Foucault, Michel 105
France 82, 96
free-market ideology 102, 158n3, 168; *see also* market economics
freight 12, 26, 38, 39, 40–42, 79; *see also* logistics
Friends of the Earth 134
fuel cells 60, 61
fuel prices 43, 49, 77, 109
fuel taxes 8, 76, 79, 148, 149
fuel use 23
future scenarios 136–138, 139

game theory 95
Garreau, Joel 116–117
Gartman, D. 107, 118
GDP *see* gross domestic product
Geddes, Patrick 125
gender 43, 44, 115, 116–117, 120n5, 120n6
General Motors (GM) 108, 110
geographic information systems (GIS) 58, 60, 63
geography 15, 16, 125–126
Germany 25, 96, 140n5, 153
Giddens, A. 127–128
GIS *see* geographic information systems

global positioning systems (GPS) xiv, xvi, 7, 58–60, 63, 148, 164
global trends 36, 39–45
globalisation xviii, 107
GM *see* General Motors
Goodwin, Philip 74, 75, 78–79, 86
Google 58, 60, 62
GPS *see* global positioning systems
green belts 20
green field sites 85
greenhouse gases 20, 21, 22, 24–26; manifesto for sustainable mobility 162; Stern Review 81; technology 64; *see also* carbon emissions
gridlock 13, 19, 20, 145, 157
gross domestic product (GDP) 23, 26, 51, 81

Habermas, J. 104n6
Hamburg 18
Hardin, Garrett 11
Harvey, D. 125, 133, 135–136, 137, 139, 156
Hatfield rail accident 77
Headicar, P. 77
high-occupancy toll (HOT) lanes 9
high-speed rail network (HS2) 86, 156
Highways England 150
Highways Agency 150
Hobbesian society 137, 138
Hobsbawm, Eric 115
Holden, E. 26
home shopping 7, 78
Hong Kong 7, 18
housing 17
HS2 project 86, 156
Hungary 50
hybrid cars 61, 82, 109, 164, 165, 168
hypermobility 15, 37, 61, 105, 111, 133, 137

ICT *see* information and communications technologies
identity 107, 126
Independent Commission on Transport 27–28, 66–67
independents, mobile 130, 131–133, 135, 136, 137, 139

India xviii, 36, 109
individualism 110, 114, 123
inequality 43, 130
information and communications technologies (ICT) 20, 57, 58, 65, 69–71, 160
information technology (IT) 38, 125
infotainment services 120n7
infrastructure 33, 100; Age of Road Infrastructure 66; CILT report 38, 39; electric vehicles 61; investment in 155–156, 158n8, 167; local transport plans 45; London 50–51; manifesto for sustainable mobility 165; mobility management 157; *New Deal for Transport* 76; northern England 72; Scotland 98; social investment 138; United States 45, 108, 109
injuries 3, 36, 162, 164, 169n1
INRIX 50–51, 52n4, 52n5
Institute for Public Policy Research (IPPR) 72
institutionalism 97
intelligent mobility 64–65
intelligent transport systems (ITS) 45, 57–58, 62, 125, 162
International Transport Forum (ITF) 39–42
internet 27, 31, 118, 119, 120n7, 126
interventionism 96, 140n5
investment: CILT report 38; Coalition Government 85; decision making 99–100; infrastructure 155–156, 158n8, 167; realists 87; Road Investment Strategy 150; Scotland 98; social 6, 100–102, 106, 138–139; US *Urban Mobility Report* 49
IPPR *see* Institute for Public Policy Research
'Iron Law of Congestion' 9
IT *see* information technology
Italy 96
ITF *see* International Transport Forum
ITS *see* intelligent transport systems

Jacobs, Jane 19
Japan 140n5, 161

Johnson, Boris 73, 99
Jones, P. 120n6
journey times 9–10, 12, 28–30, 33, 151; freight transport 38; logistics 63; manifesto for sustainable mobility 162; US *Urban Mobility Report* 46, 47, 49

Kaufmann, V. 16–17, 117, 123–124, 130, 140n3
Kenya 23, 24
Kerr, J. 107
Kinnock, Neil 115
Kunstler, J.H. 111
Kyoto Protocol 21, 24–26, 34, 39, 42, 44, 77, 80, 162

Labour 69, 74, 110, 115; *see also* New Labour
Ladd, Brian 109
'laissez faire' culture 96
land use 17, 20, 27, 75, 125, 128
Latham, R. 107
Le Corbusier 33, 161; *see also* Corbusier society
Le Vine, S. 120n6
Leeds 18, 74, 156
Lefebvre, H. 125, 133, 156
legislation 21, 67, 71, 76, 77, 84; *see also* policy; regulation
legitimation 127–128
LEPs *see* local enterprise partnerships
Level of Service (LOS) standard 21–22
Levinson, D. 151
Lewis, D. 8
Lewis-Mogridge Position 8–9
Liberal Democrats 68, 74, 110
libertarianism 110
lifestyle changes 117
light rail 33
Linerrud, K. 26
liquefied petroleum gas (LPG) xiv, 61
Litman, T. 50, 151
'liveable streets' 112
Livingstone, Ken 99
lobbies 11, 69, 76, 87, 95–96, 97, 110, 133–134

local enterprise partnerships (LEPs) 99, 101
Local Sustainable Transport Fund (LSTF) 21, 73, 78, 85, 86, 99
Local Transport Act (2008) 71, 84
local transport bodies (LTBs) 52n3, 84, 99, 101
local transport plans (LTPs) 28, 34n4, 45, 52n3, 76, 84–85
localisation 99–100
location technologies 57, 58–60, 145, 162
logistics 7, 26, 39, 145; CILT report 37; scheduling 63–64; travel demand logistics management 146–147, 160, 166–167, 168–169; *see also* freight
London 7, 9–10, 18, 50–51; Age of New Realism 68; Age of Transport Revisionism 66, 67; attraction of talent and investment 19; bus transport 67; car use 17, 43, 44, 154; congestion charging 5, 11, 100, 128, 148, 149, 152, 153; Crossrail 136, 156; 'cyclenistas' 134, 135; exceptionalism 71–74, 102; Oyster card 85; rail transport 44; role of Mayor 99, 104n4
London Underground 10, 100, 163
LOS *see* Level of Service standard
Los Angeles 18–19, 108
low-income groups 30, 112–113, 114, 128, 132, 151–152
LPG *see* liquefied petroleum gas
LSTF *see* Local Sustainable Transport Fund
LTBs *see* local transport bodies
LTPs *see* local transport plans

M6 Toll Road 150
Mackie, Peter 86
'managed' capitalism 140n5
Manchester 11, 18, 28–29, 50, 72, 74, 104n4, 128, 149, 156
market economics 5, 133, 158n3; *see also* free-market ideology
Marx, Karl 98, 126, 129–130
Marxist theory 98, 104n3, 106, 125–127, 137

mass mobility 36–37
mechanised modes of travel 21
media 95–96, 103
megacities 16
Melbourne 18
meritocracy 114
meta-mobility 16, 17, 20, 32, 124, 157, 168
Metz, D. 34n3
Microsoft 58
Middle East 138, 161
Mies van der Rohe, Ludwig 33
migrants 16
Milan 50
Milton Keynes 18
mitigation measures 48, 49
mixed land use 17, 112
mixed scanning 95–96
MMI *see* Mobility Management Institute
'mobile rules' 123
mobile technologies 58, 162; *see also* smartphones
mobilities paradigm 71, 88, 122–125, 129
mobility diversity 119, 126
mobility domains 129–133, 139
'mobility gap' 13, 31
mobility management xviii, 7, 145–146, 156–157; manifesto for sustainable mobility 160–169; travel demand logistics management 146–147, 160, 166–167, 168–169
Mobility Management Institute (MMI) 166, 167
mobility managers xiv, xvi–xvii, 147, 162, 163, 164, 165–166
mobility miles xvii, 146, 157n2, 162, 164, 165, 166
mode switching 78–80, 109, 156, 157
Mogridge, M.J.H. 8–9
Monbiot, George 110, 114
Moses, Robert 108
motility 27, 117, 119, 123–124, 129–130, 139, 139n2, 140n3
motorbikes 120n4
motorways: active traffic management 22, 57; Age of Road Infrastructure 66; auto-travel xv, 164; *New Deal for Transport* 76; protests against 103n2; Scotland 98
multimodal transport 21, 22, 162
Mussolini, Benito 110

Nair, C. 13n2
NATA *see* New Approach to Appraisal
National Centre for Social Research 113
National Cycling Strategy 76
National Road Traffic Forecast (NRTF) 43, 52n2
National Travel Survey (NTS) 80
nationalisation 69
neo-liberalism 102, 110, 111, 140n5
neo-Marxist perspectives 106, 125–127, 135
Netherlands 25, 34n5, 50, 112
network capital 129–131, 133, 136–137, 139, 140n4, 168
Network Rail 100, 150
networks 16, 129
New Approach to Appraisal (NATA) 85–86
New Deal for Transport 68, 75–77, 87, 128
New Labour 68, 69, 75–77, 88, 115, 128
New Mobility agenda 124–125
new realism 87, 90, 97, 138; *Action for Roads* 150; mobilisation of bias 96; *New Deal for Transport* 76; paradigm shifts in transport planning 66, 68, 69, 70, 71, 74–75; policy discourses 106; smarter choices 154; soft measures 77; US *Urban Mobility Report* 50
new urbanism 13n1, 17, 45, 112
New York 7, 18, 19, 108, 109
New Zealand 137–138
Newcastle 74
Northern Ireland 98, 102
Norwich 18
Nottingham 11
NRTF *see* National Road Traffic Forecast
NTS *see* National Travel Survey

Oregon 148
Organisation for Economic Co-operation and Development (OECD) 37, 39–42, 44, 45, 81
Orwellian society 137, 138, 139, 157, 160–161
Oslo 9, 148
Oyster card 85

Pahl, R.E. 20
paradox of mobility 8–9, 10, 138, 155
Paris 9, 17, 18, 51
parking xv, 76, 154
passenger transport: CILT report 38; global trends 42; scheduling 63–64; *Transport Outlook 2011* report 40–41; *see also* public transport
payments xvi
'peak car' travel hypothesis 42–44, 68, 120n6, 154
peak oil production 12
personal mobility 102
Peterborough 78
Phoenix 18
planning: CILT report 38; Eddington Transport Study 83; mobilities paradigm 124, 125; paradigm shifts in 66–71; Planning Act 84; travel demand logistics management 146, 147; UK/US comparison 46
Planning Act (2008) 84
planning policy guidance (PPG) 75
pluralism 95
policy 4, 7, 12, 95–97, 168; central-local relations 98–102; CILT report 38; discourses 105–106, 168–169; lack of consensus 51–52; lobby groups 134; paradigm shifts in 66–71; planning 20; United Kingdom 66–91; *see also* legislation; regulation
political cultures 96
political economy 3, 12, 60, 95–104, 136, 138, 168–169
political pressures 11, 69, 103, 110, 113
pollution xviii, 3, 4, 6, 39, 103; Europe 51; hypermobility 111; Los Angeles 19; *see also* carbon emissions; greenhouse gases
popular culture 107
population growth 10, 12, 33, 138, 155; future scenarios 137; global trends 37, 42; London 50; US *Urban Mobility Report* 49
Portugal 25, 50
postmodernism 33, 107, 118, 119
power 95, 96–98, 100, 104n3; Giddens 128; neo-Marxist perspectives 126; network capital 130, 139; policy discourses 105–106
PPG *see* planning policy guidance
pragmatists 87, 88
'precariat' 136
'predict and provide' 17, 45, 57, 71, 88, 155; CBI model 150; critiques of 74, 95; local transport bodies 52n3; London 72; New Mobility agenda 125; public transport 156; US *Urban Mobility Report* 50
Prescott, John 68
pricing xv, xviii, 38, 145, 166; *see also* congestion pricing; road pricing
privatisation 5, 67, 69, 70
public expenditure 72, 73, 102
public transport xv–xvi, 4, 17; accessibility 27, 28–30, 31; Age of Transport Revisionism 66–67; capacity 37; capitalist cities 7; convivial transport 5; Downs-Thomson paradox 8–9; elderly and disabled passengers 31–32; investment in 17, 156; journey speeds 9–10; lack of availability 113; Lewis-Mogridge Position 9; London 50–51, 71–74; Los Angeles 18, 19; manifesto for sustainable mobility 162–163, 164, 165, 166; mobility management 157; motility 124; Netherlands 34n5; new realism 74; planning policy guidance 75; realists 87; scheduling 63–64; segmentation studies 132; smarter choices measures 79–80; technological developments 62; Thompson's typology of cities 18; transport

intensity 26; travel demand logistics management 147; United States 48, 49, 108, 109; Wales 98; *see also* bus transport; rail transport

Quality Contracts 71–72, 76
Quality Partnerships 71, 76
quotas xvii

RAB *see* regulated asset base model
RAC Foundation 79, 88–89, 112, 120n3, 131, 152–153, 155–156, 158n6
radicalism 133–135
rail transport xv–xvi, 12; Age of Austerity 68; Age of New Realism 68; Age of Road Infrastructure 66; allocation of demand 146; business travel 119; CILT report 37; Coalition Government 85; Crossrail 136, 140n6, 156; electric 82; Hatfield rail accident 77; HS2 project 86, 156; investment in 38, 100, 102, 156; London 72; manifesto for sustainable mobility 163; mobility miles xvii; *New Deal for Transport* 76; northern England 72; post-modern urban design 33; privatisation 67, 69; realists 87; scheduling 64; Scotland 98; smarter choices measures 79–80; sub-cultural enthusiasm for 106; trends 40–41, 43, 44; United States 108; Wales 98
rationing xvii, 60, 145, 146, 165
Rees Jeffreys Road Fund (RJRF) 74
regional transport plans (RTPs) 45, 46
regulated asset base (RAB) model 149–150, 168
regulation 96, 145; *see also* legislation; policy
renewable energy xiv, 61, 64
reservation systems xv–xvi, 162–163, 165
reversibility 17, 34n1, 140n3
RJRF *see* Rees Jeffreys Road Fund
road pricing xviii, 5, 113, 148–154, 156, 168, 169; CILT report 38; Eddington Transport Study 83; Goodwin's review 79; GPS technology 59; infrastructure investment 155; *New Deal for Transport* 76; regressive impact of 26–27; road lobby against 87; *see also* congestion pricing
roads: accessibility 130; Age of Austerity 68; Age of Contestability 67; Age of Road Infrastructure 66; allocation of demand 146; critique of 'predict and provide' model 74; investment in 38, 100, 102, 155–156, 158n8; Lewis-Mogridge Position 8–9; lobbying impact on policy 95–96; manifesto for sustainable mobility 162, 165; *New Deal for Transport* 76; northern England 72; realists 87; United States 46; *see also* cars
routing 63, 65
Royal Automobile Club 134
RTPs *see* regional transport plans
rural areas xvi, 20; accessibility 27; CILT report 38; manifesto for sustainable mobility 165; travel zones 163; Wales 98
Russia xviii, 36, 138, 161

safety 64, 83, 89, 164; *see also* accidents
San Francisco 18, 109
satellite navigation (satnav) 57, 58, 63
Saunders, P. 100–101
scheduling 63–64, 65, 146, 147, 162
Schumacher society 137–138
Schweitzer, L. 153
Scotland 98, 102, 104n7, 132, 168
segmentation studies 132
shared-space schemes 112
Shlomo, A. 13n3
shopping centres 111
signification 127–128
Singapore 9, 13n2, 140n5, 148, 161
smart ticketing 85
smarter choices 11, 13n1, 77–80, 82, 86–87, 102, 105; car use 113; funding 73, 99; limitations of

154–155, 156; local transport plans 45; mainstreaming 167; manifesto for sustainable mobility 164; mobility management 157; new realism 106; paradigm shifts 70; public attitudes 168; social structures 127
smartphones 119, 147, 163, 166
social capital 123, 128, 140n3, 140n4, 168
social cohesion 36
social consumption 6, 100–101, 102, 106, 138–139
social exclusion 28, 30, 61, 75, 83, 113
social impacts 26–27
social investment 6, 100–102, 106, 138–139
social marginal cost 148
social media 118, 120n7
social mobility 15, 30, 114–115, 123, 135
social movements 133–135, 139
social production of space 125–126
social relations of production 129–130, 133
social structure 127–128, 129
sociology 15, 16, 97, 122–141; future scenarios 136–138, 139; Marxist and neo-Marxist perspectives 125–127; mobilities paradigm 122–125, 129; mobility domains 129–133; radicalism and social movements 133–135; social structures 127–128; urban capitalist transport system 135–136
South Africa xviii, 36
South Korea 161
South Pacific Islands 137–138
space, social production of 125–126
spatial mobility 15, 30, 122, 123, 124
spatial transformations 122
special interest groups 95–96
speed cameras 8, 22, 87
speed limits 22, 34, 164
status 107, 123
Stern Review (2006) 80–84, 88, 89
Stockholm 18, 148, 152

STPM *see* sustainable transport and potential mobility
Stradling, S. 132
streetcars 108
strip malls 111, 112
structuration 127
subsidies 44–45, 72, 102, 165
suburban areas xvi, 17, 26, 38
SUMPs *see* Sustainable Urban Mobility Plans
supply chains 38, 39, 63, 146
surveillance 138, 160–161
sustainability 20–21, 33, 39, 70, 74; equity 26; mobility management 157; *New Deal for Transport* 76; UK/US comparison 45, 46
sustainable mobility 22–23, 74, 139, 145; future scenarios 137, 138; manifesto for 160–169
sustainable transport x–xi, 4–5, 6, 13n1, 20, 22, 34; attitudes to 168; CILT report 37, 39; 'cyclenistas' 134–135; discourse of 105–106; electric vehicles 61; mobilities paradigm 124; mobility management 156–157; political economy of 95–104; UK policy 66–91
sustainable transport and potential mobility (STPM) 22–26, 50
Sustainable Travel Towns 78, 79
Sustainable Urban Mobility Plans (SUMPs) 21
Sustrans 134
Sweden 96, 140n5
Switzerland 158n6
Sydney 18

taxis xvii, 63–64, 163
Taylor, B.D. 153
TDLM *see* travel demand logistics management
technology xiv, 7, 15, 57–65, 69–71, 145; CILT report 38; congestion pricing 148, 151; future scenarios 138; intelligent mobility 64–65; intelligent transport systems 57–58; location technologies 57, 58–60, 145, 162; logistics 63–64; mobility

management 157; New Mobility agenda 124–125; optimistic views on 52; pollution 39; surveillance 161; vehicle 60–63; *see also* information and communications technologies
telematics xv, xvii, 57, 62–63, 147, 164
teleworking xvi, 78
Texas A&M Transportation Institute (TTI) 22, 37, 46–50, 149
TfL *see* Transport for London
Thatcher, Margaret 67, 69, 76, 77, 110
Thompson, J. Michael 17–18, 19, 33
time-space relations 127, 128, 130
tolls xviii, 8, 9, 146, 148, 150–151, 168
total journey management xvi
tourism 36, 119, 120n8, 128, 130
tracking 60, 62–63, 147
Traffic in Towns (1963) 3, 66
traffic management 3, 4; *see also* active traffic management
'tragedy of the commons' 11, 52
'tragedy of the highways' 11
trains *see* rail transport
Transport Act (1985) 67
Transport Act (2000) 71, 76, 77
Transport for London (TfL) 71
Transport Outlook 2011 report 39–42
Transport Planning Society 134
travel demand logistics management (TDLM) 146–147, 160, 166–167, 168–169
travel tourism 36, 119, 120n8
travel zones (TZs) xiv–xv, 30, 147, 163
trends 36–53; international 39–45; mass mobility 36–37; United Kingdom 37–39, 43–44; United States 45–50
trucks: carbon emissions 44; lorry-charging schemes 153; trends 41–42; US *Urban Mobility Report* 47
TTI *see* Texas A&M Transportation Institute
Tyme, J. 96
TZs *see* travel zones

ubiquity, mobile 131, 132, 136–137, 139, 160
UMR *see* Urban Mobility Report

United Kingdom: car culture 110, 111–113, 114–116; central-local relations 98–102; cycling 134–135; elitism 114; free-market ideology 102; greenhouse gas emissions 21, 25; INRIX 50; local transport plans 28, 34n4, 45, 52n3; mobility domains 131; National Road Traffic Forecast 43, 52n2; planning regime 46; political-economic cultures 96; road investment 150; road pricing 149, 152, 168; shared-space schemes 112; Social Inclusion unit 28; STPM index 23, 24; transport policy 66–91; trends 37–39, 43–44; women's car use 116
United States: automatic highway project 62; car culture 108–109, 110, 111; cost of congestion 149; GPS technology 58–59; greenhouse gas emissions 24, 25; 'laissez faire' culture 96; Level of Service standard 21–22; mobility trends 45–50, 51; New Mobility agenda 124–125; new urbanism 112; road pricing 148–149, 150–152; STPM index 23, 24; women's car use 116–117
urban areas *see* cities
urban design 33–34, 125
Urban Mobility Report (UMR) 22, 46–50, 51, 149
urban sprawl 3, 15, 17, 18–19, 20; car culture 61; UK planning policy 85; United States 108, 111, 112
urbanisation 135
Urry, John 107–108, 118, 122, 124, 128, 129–130, 133, 137–138, 139, 156

Vanderbilt, Tom 109
vehicle kilometres of travel (VKT) 23, 26
vehicle miles of travel (VMT) 148–149
vehicle tax 149–150, 165
vehicle technology 60–63
Vienna 18
Vietnam 161
Vigar, G. 97, 105, 127

vignette schemes 158n6
virtual mobility 27, 118
Vision 2035 report (CILT) 37–39, 43
VKT *see* vehicle kilometres of travel
VMT *see* vehicle miles of travel

Wales 98–99, 102
walking xvii, 12, 17, 19; active travel discourse 118, 133; Age of New Realism 68; Age of Transport Revisionism 67; carbon reduction 38; convivial transport 5; manifesto for sustainable mobility 162, 163, 164; post-modern urban design 33; realists 87; segmentation studies 132; smarter choices measures 78, 79–80; transport intensity 26; Wales 98–99
Walsh, Margaret 116, 117
Washington DC 109
Weber, Max 125, 127
Wollen, P. 106–107
women 43, 44, 112, 115, 116–117, 120n5, 120n6
Worcester 78

York 18
young people 118, 119, 154

Zielinski, S. 124–125
zoning xiv–xv, 30, 147

eBooks
from Taylor & Francis

Helping you to choose the right eBooks for your Library

Add to your library's digital collection today with Taylor & Francis eBooks. We have over 50,000 eBooks in the Humanities, Social Sciences, Behavioural Sciences, Built Environment and Law, from leading imprints, including Routledge, Focal Press and Psychology Press.

Choose from a range of subject packages or create your own!

Benefits for you

- Free MARC records
- COUNTER-compliant usage statistics
- Flexible purchase and pricing options
- All titles DRM-free.

Benefits for your user

- Off-site, anytime access via Athens or referring URL
- Print or copy pages or chapters
- Full content search
- Bookmark, highlight and annotate text
- Access to thousands of pages of quality research at the click of a button.

REQUEST YOUR FREE INSTITUTIONAL TRIAL TODAY

Free Trials Available
We offer free trials to qualifying academic, corporate and government customers.

eCollections

Choose from over 30 subject eCollections, including:

Archaeology	Language Learning
Architecture	Law
Asian Studies	Literature
Business & Management	Media & Communication
Classical Studies	Middle East Studies
Construction	Music
Creative & Media Arts	Philosophy
Criminology & Criminal Justice	Planning
Economics	Politics
Education	Psychology & Mental Health
Energy	Religion
Engineering	Security
English Language & Linguistics	Social Work
Environment & Sustainability	Sociology
Geography	Sport
Health Studies	Theatre & Performance
History	Tourism, Hospitality & Events

For more information, pricing enquiries or to order a free trial, please contact your local sales team:
www.tandfebooks.com/page/sales

www.tandfebooks.com